THE IRISH TIMES BOOK *of the* YEAR

2005

EDITED BY
PETER MURTAGH

Gill & Macmillan

Gill & Macmillan Ltd
Hume Avenue
Park West
Dublin 12
with associated companies throughout the world
www.gillmacmillan.ie

0 7171 3935 2
Design by Identikit Design Consultants, Dublin
Print origination by Carole Lynch
Index compiled by Helen Litton
Printed by Butler & Tanner, Frome

The paper used in this book is made from the wood pulp of managed forests. For every tree felled, at least one tree is planted, thereby renewing natural resources.

A catalogue record is available for this book from the British Library.

1 3 5 4 2

Contents

Introduction

It's been another year in which foreign events have seemed to dominate the news agenda. Events in, and related to, the middle east; the re-election of a US president whose views are anathema to many outside America; the death of a charismatic but controversial pope; the popular rejection of a political elite's grand design for Europe; and natural disasters at opposite ends of the earth: abrupt reminders that nature, not man, rules our planet.

In October 2004, the people of Afghanistan displayed bravery in the face of sometimes murderous opposition to choose a president in the nearest test of opinion to free elections that country had seen in decades. Even greater fortitude was shown by the people of Iraq in January this year when, in their millions, and contrary to predictions of chaos, they elected an interim assembly charged with drawing up a constitution. But shocking violence continued to plague the country throughout the year. The consequences of one variation of the violence – excessive force employed by apparently ill-trained and jittery US soldiers – was witnessed by photographer Chris Hondros, whose images and account of a family car being shot to pieces have, with the passage of time, lost none of their power to shock.

And yet despite the war, George Bush was re-elected to the most powerful political position in the world. The major cities of the United States, together with the east and west coasts, went against him but Bush commanded solid and convincing support across middle America. Much of the rest of the world looked on, incredulous. The polemicist Mark Steyn gives some insight into the mindset of those in the US who feel that Bush is correct, whatever anyone else may think.

Partisan advocates insist things are improving in the middle east. Arafat is dead and a new Palestinian order has emerged with which Israel says it can do business. Israel has withdrawn from Gaza – too late for 13-year-old Iman, a schoolgirl in Rafah shot dead by Israeli soldiers without apparent reason – in the teeth of opposition, though less serious than expected, from settlers who assert a right to live on land based on biblical writing.

At times during the past 12 months, it seemed as though the potent mix of religious fervour laced with political conviction was little different – in essence if not expression – in otherwise apparently different parts of the world. Islamic radicals promoting theocracy made their presence felt in the middle east and in London, hardline settlers in Israel and the occupied territories believe Ariel Sharon has betrayed them, and evangelical Christian voters in middle America all believe they too have God on their side. Many who do not share such convictions watch, horrified but impotent, at the unfolding consequences.

These world events and more – the funeral of Pope John Paul II, the tsunami disaster in south east Asia, the hurricane devastation in New Orleans, the French and Dutch rejection of the proposed EU constitution – dominated much of what *Irish Times* foreign correspondents wrote about over the past 12 months. Samples that I hope read as well now as when first published are contained in these pages.

Closer to home, who would have predicted that Bertie Ahern would out himself as a socialist? Or that a former senior government minister branded corrupt would be jailed for tax offences? President McAleese was returned to office unopposed in the face of overwhelming popularity. *I Keano* had audiences rolling in the aisles; Kevin Myers had (some) readers frothing at the mouth but others entertained or confirmed in their views.

A year cannot adequately be summed up by the big news events that punctuate the days. Many readers will sooner recall a finely crafted individual story illustrating a social problem, or words describing the winter solstice. For many, Róisín Ingle's Magazine column is compulsory Saturday morning reading before anything on the front page. And so it is: readers dip in and out of features, arts, sports, opinion and business columns in ways that defy blanket stereotyping. Some readers buy *The Irish Times* for Simplex and Crosaire. Some readers reserve all their cross words for Kevin Myers and John Waters.

The selection is not comprehensive and could never be. *Irish Times* writers and photographers cover such a multiplicity of events six days a week that an anthology such as this can only ever be a smattering of what is available day by day. The selection is mine alone and is therefore flawed and partial. Choosing what's left out is the hardest part.

Thanks as ever to colleagues who made suggestions; to the picture desk staff who helped retrieve photographs; to Rita O'Hare in the Editor's Office who made sure that vital deliveries were sent to Aoileann O'Donnell of Gill & Macmillan. Finally, a special thanks to my colleague Conor O'Clery who has retired from *The Irish Times*. Much loved by readers, Conor has been an inspiration to many journalists over many decades, not least me. His professionalism, his integrity, his ability to communicate and his grace under pressure are second to none.

Peter Murtagh
The Irish Times
September 2005

Journalists and Photographers

David Adams is an *Irish Times* columnist.

Paddy Agnew is Rome Correspondent of *The Irish Times*.

Eileen Battersby is Literary Correspondent of *The Irish Times*.

Alan Betson is a staff photographer with *The Irish Times*.

Maeve Binchy is a novelist and former *Irish Times* feature writer.

Rosita Boland is a feature writer with *The Irish Times*.

Mark Brennock is Chief Political Correspondent of *The Irish Times*.

Anna Carey is a freelance feature writer.

Tony Clayton Lea is a rock journalist.

Marc Coleman is Economic Editor of *The Irish Times*.

Clifford Coonan is a freelance journalist based in Beijing.

Paul Cullen is an *Irish Times* reporter and Development Correspondent.

Deaglán de Bréadún is Foreign Affairs Correspondent of *The Irish Times*.

Eithne Donnellan is Health Correspondent of *The Irish Times*.

Keith Duggan is an *Irish Times* sports journalist who specialises in Gaelic Games and also writes a column, Sideline Cut, in the sports supplement.

Michael Dwyer is Film Critic of *The Irish Times*.

Jack Fairweather is a freelance journalist who reported from Iraq for *The Irish Times* and *The Daily Telegraph* of Britain. He has now left the country.

Hilary Fannin is the *Irish Times* TV critic.

Brenda Fitzsimons is a staff photographer with *The Irish Times*.

Godfrey Fitzsimons is an *Irish Times* sub-editor.

Peter Hanan is a freelance caricaturist who illustrates the Saturday Profile in the Weekend supplement.

Nuala Haughey is a former *Irish Times* staff journalist now working freelance in Israel, the Gaza Strip and the West Bank.

Shane Hegarty is a feature writer with *The Irish Times*.

Mark Hennessy is Political Correspondent of *The Irish Times*.

Kitty Holland is an *Irish Times* reporter.

Chris Hondros is a staff photographer with Getty Images. In 2004, he was nominated for a Pulitzer Prize, America's highest honour for a journalist, for his work in Liberia. He has worked in Iraq for several periods since the US invasion.

Tom Humphries is a sports journalist and also writes a weekly column, LockerRoom, in the Monday sports supplement.

Róisín Ingle is an *Irish Times* feature writer and columnist in the Saturday Magazine. Her first book, *Pieces of Me: A Life-in-Progress*, was published in September.

Matt Kavanagh is a staff photographer with *The Irish Times*.

Douglas Kennedy is an American-born novelist and occasional *Irish Times* reviewer. He studied in Trinity College, Dublin, and lives in London.

Conor Lally is an *Irish Times* reporter.

Mark Lawrenson is *Irish Times* soccer analyst.

Hugh Linehan is editor of The Ticket, the entertainment and review supplement published on Fridays.

Eric Luke is a staff photographer with *The Irish Times*.

Dara Mac Dónaill is a staff photographer with *The Irish Times*.

Don MacMonagle is a freelance photographer based in Killarney.

Dan McLaughlin is a freelance journalist based in Budapest, Hungary, from where he reports on eastern Europe for *The Irish Times*.

John McManus is Business Editor of *The Irish Times*.

Frank McNally is an *Irish Times* reporter. He also writes a weekly column, The Last Word, in Saturday's Weekend section.

Cathal McNaughton is a photographer with the Press Association of London.

Fionola Meredith is a freelance feature writer.

Frank Millar is London Editor of *The Irish Times*.

Frank Miller is a staff photographer with *The Irish Times*.

Brendan Moran is a photographer with the Sportsfile agency of Dublin.

Gerry Moriarty is Northern Editor of *The Irish Times*.

Orna Mulcahy is Property Editor of *The Irish Times* and she also writes the Irish Lives column in the Saturday Magazine.

Kevin Myers writes An Irishman's Diary.

Breda O'Brien is an *Irish Times* columnist.

Bryan O'Brien is a staff photographer with *The Irish Times*.

Carl O'Brien is Social Affairs Correspondent of *The Irish Times*.

Tim O'Brien is Regional Development Correspondent for *The Irish Times*.

Conor O'Clery was North American Editor of *The Irish Times* until mid-2005 when he retired.

Lynne O'Donnell is a freelance journalist.

Sean O'Driscoll is a freelance journalist based in New York.

Shelia O'Flanagan is a novelist and financial columnist with Friday's Business This Week supplement.

Pól Ó Muirí is editor of Tuarascáil, the weekly Irish language current affairs column published on Wednesday.

Ian O'Riordan is an *Irish Times* sports journalist, specialising in athletics.

Joe O'Shaughnessy is a freelance photographer based in Galway.

Fintan O'Toole is an *Irish Times* columnist and the paper's theatre critic.

Mary Raftery is an *Irish Times* columnist.

William Reville is associate professor of biochemistry and public awareness of science officer at University College, Cork, and writes a column for Science Today published on Thursdays in *The Irish Times*.

Barry Roche is Cork Correspondent of *The Irish Times*.

Kathy Sheridan is a feature writer with *The Irish Times*.

David Sleator is a staff photographer with *The Irish Times*.

Denis Staunton was Europe Correspondent for *The Irish Times* prior to his appointment in September as Washington Correspondent in succession to Conor O'Clery.

Chris Stephen is a freelance journalist based in Moscow. He has written extensively for *The Irish Times* from the Balkans and from the international war crimes tribunal in The Hague.

Mark Steyn is a Canadian-born columnist living in New Hampshire. He writes a weekly column for *The Irish Times* and several other publications in America and the UK.

Joe St Leger is a freelance photographer.

Sylvia Thompson is a feature writer who specialises in health matters.

Michael Viney writes Another Life, a column in Saturday's Weekend supplement about the natural world and his life on the western seaboard in Co. Mayo.

Dominick Walsh is a freelance photographer based in Kerry.

John Waters is an *Irish Times* columnist.

Arminta Wallace is an *Irish Times* feature writer.

Haydn West is a London-based photographer.

Grania Willis is Equestrian Correspondent of *The Irish Times*.

FRIDAY, 1 OCTOBER 2004

Loyalty Dependent on Improvement in FF's Fortunes

Mark Hennessy

Politics is a zero-sum game. For one TD to gain, another must lose. Nevertheless, the sum of unhappiness within Fianna Fáil is no larger than usual. It is just that different people are unhappy.

Backbench FF TDs yesterday quietly gathered in small groups to mull over the Taoiseach, Mr Bertie Ahern's ministerial reshuffle. Listening to third-hand gossip around the corridors of Leinster House yesterday, one could have been forgiven for thinking that a rebellion was quietly smouldering.

In reality, it is not a rebellion, or even the threat of one, but more than a few TDs, particularly those elected in 1997, are simply gutted.

However, there is one major caveat: the loyalty of backbenchers is now dependent upon a significant improvement in FF's fortunes in coming months.

Leinster House's Merrion Square car park told its own story yesterday afternoon, as FF TDs began to drift away early for their constituencies. 'Guys are going to be busy looking after their seats. But if they see that improvements are not coming by next year, then it will be every man for himself,' warned one TD.

Though few TDs expected Mr Ahern to make any more Cabinet changes than he did, they did

Mary Coughlan, Minister for Agriculture, at the National Ploughing Championships in Tullow, Co. Carlow, with draught mares Molly and Dolly. Photograph: Brenda Fitzsimons.

feel that he had promised to free up Minister of State spaces.

However, FF TDs have been here before, and they knew it yesterday: 'He always does this. He creates expectation and then disappoints,' grumbled one backbencher.

The lack of an observable geographical logic to his choices irritated, even though many of the same complainants would be equally bitter if geography alone dictated events. Said one TD: 'Look, there are two jobs in Clare. That won't do anything for seat numbers, no matter how much people might like Tony Killeen.' The performance of the Department of Health under the Tánaiste, Progressive Democrats leader Ms Harney, will play a key role. For now, FF TDs admire her guts, nervously wonder what she will do, and quietly emphasise that they will not tie their fortunes to her if she goes too far.

'Believe me, we will not be defending Harney if this goes wrong. But one could not but be impressed by the passion in her speech on Wednesday night,' said one Dublin TD. The key will be her handling of the Hanly Report: 'There would be a residual loyalty to an FF minister implementing it, but she won't have that,' said another. However, most of them believe that a wily operator such as the Tánaiste will work hard to avoid standing on observable landmines.

Still pondering the make-up of the Cabinet and the Ministers of State, most TDs believed that Mr Ahern's grand design suffered last-minute complications. 'He could not have planned it to come out this way. Sure, it avoids making too many new enemies, but there is no coherence to the juniors,' said another TD.

Most colleagues feel sympathy for sacked Minister of State, Mr Jim McDaid, even if only for the fact that he was singled out for removal. For months, colleagues believed that Mr Ahern had guaranteed Mr McDaid that he would survive as a junior if he ran in the European Parliament election and lost. However, this appears not to have been the case, according to one source with close knowledge of another FF TD's Euro campaign: 'There was no such deal sought, or offered.'

Though they lacked hard information, most FF TDs believe that Mr Ahern had originally intended to fire Mr Séamus Brennan and to bring in somebody else.'Whatever happened to Séamus Brennan had a domino effect, I'm sure of that,' said one FF TD, who warned about the party's future in the next elections.

The lack of senior Cabinet representation on Dublin's northside, bar the Taoiseach himself, is now seen by some as a serious problem for Fianna Fáil. In Dublin North East and Dublin North West, FF currently holds two out of three seats, while it also has two in North Central, which is being cut to a three-seater next time. In each, FF will face a battle.

In North Central, Minister of State Ivor Callely and Mr Seán Haughey, Fine Gael's Mr Richard Bruton and Independent Mr Finian McGrath will be in contention. In North East, FF currently has Dr Michael Woods, who will be 70 next year, and Mr Martin Brady, though Sinn Féin's Mr Larry O'Toole must surely pose a serious threat next time. In North West, Minister of State Noel Ahern and Mr Pat Carey are sitting tenants in a constituency where Sinn Féin's Mr Dessie Ellis should offer serious competition.

Clearly disappointed, one TD said: 'People will wait for the Budget to see what it throws up. Otherwise they will start thinking about their own re-election. That's where it gets messy. If one guy goes out on a local hospital issue, then everybody else will have to do so. It creates a dynamic.'

SATURDAY, 2 OCTOBER 2004

Woman of Contradictions

Fintan O'Toole

Last Wednesday was a light day for the President, Mary McAleese. In mid-morning, she drove the short distance from Áras an Uachtaráin to the Royal

President McAleese in her official residence, Áras an Uachtaráin, in the Phoenix Park, Dublin. Photograph: Bryan O'Brien.

Hospital in Kilmainham to make a short speech at the opening of a conference on lifelong learning. In mid-afternoon, she had a photocall at the Áras with the winners of the EU Young Scientists competition. The next day was also going to be an easy one, with nothing more onerous on the agenda than a visit to the National Ploughing Championships.

It was becoming more and more obvious that she was going to be re-elected unopposed and that she didn't have to worry about an election. So there was no obvious reason why she should have declined an invitation for Wednesday evening.

On the face of it, it was an invitation she ought to have welcomed. In perhaps the most combative speech of her presidency, delivered to a conference in Charlottesville, Virginia, last year, she had spoken of how, in Ireland, 'carefully hidden stories ... are coming out of the shoe-boxes in the attic and into daylight'. The event she was invited to open was certainly about taking the shoe-boxes out of the attic. Gerard Mannix Flynn's play and exhibition, entitled *James X*, at Liberty Hall in Dublin, is an extraordinarily graceful exploration of his own experiences, from his early childhood onwards, at the hands of the State which committed him to its industrial schools and prisons. It is an event of great symbolic importance: an attempt to heal a hurt that runs very deep and that, as the Catholic Archbishop of Dublin, Diarmuid Martin, remarked last week, we are still struggling to come to terms with.

One of the differences between President McAleese and her predecessor is that Mary Robinson would have jumped at the chance to open Mannix Flynn's show. She would have seen it as an opportunity to use the presidency in a way that avoided party politics but that was nevertheless deeply political. She would have understood that the mere presence of the head of State at such an event would have made an eloquent statement. It seems, however, that the event, and the subject, was just too sharp, too dangerous, too angular for President McAleese. For those who accuse her of blandness, here was evidence for the prosecution.

Yet that speech in Virginia in May last year, when she spoke of the hidden stories coming into the daylight, was another side of Mary McAleese. The manner of its delivery showed why she has been such a popular president. Her bearing was in sharp contrast to that of the shy, sometimes awkward Mary Robinson.

President McAleese has an uncanny ability to be both lofty and warm, both regal and populist, both head of State and national mammy. She can put an audience at its ease while keeping an element of dignified distance. She can deliver long and complex sentences in a conversational tone and a mellifluous voice. And she is, on her day, one of the most accomplished public speakers in global politics. That day in Virginia, she stuck to a long script without once giving the impression that she was reading. Fluent, intelligent, always in touch with her listeners, she held a tough audience of academics, journalists, students and locals in the palm of her hand. When she had finished, one member of the entourage of the governor of Virginia sighed, looked around at the others at her table and whispered in a voice hovering between awe and despair: 'You know, our president couldn't speak even one of those sentences.'

Nor was that speech just a matter of style. She gave a much more nuanced and hard-edged version of the Ireland she so often celebrates in a language of airy uplift.

'More money in pockets has visibly lifted standards of living, but it is being badly spent too, on bad habits that have never gone away,' she said. 'The Irish love of conviviality has its dark side in the stupid, wasteful abuse of alcohol and its first cousin, abuse of drugs. They chart a course of misery and malaise so utterly unnecessary that we need to re-imagine an Ireland grown intolerant of behaviour which it has too benignly overlooked for too long.'

While those comments successfully ignited a debate back home, McAleese also commented wryly on the inequalities of the new Ireland.

'The widespread embrace of prosperity has been a wonderful and heartening phenomenon,' she said, 'but if you are still marooned on the beach and the uplifted boats are sailing over the horizon, the space between can seem a frightening, unbridgeable chasm.'

SO WHICH IS the real president? The one who often avoids awkward occasions and who sometimes uses her extraordinary powers of eloquence to dignify boilerplate feel-good rhetoric about how 'Ireland still has a story to tell which is the envy of almost all others' and how, as she informed the Oireachtas on the eve of the millennium, 'today where the name of Ireland is spoken, the word success is close behind'? Or the sparky, feisty woman who could deliver a lecture to lawyers, as she did at UCD in 1999, and excoriate her own profession as 'a closed shop and an often pedantic and precious institution' with a 'gravitational tendency towards vanity'?

Part of the problem in answering such questions is that at times Mary McAleese has seemed to be weirdly disconnected from life in the Republic in a way that is not perhaps surprising for someone who has spent so much of her life outside the State.

This is a president who kicked off her term of office with an inaugural speech in which she talked about how 'At our core we are a sharing people. Selfishness has never been our creed'. It was a strange statement at a time when the McCracken tribunal report, with its details of the Ansbacher scam, was still being digested and a report by the Comptroller and Auditor General, showing massive and largely unpunished tax evasion to be rife, was making the headlines.

Another example came in April 2002. At the time, the Government had been forced to withdraw its Disability Bill in the face of a storm of anger from people with disabilities and their families. That same month, the United Nations Committee on Economic, Social and Cultural Rights was considering the appalling practice in Ireland of incarcerating people with intellectual disabilities in mental hospitals. So when President McAleese agreed to open a seminar for the group, Disabled People of Clare, she was widely expected to take the opportunity to respond with a statement of the basic values of equality. What did she say?

'It is thankfully reassuring to see how much progress has been made in the care and treatment of people with disabilities in recent years.'

The dreamy optimism of President Pangloss, in which all seems to be for the best in the best of all possible worlds, reached its height in her address to the Oireachtas on the eve of the millennium. It presented a vision, the like of which has not been heard since the heady days of the Irish Revival in the late 19th century, of an ideal Ireland that was destroyed by filthy foreigners and might be born again. She evoked, to the hilarity of medieval historians, a lost 'golden age' of a near-perfect Christian civilisation 'in the middle part of the first millennium'. This golden age 'fell victim to the Viking invasion' and was followed by an unending succession of 'wars, invasions, rebellions, plantations and plagues'. But, she hinted, the golden age was at hand again. A new 'age of miracles' was about to begin.

There is a naïvety to this side of McAleese that, at its worst, makes her sound like a mixture of a Madison Avenue advertising maestro and an old Communist dictator spouting about Utopia while the people mutter darkly behind their hands. Yet there is something real behind it, a genuine source of passion and conviction. Her difficulty is that it is a source she is reluctant to reveal too clearly.

Mary McAleese is a deeply committed Catholic. Probably the most personal speech of her presidency was one she gave in 1999 in Florence to the conference of the World Community for Christian Meditation. It is fascinating because it is the speech not of a head of State, but of a believer among believers. Its vision is deeply and utterly religious, a 'vision of how Christ's message of love and unity can be realised' in this world. Its answer to the world's conflicts and problems is 'our faith in God, in His infinite love'.

Her great difficulty is that she came to office at the worst possible time for a missionary Christian, a time when the public is less comfortable with a religious definition of the State than at any other period in its history.

IT IS NOT accidental that Mary McAleese became a widely accepted president through a religious act – the taking of communion in a Protestant church. She clearly knew what she was doing when she openly took the bread and wine at Christ Church Cathedral in Dublin a few weeks after taking office. Before that moment, she was the woman who had represented the Irish Catholic bishops in a hardline presentation at the New Ireland forum in 1984. After it, she was the woman who had infuriated and upset the Catholic Archbishop of Dublin, who denounced her action as a sham. As a political manoeuvre, it was brilliantly conceived and nervelessly executed. But it was also a lesson in how dangerous and unsettlingly divisive religious symbolism could be. In the long term, it probably discouraged her from appearing as an openly religious figure.

Another reason not to do so, of course, was her quiet work alongside her husband in reaching out to Loyalist communities in Northern Ireland. The theme for her presidency, as she has stressed ad nauseam is Building Bridges, and one of her problems is that Building Bridges is not in fact a theme, merely a slogan. Yet the one area in which she has given it real substance has undoubtedly been her work with the North's Protestant community.

Though her manner of expressing it yesterday was a little embarrassing (the thought of anyone weeping for joy at the sight of Ian Paisley is rather disturbing), her excitement at the possibility of a genuinely inclusive settlement in Northern Ireland is clearly real. Constantly reminding Northern Protestants of her own religious feelings, however, might have put an obstacle in the way of that work.

All of this, though, raises important questions for her second term. Is it really fair to blame Mary McAleese for being bland and then to want her to keep quiet about the things she feels most deeply about?

There is surely a connection between her tendency to make vacuous statements full of generalised uplift and the fact that the things that really animate her vision – her faith in Christ and her desire for a world that matches that faith – are mostly thought to be too embarrassing for the head of a secular state to utter. If the Church were not so sexist, she would have made a wonderful bishop, and it may well be that part of her appeal for very many people is that she is in fact, at a time when the authority of the hierarchy has been so badly damaged, a kind of alternative bishop. That might not be such a bad thing for a president to be.

The question is whether a secular state can tolerate someone at its head who feels confident enough to express herself in the religious language that clearly makes the deepest sense to her. If the answer is yes, that in itself might symbolise the emergence of a more tolerant society.

MONDAY, 11 OCTOBER 2004

Afghan Voters Defy Murderous Threats

Kathy Sheridan, in Kabul

In the end, they defied the odds. Afghanistan faced up to the murderous threats of the Taliban and al-Qaeda and humiliated them both. Dust storms meant the sun never broke through, making election day the coldest, dustiest and most unpleasant of the year. But still the people came, cheerful and resolute. Not only did they defy months of threats and intimidation. On election day in the north, they braved a metre of snow; in the south the oppressive heat; in the centre, air so dust-laden that it was difficult to breathe.

In Kabul province, a line of voters confronted with aggressive and voluble threats to vote for a minor candidate, suddenly turned on the aggressors and the army had to intervene. It may well have been a turning point for a long-oppressed people.

Later, a young Afghan soldier would be killed after hitting a landmine in the Kandahar region and three police would die in Uruzgan while transporting ballot boxes to a count centre. Meanwhile, high up in some of the world's remotest regions, hundreds of donkeys laden with ballot boxes were crossing rivers and dirt tracks, their drivers equipped with GPS signals, at the start of their long and lonely trek towards trucks bound for the count centres and a new era for Afghanistan.

Earlier, in the dawn half-light, local election officials at a school in central Kabul, solemnly, nervously, pulling on their blue UN vests at 6 a.m. – 'to help to choose a president for our country after 23 years of war', said a young woman teacher, Parween Dalilee – were a sight to jolt the most dead-eyed cynic.

The pay was $40 (including three days' training), good money in Afghanistan, but they would do it for nothing, exclaimed Parween and her 18-year-old colleague, Zohra. 'We want to help our country,' said Zohra, like so many young Afghans, serious and reflective beyond her years. Her parents were at home praying for her protection from the Taliban and al-Qaeda, she admitted, but 'this is not a day to give in to fear'.

Across town, at the city's Aedgha Mosque, within sight of the stadium where only a few years ago the Taliban summoned Kabulis to watch summary executions of men and women, a sole woman in a burka walked swiftly up to the

Afghan refugees queue to cast their votes in Chaman, a town on the country's border with Pakistan. The first vote in the presidential election was cast by a 19-year-old woman refugee. Photograph: Saeed Ali Achakzai/Reuters.

women's polling station at 6.50 a.m. and waited patiently while officials carefully arranged indelible pens and ink on the tables, like children on their first day at school. Basic as they are to indulged western eyes, those pens and ink were vital tools in establishing the legitimacy of this election.

Misunderstandings over the registration process and outright fraud meant that countless numbers had received multiple registration cards. When asked about this in August, the outgoing president, Hamid Karzai, at a news conference with Donald Rumsfeld, commented airily that 'people are enthusiastic and they want to have cards. It doesn't bother me. If they want to vote twice, they're welcome.' Later, he back-pedalled, noting that every voter's thumb would be marked with indelible ink to prevent them voting twice.

But on Saturday, it was immediately obvious that someone in the Joint Electoral Management Body (JEMB) had skimped on the cheapest essentials for officials. A single pen for each. And although there was no doubting their enthusiasm, some staff were so poorly trained that they confused the marker (for the ballot paper) with the indelible pen (for the fingers). Even the ink – to load the fast-drying pens – came in tiny quantities. Worse, some of it was washable. In some areas, voters coming back for a second bite (he liked two candidates, explained one voter cheerfully) demonstrated a perfectly clean thumbnail.

Within a few hours, some polling stations had to close to allow officials to sort out the problem. But in terms of perception, the damage had been done. Minor candidates, and anyone seeking a stick with which to attack the process, were handed one, trimmed and sharpened. Candidates, including the high-profile Yunuz Qunooni, whose men had been intimidating voter queues in Kabul province an hour earlier, were suddenly demanding a boycott of the process on the grounds of fraud.

Yesterday, games of brinkmanship were being played out at several levels. Would those candidates persist in their calls for an investigation, knowing that their own election day violations would be trumpeted? And while the Americans and others would like nothing better than to head off an investigation, can they do so without weakening the perceived legitimacy of the new president, who no-one doubts will be Karzai? The Free and Fair Elections Foundation of Afghanistan (FEFA), which had placed 2,300 observers in all 34 provinces, was taking a cautious line, going with the headline 'FEFA congratulates Afghans for having peaceful elections.'

The Organisation for Security and Co-operation in Europe (OSCE), which had 40 election experts here and noted rather more sinister breaches, such as observers being ejected from some polling stations before ballot boxes were sealed, also focused on the 'millions of Afghan men and women [who] turned out ... in Iran and Pakistan as well as Afghanistan ... We do not yet know what their choices are, but we know they should be respected.'

Meanwhile, no-one is prepared to take bets on the final turn-out figure. Voters were allowed to ballot wherever they found themselves, so no polling station had a fix on expected numbers. An American observer on Saturday was estimating it at 60 to 65 per cent.

Only one thing is certain at this stage. The people of Afghanistan played their part. Some 20 miles outside Kabul, past the checkpoint where a long line of trucks have been detained until this tense day ends, up a stony dust-track best negotiated by a tractor or four-wheel drive, past the graves of war 'martyrs', grapevines and herds of goats and sheep, old and young were trudging more than four kilometres to mark their papers in the school and mosque. This lovely old village was destroyed by the Taliban, the buildings blown up, the crops burned and the people forced to flee north.

The shiny village well, installed by a Danish NGO when the villagers returned three years ago, has stopped working and they're back to drawing their water from the river, 10 minutes away by donkey. But, says their friendly, courteous leader, Mahommad Ullah, 'We want just freedom ... We want peace, not the Americans but the ISAF force in Afghanistan. Today, the people are very happy indeed'.

MONDAY, 11 OCTOBER 2004

If Kerry Wins, I'm Going to Quit *Irish Times*

Mark Steyn

It was sobering, on reading the recent flurry of letters in this newspaper under the heading 'Balancing The US Debate', to discover that it was this column that had single-handedly unbalanced it.

'If Steyn represents the American right, where is the spokesperson for the American left?' demands Conor McCarthy of Dún Laoghaire. The hitherto perfectly poised see-saw of press coverage of the US is apparently all out of whack because my corpulent column is weighing down one end while on the other up in the air are the massed ranks of *Irish Times* correspondents, RTÉ, the BBC and 97 per cent of the European media class, plus Anthony O'Halloran, who opined in these pages a few days ago that 'anyone who cares to visit a small town in the Midwest will encounter what can only be described as ultra-right-wing thinking.' Prof O'Halloran didn't cite any examples of this 'ultra-right-wing thinking', secure in his assumption that most readers would know the sort of thing he had in mind.

As the *ne plus ultra* of unbalanced right-wing thinkers, it's not for me to suggest how the US debate might be balanced in these pages.

I have only one theory on column-writing, which is this: at a certain basic level, a columnist has to be right more often than not, otherwise the reader (I use the singular advisedly) is just wasting his time. If I were Robert Fisk, the famed foreign correspondent with decades of experience in the Muslim world, I'd be ashamed to leave the house. Sample Fisk headlines on the Afghan war: 'Bush Is Walking Into A Trap', 'It Could Become More Costly Than Vietnam'. Sample insight on the Iraq war: when the Yanks announced they'd taken

Baghdad International Airport, Fisk insisted they hadn't and suggested they'd seized an abandoned RAF airfield from the 1950s by mistake. It's this kind of unique expertise that has made him so admired around the world, not least in Ireland.

By contrast, readers of this column may have gained the impression that George W. Bush will win the presidential election on November 2nd. If he doesn't, I shall trouble readers of this newspaper no further. It would be ridiculous to continue passing myself off as an incisive analyst of US affairs after I've been exposed as a deluded fool who completely misread the entire situation. In the bright new dawn of the Kerry Administration, you'd deserve better. If that's not an incentive for Irish citizens to smuggle a few illegal campaign contributions the senator's way, I don't know what is.

But, if, on the other hand, Bush is re-elected, I make one small request of the Irish and European media: you need to re-think your approach to this presidency. Consider, for example, the two elections this weekend: Afghanistan and Australia. In the former, they held the first direct presidential election in the country's history. Hitherto, if you wanted to become president of Afghanistan, you had to hang around till the incumbent's term expired, which was generally when he did, usually at the next guy's hand. King Zahir was deposed in 1973 by his cousin Daoud, who was killed by his successor Taraki, who was suffocated by his successor Hafizullah Amin, who was executed by the Soviets, who installed Babrak Karmal, who died in a Moscow hospital but in a rare break with tradition managed to outlive his replacement, Najibullah, whom the Taliban wound up hanging from a traffic post. So, in a break with tradition, Hamid Karzai is now the first elected head of state in the country's history.

A black-headed gull washes itself in the lake in St Stephen's Green in Dublin. Photograph: Cathal McNaughton/PA.

And yes, it was a flawed election: it emerged on polling day that the indelible ink used to mark voters' thumbs could be rubbed off. And whose fault is that? Well, the election was managed by the UN, which evidently got its indelible ink from the book-keeping department of its Oil-for-Food programme. That's one more reason, in case we needed any, to dismantle the UN and all its bloated works.

But, UN incompetence aside, Afghanistan is making steady progress, no thanks to the media naysayers, who assured us nearly three years ago that Karzai was little more than a ceremonial mayor of Kabul and as soon as one of his many enemies got a good shot at him the country would be plunged back into its 1980s chaos. He represented nobody, he spoke for nobody. Robert Fisk again, in March 2002: 'Hamid Karzai can scarcely control the street outside his office.' Oh, really? Events in Afghanistan seem to be going Bush's way, rather than Fisk's.

Same in Australia, where John Howard's conservative coalition was re-elected. It was supposed to be close, but Howard won comfortably, prefiguring similar victories to come by his fellow doughty warriors of the Anglosphere, Bush and Blair. Had Australia's government gone the way of Spain's, you can bet CNN and co would have played it up as a big loss for Bush, in the same way that they focused on those smudgy Afghan thumbs rather than the joyous Afghan faces – the young women voting for the first time on a polling day almost wholly free of violence.

This was a remarkable weekend, but also a typical one, in that all the movement is in Bush's direction. For a supposed 'unilateralist' who's turned 'the world' against America (the basic Kerry indictment), he has a lot more reliable pals right now than, say, Jacques Chirac. The French president's closest ally, Gerhard Schröder, is unlikely ever again to be booking the room for an election-night victory party. Some US presidents are content to enjoy the perks and treat their term as one long holiday weekend (Clinton); others see their task as one of managing historically inevitable decline (Carter) or living with an unsatisfactory *status quo* (Eisenhower). But Bush, like Reagan and Roosevelt, is a transformative president. When he leaves office in 2009, the world will be very different.

And that's all I'm asking for after November 2nd – that the Euroleft chuck the tired gags about 'Shrub' the moron, the idiot, the stupid white man that saw them through his first term. Stow the pop psychology, too – the cracks about the 'daddy complex' that supposedly led him to topple Saddam. It's already obvious the 43rd presidency is far more consequential than the 41st: George Bush snr's place in history will mainly be as the guy who warmed up the name for George Bush jnr. If you're not prepared to give serious thought to the challenge Bush poses to the UN and EU complaceniks, you're never going to understand the times we live in.

If Kerry wins, I'm outta here. If Bush wins, eschewing lazy European condescension for the next four years would be the best way of 'balancing the US debate'.

FRIDAY, 22 OCTOBER 2004

Kiss me Kate

Donald Clarke

'Could you do me a favour?' Kate Winslet asks me. Lie in front of a train? Ram my arm into a threshing machine? Watch two Ben Affleck films back-to-back? Anything.

It transpires that Kate has become involved with a competition named Bounty Hunter on some radio station or other. As I understand it, members of the public arrange for a celebrity acquaintance to phone the relevant show. A poll is then carried out to determine which entrant has delivered the most impressive famous person. The winner receives £10,000 with £1,000 being

Kate Winslet as Sylvia Llewelyn Davies in a scene from the film Finding Neverland.

awarded to a charity of the celebrity's choice. As we speak it is a three-way-tie between Kate, the guy who played Zammo on Grange Hill and Angelina Jolie.

'But it was Angelina's personal pilot who phoned in,' she explains. Well, he can't need the money. 'That's what I thought. But my friend is about to get fired, so she really needs the ten grand.' I hand her a pen. 'OK. So this is the website and you have to tell all your friends to vote for Kate Winslet.' She writes her name clearly on the card before, with surreally unnecessary precision, adding: 'That's me. Kate Winslet.' I'm so glad she has turned out to be a good egg. We have got used to the fact that Bing Crosby wasn't such a lovely old buffer and that Arnold Schwarzenegger isn't a robot from the future, but it really would be too much if Kate Winslet, with her upside-down smile and her slightly clumsy physical manner, turned out to be a self-absorbed toad.

Winslet's more easily upset fans should, despite its being a very enjoyable middle-brow entertainment, approach her new film, *Finding Neverland*, with a modicum of caution. Telling the story of the relationship between J.M. Barrie (Johnny Depp), the author of *Peter Pan*, and the young widow whose children became the inspiration for *The Lost Boys*, the picture begins amiably enough. Then, about half-way through, Winslet begins coughing into a hankie. When people cough in the movies, they never have a cold.

'Did you cry?' she asks.

Like Paul Gascoigne. Like Tiny Tears. Like Johnny Ray. People were pointing and laughing.

Kate punches the air and makes a 'woo hoo' noise. 'That's what we want: more grown men crying. I think it is good for a man to have a cry now and then. Excellent!'

You can see why Winslet is so popular with the lads (interestingly, women's magazines have often been a bit snitty about her). She gives the impression of being rather good fun in a way that, say, Nicole Kidman does not. I bet she likes a game of Subbuteo now and then. I can imagine her betting her husband, the director Sam Mendes, that she can spit farther or hold her breath longer. I suspect Juliette Binoche never says 'woo hoo' in interviews.

She is, of course, also rather easy on the eye. Dressed today in a black halter-necked top and blue jeans, blonder than she has sometimes been, she looks ... well there is nothing more nauseating than an interviewer going on about how ravishing some movie star is, so I won't. Not that Winslet would describe herself as a movie star. Indeed, when I say those words she visibly winces. Come along, she is in the Dorchester Hotel promoting a film starring Johnny Depp. Get real!

'This is where I get so embarrassed,' she says. 'A movie star? I just don't feel I belong here at all. I find myself in the Dorchester, some posh hotel I never thought I would be in. I still find it all so exciting.'

Kate was born to theatrical parents in Reading in 1975. She acted throughout her teens, but, aside from a brief appearance alongside the Honey Monster, never made much noise as a juvenile. Her big break came in 1994 when she was cast in Peter Jackson's *Heavenly Creatures*, the true story of a notorious murder in 1950's New Zealand. Then came Ang Lee's *Sense and Sensibility*, Kenneth Branagh's *Hamlet* and some film about a boat.

'I was completely at a point after *Titanic* where doing things like this – coming to the Dorchester – was becoming a bit of a drag and I didn't even look at the wallpaper or what lovely drinks I could order or how comfortable the seats were. It was just like walking through an airport terminal and not looking right or left. During filming, people were saying: 'How will this change you?' And I was adamant that it wouldn't change me. But the truth is it was hard to live a normal life in my little flat in London N7 after that. I was being door-stepped. My car was chased. It was horrible.'

I wonder if her decision to follow up *Titanic* with smaller, more eccentric pictures such as Jane Campion's *Holy Smoke* and Gillies MacKinnon's *Hideous Kinky* was part of a conscious attempt to get back to basics.

'Oh definitely,' she says. 'Very much so. That was about survival. Not to mention that I really liked those scripts and often the big-budget films these days don't have such great scripts.'

What was the dumbest thing she was offered? 'Oh something with robots, I think. I am not really the action movie type. I was running around a lot in *Titanic*. But my wobbly bottom was corseted in.'

It is easy now to forget that during the production of *Titanic*, movie pundits, often using the real ship's demise as a clumsy analogy, consistently suggested that the film might prove to be the biggest flop in Hollywood history. The production was way over budget. Chaos reigned on the Mexican set. And Kate spent much of the shoot waist deep in icy cold water.

'It was part of the job. It just didn't occur to me that it was odd,' she says. 'It wasn't like we were being mistreated; that was just part of the job and we happened to be shooting in ice cold water that day. But we British actors are relatively uncomplaining. What you see is what you get with me. I am the same on set as I am right now, I hope. As far as all the press speculation went, we didn't really hear much of it.'

In the aftermath of *Titanic*'s success, a recurring strain in press coverage of Winslet made its first appearance: musings on her weight. Honestly, to read some of the coverage at the time you'd think she was the size of Hattie Jacques and that comical tuba music greeted her entrance into any room. Firstly, she was portrayed as a proud defender of a woman's right to be curvy. Then she was, apparently, a little too fat. Then she was a traitor for giving in to the system and losing weight.

'I am afraid that still goes on a bit,' she says. 'My agent will get phone calls from cosmetics companies and the first thing they say sometimes is "How is her weight currently?" And my agent will just say thank you and put the phone down. And what is so annoying is that I don't have a weight problem now. I was a chubby teen and after *Titanic* my weight went up and down for a year and then I had a child. When they called me Weighty Katy it did hurt, because there were times as a teenager when I was eating less than was healthy. I had to be careful that didn't happen to me again. But at least it was just that from the press and not me being photographed in the gutter after the latest orgy of cocaine. I have, thank goodness, never been that sort of person.'

And then there was the bizarre incident last year where photographs accompanying an interview in *GQ* magazine were touched up and morphed to the extent that she ended up looking like an eight-stone giant. 'Oh that thing was really pointless,' she sighs. 'I think they just did it to create a kind of controversy. But there was an assumption that I would be happy about it; that's what drove me the craziest. I was very unhappy about it. All magazines tend to do retouching to get rid of moles and so forth. But the people that buy the magazines don't necessarily know they are retouched and therefore a lot of women will look at them and say: that's how I want to look.'

In 1998 she married James Threapleton, who had been an assistant director on *Hideous Kinky*, and in 2000 they had a daughter, Mia. Initially, the press was back on her side: how refreshing that she was dating 'below the line' (industry speak for the less starry members of the cast and crew); wasn't it great that they had bangers and mash at the reception? Then things turned ugly when the marriage broke up. Rumours abounded that the relationship fell apart because one partner was a little too famous for comfort. It was further suggested that she had begun dating Mendes, the director of *American Beauty* and *The Road to Perdition*, while still with Threapleton.

'On the whole, I don't talk about that,' she says. 'All I can say is that stuff was all rubbish. That stuff was a bitter pill to swallow, but divorce itself is a difficult pill to swallow.' Things seem to have worked out OK. In June 2003, she and Mendes were married in the West Indies and later that year she had a son, Joe. So tell us all about how terrific Mr Mendes is.

'Oh, well, look. I just really don't talk too much about my private life.' She suddenly looks enormously uneasy. Curling up on the sofa she focuses acutely on the floor and begins twisting one hand about another. 'Well, er, um. It is just great. What can I say? I am very lucky, very happy. We have the two most wonderful children. He is such a brilliant dad and a great step-dad. We are really happy. What else to say?' Rescuing her from obvious discomfort, I ask her to tell us about her extraordinary ability to injure herself on set. She has just finished shooting John Turturro's bizarre sounding musical, *Romance and Cigarettes*, with James Gandolfini, Susan Sarandon, Christopher Walken, Eddie Izzard and everybody else. Somehow she managed to do something ghastly to her ankle.

'Oh God, that was awful. I was dancing in four-inch heels and just tore all the ligaments in my leg,' she says. 'But something always happens to me. I was battered by fake rain in *Sense and Sensibility* and fainted from the cold. I have scars everywhere. I have scars on my knees from falling on the deck on *Titanic*. Here look at this.' She leans forward and rolls back her sleeve to reveal a pale, thin line on her wrist. 'That was from *Holy Smoke*. It was this scene where my sari was being pulled and it was pulled over my wrist and burnt me.' I suddenly feel as if I am in the scene from *Jaws* where Robert Shaw and Richard Dreyfus compare wounds. I suppose it would be highly inappropriate if I showed her one of my scars.

'Oh don't worry darling. I've seen it all.'

Like I said, she really does come across as one of the lads. The listeners to X-FM seem to agree and, holding off a late surge from Dame Judi Dench, her co-star in Richard Eyre's *Iris*, she triumphed in *Bounty Hunter*. Zammo held on to the third spot. Angelina was nowhere.

MONDAY, 25 OCTOBER 2004

Modern Life is Breeding Intolerance

John Waters

On certain issues, rational debate becomes impossible because of a polarisation of viewpoint between prejudice and platitude. The 'debate' about immigration is developing along these lines, with the stage now left to those who see only negatives in immigration and those – usually insulated from any direct consequence of their opinions – who advertise their virtue by denying the existence of any difficulty at all. The middle ground is vacated and, since this is where workable solutions are invariably found, the outcome is predictable.

If we have difficulty envisaging where this leads to, we need only look to Dunsink, the latest flashpoint in an analogous matter. Public discussions about Travellers have long been characterised by this prejudice-platitude dichotomy. A survey some years ago indicated that two-thirds of Irish people are 'ambivalent' about Travellers, with just 20 per cent expressing outright negative feelings. Hence, most people acknowledge that Travellers have difficult lives and are willing to help.

Instantly recognisable, even from the rear. Ian Paisley sits across the table from Taoiseach Bertie Ahern, foreign minister Dermot Ahern and government officials, when they met to discuss the future of the suspended power-sharing executive in Northern Ireland. Photograph: Haydn West/PA.

This comes unstuck, however, because pro-Traveller arguments are usually advanced in such a hectoring manner that the goodwill is lost. For all that this society may appear to be highly prejudiced against Travellers, there is this interesting contradiction: on the one hand, most people are not prejudiced and, on the other, almost every public utterance takes the high moral ground against anyone who argues that the presence or lifestyles of Travellers presents any kind of problem.

Legitimate worries and concerns about litter, crime, violence, roaming animals or the adverse effects of halting sites on house values are dismissed as, for example, 'nimbyism'. The result is that the two-thirds of people who are appalled by the living conditions of many Travellers, and who perceive in this an absolute human rights dimension, are driven into the arms of the 20 per cent already lost to prejudice. In the absence of a fluid and open debate, the issue is reduced to the simplicities of its extremes, one catcall met with another and all possibility of compromise lost.

The official response is often to employ moral bullying to enforce a solution, with any objections perceived ipso facto as 'anti-Traveller' or even 'racist'. A stand-off ensues, characterised by an increased wariness and an entrenchment of the determination to shunt the problem on. And so we lurch on to the next flashpoint and the inevitable official heavy-handedness on display at Dunsink.

The lives of many Travellers are appalling. Their infant mortality rate is 150 per cent higher and their life expectancy roughly a decade less than the general population. More than 1,000 families live by the roadside without electricity, running water or sanitation. But there are legitimate questions to be asked about the balance of responsibility for this state of affairs.

When I was a child, relationships between Travellers and what is now called the 'settled' community were characterised by a mixture of wariness and respect. There was a roadside site close to the house of an aunt of mine in the countryside, to which Travellers would come once a year, stay for a while and move on. While there, they would call to local houses and exchange buckets and cans for food. The two communities functioned in relative harmony, though no great love was lost on either side.

Today we live in a very different society. The insistence on a cultural entitlement to travel may well have a persuasive historical and philosophical basis, but is arguably in conflict with how this society has developed. Half of Irish Travellers live in the four main urban centres of Dublin, Cork, Galway and Limerick. In an urban setting, space is at a premium, houses and land wildly expensive and the ecological balance of such a delicate nature that it is an open question whether nomadism is compatible with such modes of living at all.

Every motorist knows how much the concept of space has become circumscribed in the urban environment, with traffic wardens and clampers skulking around every corner to impose financial penalties on those who step out of line.

These and other phenomena tell us that we face a dwindling of the non-monetary elements of public exchange, in a society in which almost everything, including prejudice and goodwill, has a financial cost. And whatever morals might be extracted from this by priest or pundit, the reality is that the ordinary citizen is more and more hard-pressed to maintain a hold in a society which, daily, becomes more unfriendly. The citizen sees his life occurring beyond his control and barely within his means. He sees himself as paying through the nose for everything, usually more than once. However much he may sympathise with those who are much worse off, he feels little capacity to create space or compassion for a lifestyle which has the hallmarks of self-inflicted misery. In his gridlocked life, facing his mortgaged future, he listens to the platitudes and moral bullying of the public Pilates and delves into himself to discover a prejudice he never knew he had.

SATURDAY, 30 OCTOBER 2004

My Lost Weekend

Brock the Jack Russell

My name is Brock. I am a Jack Russell terrier, aged one-and-a-half. I live in a country called Ballyfermot, with a good family. Ballyfermot is a nice place, with many cats to chase. I was very happy there for a while. But then the war came.

I don't remember when it began. All I know is, one night, explosions started going off all over the neighbourhood. I hid under a blanket, but the bangs continued. It was the same every night. Mum laughed and said, 'Poor Brock, he's scared of the fireworks!' But many humans were scared too.

Brock … the opposition totally out-run. Photograph: Haydn West/PA.

I think now that the explosions made me a little crazy. I heard one of the older dogs say something called 'Hallowe'en' was coming. I thought: if it's this bad before it comes, I'm not waiting for the invasion. I decided to leave Ballyfermot. I knew some dogs in a country called Inchicore, so I thought I'd go and stay with them for a while. But the war was in Inchicore too, and my friends were in hiding. I had no choice but to keep travelling. Somewhere further on, I saw people running for a train and I ran after them.

The train was called Luas. It was fun. The passengers liked me. There was an invisible woman making announcements and when I barked at her, everyone laughed. I got off the Luas eventually. The passengers waved. The driver waved. Everybody seemed happy. Then a car crashed into the train.

My first night away, I met some rough-looking dogs. They smelled my bottom and, just to be polite, I smelled theirs. But when they asked me where I was from and I told them, they said I was a 'culchie'. The mood was very threatening. Luckily a cat appeared, and after we chased it down an alleyway together, they said I was 'sound'. I stayed with them for the night.

The next morning they were gone, and I had fleas. I wandered aimlessly. There were many strange sights. I saw arms dealers selling explosives on the streets! 'Get the last of the bangers,' they shouted. I barked at them angrily and ran. Some time later, I noticed crowds of people walking hurriedly, and I followed. They must be refugees from the war, I thought. But they led me into a giant stadium, where a group of children – very big children – were chasing a ball. There was also a man blowing a whistle. At first I thought I misheard, so I listened to the whistle carefully, and there was no mistake about it. It was inviting me to join in! I couldn't believe my luck.

Anytime I ran onto a pitch in my home country, I would get – as Ballyfermot people say –

Brock breaks away from Tadhg Kennelly of Ireland and Jude Bolton of Australia in the second test of the Coca-Cola International Rules Series between the two countries at Croke Park in Dublin. Photograph: Brendan Moran/Sportsfile.

'a boot up the hole'. But the humans in the big stadium were great. They let me play for ages. Finally somebody took me off. He said it was nothing personal, that I'd played well, but they just needed to 'change things around tactically'.

After that, I ended up in a place called Drumcondra. I met a gang of cross-breeds, who claimed to be the famous 'dogs in the street'. They were full of stories, mostly about a man called 'Bertie'. But none of it made much sense. So I started wandering again.

I walked down a big wide street, with a huge silver spike. I had no idea what this thing was, but I peed against it anyway, just to be on the safe side. I walked and walked. Night came, and the explosions started again, but I was too tired and hungry to care. I tried stealing sausages from a butcher's shop, half-hoping I'd get caught. I had hit rock bottom. I sat down and howled. Luckily, some children took pity. They brought me home and fed me and said I was theirs now. I knew it was wrong, but I just let it happen. They bought me a collar, and gave me a nice bed to sleep in. The next day, my new dad brought home the newspaper and – guess what? I was on the front page! So was my real family. One thing led to another. And soon I was back in Ballyfermot.

Although I miss my new friends, I'm glad to be in my own house again. I'm famous now, but it hasn't changed me. My experience has made me appreciate how lucky I am. All I wish now is for peace in our country soon.

In conversation with Frank McNally

SATURDAY, 30 OCTOBER 2004

Witness to a Convoluted Century

The Life of Graham Greene Volume Three: 1955-1991 By Norman Sherry

Douglas Kennedy

God, it's long. And God, it's detailed. Deeply detailed. Then again, this is, without question, 'A Big Book'; the final instalment of a near-30-year obsession with the life and times of a writer who (for me, anyway) stands as one of the central figures of post-war literature. Now, whether you buy into the idea that Graham Greene was the great English novelist of the second half of the last century will also determine whether you'll buy into this, the third instalment of Norman Sherry's massive life of Greene.

For me, Greene was a remarkable literary hybrid who wrote hugely readable novels that also grappled with such fundamental human complexities as the obsessive nature of guilt, the impossibility of self-redemption (and of escaping one's self-imposed destiny), and the search for forgiveness in a pitiless world. As such, his central works – *The End of the Affair, The Heart of the Matter, The Power and the Glory* (to name just a few of the key novels in his hugely prolific career) – managed that remarkable trick of being simultaneously serious and popular ... a fact which made him a shady figure in the eyes of certain über-literary types.

After all, there is a school of modern critical thought which equates narrative accessibility and the use of popular genres (like the thriller or the adventure yarn) with commercialism, and which also believes that a writer who gets you to turn the page cannot really be the purveyor of consequential literature. As Greene was guilty of Accessibility and Popularity in the First Degree, the Nobel Prize committee constantly passed him over for what John O'Hara once ruefully called 'the dynamite money' (their sniffy commentaries on Greene appear in one of the appendices – alongside a list of Greene's 47 Favourite Prostitutes). And, of course, he was the subject of jeering derision by lesser writers, such as Anthony Burgess.

Still, what comes across so clearly in the sweeping narrative of Sherry's third volume is that Greene truly bore witness to the convolutions of the last century. Consider his geographic meanderings during the final third of his life. Besides his constant peregrinations within Europe (France claimed him as her own during his near-30 years of residence there, even though he denounced French corruption in *J'Accuse*, his Jeremiad against le milieu Niçois), there were travels to China, the Congo, Cuba, Dakar, Haiti, Israel, Jamaica, Liberia, Sierra Leone, the US and the USSR ... not bad for a man edging into his twilight years. The cast of characters that entered his life during this time also reads like an international who's who – from Castro to Daniel Ortega to General Omar Torrijos, to Elizabeth Taylor and Richard Burton, to Evelyn Waugh, to John Gielgud and Ralph Richardson, to Charlie Chaplin ...

Well, you get the idea. And yet, what's most intriguing about Greene (a fact that Sherry constantly points up) is that he was someone who never embraced the cult of literary celebrity, who remained intensely closed-off and adverse to public scrutiny, and who led a private life of considerable complexity and frequent self-loathing.

Indeed, having never divorced his wife, Vivian, and having jettisoned his long-term mistress, Dorothy, the great object of desire for Greene in his middle years was the very beautiful and very married Catherine Walston. This downwardly spiralling affair forms a central emotional spine to this volume.

So too does Greene's involvement with his new mistress, Yvonne Cloetta – who, like Catherine, remained very much living with her husband while also being passionately entangled with Greene. Though married women were certainly a Greene speciality, Sherry makes it abundantly clear that, when it came to la vie sexuelle, Greene had a voracious appetite – and one which was fuelled both by neediness and insecurity. Just as Sherry also repeatedly points up the depression and abrupt mood swings which shadowed so much of his life.

In short, Greene's wildly tangled emotional landscape, his restlessness, his fear of ennui, his ongoing peregrinations, and his ferociously disciplined work habits (his galvanising need to put pen to paper every day and grind out his quota of words) are great copy. And though Sherry has been widely attacked in many quarters for letting this final biographical volume drift into discursiveness and also for imposing his own personality on the narrative proceedings, the life itself is so damn interesting (and Sherry's research so comprehensive) that the biography manages to transcend such lapses in judgment.

Indeed, Sherry can be slapped on the wrist for using the personal pronoun 'I' a bit too often. Just as I was a little dubious about his decision to include a photograph of himself on a donkey in Mexico, where he followed the same route that Greene traversed while researching *The Power and the Glory*.

And yes, he is sometimes guilty of over-embellishment and dragging out a story, for example, the storm-in-a-teacup tale of Greene judging the GPA Award in Dublin, wherein all the assorted backstage machinations (largely caused by Greene himself) are endlessly detailed, for little ultimate gain (though I did have to smile when Sherry recounts that, some months after the event, Greene told him: 'Dublin killed me').

And yes, throughout this hefty tome, you sense that Sherry considers himself almost an integrated part of Greene's life – no doubt, an understandably obsessive point of view, considering that the gentleman has spent nearly 30 years following Greene's footsteps everywhere.

The tricky convolutions of the Sherry/Greene inter-relationship – coupled with the biographer's innate understanding of his subject's Chinese Box-like personality (riddled with hidden compartments and vast ambiguities) – lend this third instalment an intriguing drive. Then again, Greene lived a life of such emotional density, such professional achievement and such personal despair that it cannot but be the stuff of a compulsive narrative. This final volume might have its self-seeking idiosyncrasies, but it is still a great account of the final years of a great 20th-century life.

Douglas Kennedy's novel, A Special Relationship, *is out in paperback (£6.99, Arrow). His new novel,* State of the Union, *will be published in 2005 by Hutchinson*

THURSDAY, 4 NOVEMBER 2004

Bush's Firm Mandate

Conor O'Clery, in New York

In the end it all came down to Ohio, with its 20 electoral votes. For John Kerry it was an excruciating case of what might have been. If just 150,000 voters in Ohio out of 5.8 million had voted the other way, today he would be president-elect John Kerry.

That title must have been in the Massachusetts senator's mind for a few tantalising hours on Tuesday afternoon, when exit polls conducted for the Associated Press and the television networks by Edison Media Research and Mitofsky International showed him winning the election, not just nationally but in Ohio and Florida. The gleeful celebrations in Boston were premature.

Even if Mr Kerry had won Ohio by a whisker it would have been just as unsatisfactory a result for the country as that in the 2000 election, when George Bush took the White House while Al Gore won the popular vote. This time Mr Bush won the popular vote by a much bigger margin. More importantly, he exorcised the ghost of the 2000 Florida recount that haunted his first four years by winning with a five percentage margin in the Sunshine State.

Bush and Kerry carve up Ohio by Peter Hanan.

No more claims will be heard now about his legitimacy as President. The son of George H.W. Bush has won a firm mandate. He and his ruthless political adviser Karl Rove – who, if this was England, would surely get a knighthood for his strategic brilliance – won validation for a campaign that stressed conservative values combined with resoluteness in the war on terror.

A majority of voters said consistently that the country was going in the wrong direction but on Tuesday they declared that they did not want to change their commander-in-chief in a time of war.

Mr Kerry swept the Democratic strongholds of the north-east and California while winning the swing state of Pennsylvania, in a campaign based on criticism of the conduct of the war and the economy. But Mr Bush built up his votes in the south and the mid-west, attracting support from people for whom the moral values he espoused and leadership on terrorism were more important issues.

He won despite the war in Iraq. It was an election in which the key issues of guns, gays and God motivated Republicans as much as the anti-war sentiment motivated Democrats.

Mr Bush had the support of the Nascar dads, the security moms and the evangelicals. In the 'blue' Republican states he capitalised on a culture where people are committed to their religion, and feel sometimes looked down upon by the leaders of the liberal culture of the big cities. But in cities like New York there were also Republicans strongly supportive of Mr Bush for practical reasons, such as a desire to stay the course in the war on terrorism.

Mr Denis Kelleher, chairman and CEO of Wall Street Access, an investment company in Manhattan, also hopes that Mr Bush will be able to bridge divisions and get more done in a second term, without having to face re-election. 'Bush has no vice-president that he has to protect,' he said. 'He can bring the country together, not wondering how it would affect his re-election effort. He will want to be judged as a statesman.'

He would also want to heal frayed relations with allies.

The election also increased the Republican Party's majorities in the House of Representatives and the Senate. Voters in post-9/11 America declined to renew their traditional preference for a divided government, where a Congress of one party acts as a brake on a president from another.

Not for 30 years has the Republican Party enjoyed such a long period in power in the House of Representatives. This monopoly in Washington gives Mr Bush an opportunity to push forward a conservative agenda that includes making his tax cuts permanent and advancing a constitutional ban on gay marriage.

He will have an opportunity to appoint two to three judges to the nine-member Supreme Court during the next four years. All the judges are getting on in years, and Chief Justice William Rehnquist, aged 80, has thyroid cancer. If he retires, Mr Bush might appoint one of his favourites as chief justice, Clarence Thomas or Antonin Scalia, both of whom oppose Roe v Wade, the ruling which legalised abortion, and nominate a conservative judge to replace him.

Only time will tell if the President, who has so far governed to his conservative base, will reach out to become what he once promised to be, a 'uniter and not a divider'. He will certainly have to reach out to conservative-leaning Democrats in the 100-member Senate to make up the 60 votes necessary to break a filibuster on the judicial appointments he will want to make.

Given the second term that was denied to his father and a supportive Congress, Mr Bush may indeed cast an eye to history and make some tough legislative decisions, on social security and Medicare reform, for example, and try to bring down a federal deficit that will exceed $400 billion this year.

The President is also likely to shake up his team. No one in the administration paid with their jobs for mistakes and blunders in a war that has cost the lives of over 1,100 US soldiers and possibly 100,000 Iraqis – but perhaps they will now that the election is over and dumping a cabinet member will no longer be an electoral liability.

There is much speculation about who will come and go. The Secretary of Defence, Donald Rumsfeld, now in his 70s, may depart to bring new civilian leadership to the beleaguered Pentagon. Colin Powell has made no secret of his unhappiness in the administration and national security adviser Condoleezza Rice has been tipped for his job. The new team will face some harsh realities abroad.

The insurgency in Iraq gathers strength daily; the US armed forces are overstretched. The war on terrorism is far from being won. North Korea may have half a dozen nuclear weapons.

The Democrats are devastated by the result. They can only ask: what more could we have done? They energised an often fractious base in their rage against Bush, they got out a record turnout, they registered millions of new supporters. They matched the fund-raising ability of the wealthier Republicans and were helped by an election law that allows wealthy individuals such as billionaire investor George Soros to pour unlimited money into independent groups known as '527s' that could attack the opposition in TV commercials.

John O'Donoghue (right), Minister for Arts, Sports and Tourism, with John Kelly (left), host of RTÉ Radio 1's The Mystery Train *and RTÉ ONE's* The View, *at the launch of RTÉ's Moving Pictures in which members of the public record their opinion of paintings in the National Gallery in Dublin, some of which Mr Kelly will broadcast to mark the gallery's 150th anniversary. Photograph: Alan Betson.*

They had everything going for them. They took on the President at a time when Mr Bush was being battered with a steady stream of bad news. They had a candidate who won the debates with the President and managed to make it a close race, but they still lost the presidential election and they saw their numbers dwindle in both houses of Congress.

The conclusion will be drawn that they lost because the President turned out to be a brilliant, energetic campaigner, though his relentless effort to win Pennsylvania fell short despite 44 visits, more than to any other state.

They lost because the Bush-Cheney camp managed to make the election campaign a referendum on the challenger, portraying him as a flip-flopper, someone who would send mixed messages to the enemy, who represented defeatism rather than strength. No one who was in the United States during the last few months could have escaped hearing in attack ads Mr Kerry's own words to explain his protest vote against a war requisition used against him time after time: 'I actually voted for the $87 billion before I voted against it.'

They lost most of all because the Republicans matched them in energising their base and motivating supporters on issues such as gay marriages and opposition to abortion.

A debate within Democratic ranks will now get under way – it has probably started – about who will challenge the next Republican candidate for the White House in four years. If the majority in a deeply divided America has tipped towards the evangelists, what hope has a figure like Hillary Clinton, Democratic senator for New York, who has been vilified for years by the right?

There has been much talk about how the Clintons would see an opening for the former First Lady in a Kerry defeat. She may well make her long-anticipated run in four years but many Democrats will look for a more centrist champion. Her challenger in the primaries could be Mr Kerry's running mate, John Edwards, but he did not perform strongly during the campaign, and could not even keep his own state of North Carolina in line: it voted for Bush and his US Senate seat there went to a Republican.

Perhaps Mr Kerry will make another run in 2008 but defeated presidential candidates rarely get a second chance (Richard Nixon was an exception).

The deep despair of the Democrats was expressed by an Ohio Democrat, Dan Foley, the elected Montgomery County Clerk of Courts in Dayton. 'I have never seen the kind of emotion and activism on the part of Democrats in a presidential campaign,' he told me in an e-mail. 'Yesterday about 3.30 p.m. I saw a guy standing in the pouring rain with no umbrella and no raincoat holding a sign that said 'VOTE FOR CHANGE'. Sunday night I was driving home from a rally and about 10 p.m. I saw two middle-aged women putting Kerry-Edwards signs in a public right of way on a fairly busy street.

'People came to Dayton from all over because they knew they could possibly have an impact here. Bill Clinton called my house twice [via recorded message] on the day before the election telling me to vote, ACT [Americans Coming Together] called a couple of times seeking volunteers, and we had many people walking door to door for the last two months. One guy walking with me had streams of sweat cascading down his forehead last Saturday but he kept walking.

'Our county is the highest county in the state for mortgage foreclosures [as clerk of courts, I'm the keeper of the record] as a percentage of the population; we have been hit hard by manufacturing losses; my wife knows a guy who is training the new person who is taking over his outsourced job; and now my state just approved this gay marriage issue that has nothing to do with either helping the economy or moving Ohio forward in a progressive manner.

'I am almost 40 years old and I can't remember feeling this bad about a campaign result.'

FRIDAY, 12 NOVEMBER 2004

'Onward Journey' Begins with Trip to Park

Frank McNally

Mrs McAleese embarked on her second term as President yesterday, describing her inauguration as the start of an 'onward journey'.

This was also the title of a musical tribute from piper Liam O'Flynn. But the theme was almost fatally undermined when the vintage Rolls-Royce used to carry Mrs McAleese to and from Dublin Castle initially refused to make the return trip. As the President exited St Patrick's Hall, the 1948 Silver Wraith failed to respond to the urgings of veteran driver, Garda Mick O'Hora. Parked to one side of the Castle Yard and unnoticed by all but a few concerned Gardaí and journalists, the car continued to veto any further part in the proceedings for several minutes, while Mrs McAleese greeted well-wishers.

Garda O'Hora kept his cool, however, and the Rolls finally purred back into life in time to bring the President on the first leg of her onward journey – back to Áras an Uachtaráin.

It was the only hitch in an otherwise flawless ceremony. Mrs McAleese also began her second term with a backward nod to the theme of the first. Urging those who still hesitated to take the last step across 'the bridge of peace on this island', she pledged to do her best 'to make us comfortable in each other's company' on the opposite side. The DUP were not there to hear the promise, but the Official Unionists were represented among the 700 guests.

The eight church leaders to officiate at the ceremony included, for the first time, a representative of the Islamic community. Sheikh Hussein Halawa offered a prayer that the world would return 'to the path of sanity' and said to Mrs McAleese: 'We ask Allah to assist you in your efforts for the betterment of the Irish nation and the service of world peace.'

Guests at the inauguration also included 700 children, representing schools in every Irish county, who watched the ceremony on a giant screen in the Castle Yard. Fears that politics has alienated the nation's youth were assuaged when the relatively mute reception for Westlife's Nicky Byrne gave way to wild cheers for the arrival of the Taoiseach. The Bertie-mania was matched only by the reception for the President herself.

Mrs McAleese did not have to contest an election for her second term. But the winner of the competition to dress her for the inauguration – Dubliner Aideen Bodkin – secured a popular mandate in the Castle yard. The vintage look, complete with 1950s-style jacket, took off more readily than the car of the same era.

'I'm mad about fashion and I thought it was very nice – everything matched,' said Andrea Hayde (13) from Cashel Community School. Her friend Ashley Ryan (12) agreed, but thought the President even nicer than her clothes: 'She's sound out!'

President McAleese last night hosted a State reception for 2,000 guests at Dublin Castle, which was followed by a fireworks display.

FRIDAY, 12 NOVEMBER 2004

West Bank Wearily Awaits the Return of a Leader

Michael Jansen, in Ramallah

Towers of black smoke from burning tyres rose over Ramallah early yesterday morning. The Israeli checkpoint at Kalandia, the gateway from Jerusalem to the West Bank, was deserted, streets were empty, shops shuttered.

The citizens of Kalandia, Ramallah and al-Bireh, wearied by the Ramadan fast and anxiety

Mary McAleese and her husband Martin greet members of the public after her inauguration at Dublin Castle for her second term as President of Ireland. Photograph: Eric Luke.

over the health of their President, were still at home in their beds after sitting in front of their television sets all night waiting for news from Paris.

The announcement of his death came at half past four in the morning. Few were awake to hear the proclamation.

Four hours later at the presidential compound, the muqata, on the edge of Ramallah, the international media and a scattering of Palestinians were making their way down the slope to the main gate.

An old woman in long black dress, black cloak edged with white embroidery, her head covered in a black scarf, walked sedately down the slope. Her face was pale, tears glistened on her cheeks. Halfway down, the media and a few other Palestinians had begun their vigil outside the gate. Palestinian flags hung limply at half-mast. Two giant flags were draped down the side of the bank of buildings behind the muqata.

The leadership was meeting inside, preparing for his funeral and completing the succession process begun two weeks ago when Mr Arafat was flown to France for treatment. The media and populace were kept at bay by soldiers in green uniforms and dark red berets. As the gate opened to admit cars, we could glimpse bulldozers at work across the wide expanse of parking lot, clearing away the debris of the 2002 Israeli assault on the muqata, and spreading sand along the far wall.

Mr Arafat will be buried this afternoon in a temporary concrete tomb so his body could be moved to Jerusalem if and when the Palestinians establish their state and reclaim East Jerusalem as its capital. It was Mr Arafat's wish to be interred in the holy city on the Haram al-Sharif, the Noble Sanctuary, claimed by Israel as the Temple Mount. Near the grave a small mosque will be erected to replace one blown up by the Israelis.

On the doorstep of a house across from the gate sat three shebab, lads, wearing jeans, T-shirts and black-and-white checked kuffiyas on their heads. They are students at Bir Zeit University near Ramallah and members of Mr Arafat's Fatah movement. Mr Khaled Salman said they had come early in the morning and would stay until Mr Arafat returned home. 'No one asked us to come. We want to be here, to show respect,' he said.

Since many Palestinians have accused Egypt of hijacking the funeral by holding the official ceremony in Cairo, I asked if they minded that the religious service would be held there before Mr Arafat is flown by helicopter to the muqata. Ahmad shrugged. 'It is not nice for world leaders to go to Cairo, but they cannot come here because of the occupation. He will have a proper funeral here in Ramallah amongst his own people.'

Television teams, photographers and reporters ambushed Palestinian personalities as they walked along the street outside the muqata. Dr Hanan Ashrawi, a member of the Legislative Council, also commented on the decision to hold the official ceremony in Cairo. 'The Egyptians have a sense of closeness to the president and they feel they have to do him justice. The heads of state and dignitaries can go there to uphold his stature,' she said.

Dr Ahmad Tibi, a Palestinian citizen of Israel who had been an adviser to Mr Arafat for many years, observed: 'Israel lost a great opportunity to

Palestinian security guards try to protect the coffin of the Palestinian leader Yasser Arafat as it is carried through a crowd of thousands of mourners inside his compound in Ramallah on the West Bank where he was buried. Photograph: Oleg Popov/Reuters.

negotiate with Arafat for a two-state solution [involving] a Palestinian state with East Jerusalem as its capital living next to Israel. This is the only option for a solution.'

Palestinians argue that no other leader has the respect or the popular appeal to make the compromises necessary to reach a solution.

I met Mrs Rawya Shawa, a legislator from Gaza and sharp critic of Mr Arafat's rule, in the lobby of the Grand Park Hotel. 'I know the value of Arafat as a national leader and his positive effect on Palestinian life,' she said, 'but I am not certain he left us a proper administration. Of course, he is not totally to blame. We also have the occupation, but he could have left us something better.

'He could have left us law and order. Without order there could be civil war.'

SATURDAY, 13 NOVEMBER 2004

All Things to All People

Mark Brennock

In the typical Bertie interview there are a few standard statistics-based litanies: Falling unemployment, economic growth, improving pupil-teacher ratios, more money spent on health. The message is: You guys concentrate on the negative all the time. You don't point out how good things are.

In an interview to mark the 10th anniversary next week of his election as Fianna Fáil leader, he makes these points again, but there is a new message that he is keen to put across too. 'Life is still tough' for a lot of people, he says. He also remarks on the fall-off in voluntary work in support of schools, sports clubs and community organisations, which has come with growing economic prosperity. The successful must give something back to society.

His eyes have been opened, he says, by learning that the Rutland Street School in inner city Dublin has tempted children from deprived backgrounds to attend school by offering them breakfast when they get there. He was taken aback by a recent report on Travellers showing how many were still living on the side of the road. He is proud of the economic progress, but says he wants to be remembered for improving the lot of the underprivileged.

It has been said for months that the Taoiseach is genuinely surprised and annoyed that his Government is seen as right wing. After the local and European elections in June, the party decided to reposition itself as a party of social justice.

In interviews, the Taoiseach usually emphasises the first part of the party's 2002 election slogan: A Lot Done. This week he is keen to acknowledge social problems and to emphasise the second part of that slogan: More To Do.

His personal political outlook defies typecasting. He is not in the centre, but often seems to be on both sides. On every issue of importance in Irish society Bertie Ahern can convincingly give expression to apparently opposing positions. He is a traditional daily Mass-goer throughout Lent and gives up drink for the month of November. He is also a non-traditional separated man who had a long and public second relationship.

He leads a Government implementing much of the traditional right-of-centre economic agenda, but this week insists, 'I am one of the few socialists left in Irish politics.'

He led Republican Ireland to historic compromise in relation to Northern Ireland, while keeping a portrait of Pádraig Pearse above his desk. He was against the invasion of Iraq while facilitating the invaders' passage through Shannon. He led his party away from the mire of Charles Haughey, Ray Burke and Liam Lawlor, while being slow to disown them unambiguously.

He is left and right, traditional and unorthodox, religious and secular, social democrat and economic liberal, Croker and Old Trafford. Some see this as a Machiavellian riding of two horses. However, he rejects the suggestion that he deliberately positions

Bertie Ahern en route through Government Buildings to the Dáil. Photograph: Bryan O'Brien.

himself on both sides of every significant divide in Ireland. It just comes naturally, he says. 'I genuinely believe in being an inclusive person,' he says. 'I don't have to work at it because it comes naturally to me.' It's about being tolerant, and seeing things the way the other person sees them.

'For this year I have studied [Ian] Paisley. I have studied Paisley's tactics. I would, in negotiations, study the other person and try to understand their views.'

He says he knows people often demand of him that he express his own view on an issue or 'take a stand' when he is reluctant to. 'But it's not a question of what is my view. Ultimately, only things that have a consensus … are likely to succeed. Why does the European model work? Because two world wars have forced people to come together and not have wars any more, and now they try to find consensus.'

He is much more a chairman than a chief: what others call dithering, he calls consensus-seeking. This is exemplified when he is asked his view on the liberal agenda issue of the moment, gay unions or marriage. There is no consensus now, he says. He knows gay people who have other priorities in terms of taxation and inheritance rights. The Government is committed to treating gay people as equals in society. We need calm, rational debate, he says. And at the end of a very reasonable discourse on a complex subject you realise he has expressed no view at all.

It is a style that has worked well for a decade. Today, his term as taoiseach equals that of Seán Lemass. Next Friday he will have been party leader for 10 years. There is no fantastic replacement leader waiting in the wings. But he says he has no intention of pursuing Éamon de Valera's record of 21 years as taoiseach, which would require him to remain in the job until 2018, the year he turns 67. Now 53, he still intends to quit politics when he is 60 [September 2011]. 'I just think you would have been around a long time [35 years].' But he adds that his appetite for the job is as strong as ever, and while he sees things he has done, he also sees things he hasn't done.

He gives a preamble first to emphasise the positive. Gone are 'the 17 per cent unemployment, the deprivation that was in the inner city when I started being a political activist, Gardiner Street, the slums, the squalor, the 14 flats to one toilet. The changes are immense.' Emigration is now voluntary. Educational participation has shot up.

But there is now a 'new agenda' of problems. 'We have by and large created a very good corporate Ireland, a very good business Ireland. We have good sports, good leisure Ireland. But there is still a section of people, a lot of them in my own constituency; even though we are putting a lot of money into new flat blocks, life is still tough for a lot of those people.' He says there are discrepancies in the pupil-teacher ratio between schools in upper middle class areas and those in less well off areas.

In Rutland Street School, in his own constituency, 'when we started doing breakfasts in the school, the percentage of people coming with their kids went up dramatically, and that was a bit of an eye-opener for me. It wasn't the parents who brought them to the school, the kids came to the school because they were getting a breakfast.' He refers to the recent report on Travellers which talked of the number of people still living on the roadside. 'When you go to bed these nights and you think of people by the roadside it doesn't do your heart good,' he says. 'They are the kind of

Bertie Ahern at a reception in the Great Southern Hotel in Galway to mark his 10 years as leader of Fianna Fáil with (left) Emma Brennan and (right) Aoife Goloden, both members of the Cumann de Barra branch of the party at Galway University. Photograph: Joe O'Shaughnessy.

issues I would like to see through and I look forward to doing that for another seven years.'

He says that accompanying the new prosperity, the fall-off in social involvement and voluntary activity by citizens is notable. He has twice read the book *Bowling Alone: The Collapse and Revival of American Community*, by American Robert D. Putnam, on how people are becoming increasingly disconnected from family, friends, community and democratic structures, and it has struck a chord with him. There was once an Irish tradition of people giving their time voluntarily to community organisations, St Vincent de Paul, schools, sports clubs and churches. This is fading.

When he is out of the country, local diplomats are asked to find a suitable Catholic church where he can attend Mass. But religion is absent from his public persona. Asked about the recent public mixing of religion by George Bush and Rocco Buttiglione, he says: 'I'm totally opposed to wearing religion on my sleeve and I don't like that and I don't think people should do it.' He quotes a 1960 speech in which John F. Kennedy insisted there should be no barrier to his becoming the first Catholic president of the US. 'So it is apparently necessary for me to state once again – not what kind of church I believe in, for that should be important only to me – but what kind of America I believe in.' Kennedy went on to express belief in the absolute separation of church and state.

'I think religion gives you some values,' says Ahern. 'Some of them I manage to stick to and some I don't. That's for me. It's not something to push on to people. But I greatly admire people in the churches, all of them. I think they are good people. My own private faith should not impinge on my public role and it doesn't.'

After 9/11, he says, he took an interest in the Islamic world: after Omagh he took an interest in the Church of Ireland. He says as a private individual, he believes involvement in a church – whichever one – is good for people. 'I've got more and more interested in recent years in the Koran and listening to more and more Muslims around my own constituency. You do get a sense of security and support from being close to a church. That's not craw-thumping ... When times are rough for people, if it's a bereavement, a difficulty at work, a difficulty with relationships, listening to the analysis given by church people is a good thing,' he says.

The private Bertie tends to remain private. The message before every interview with the Taoiseach is that he won't discuss his personal life. His separation from his wife Miriam and the end of his long-term relationship with Celia Larkin are well known. Asked whether his own experience of being in public life makes him believe Irish people are tolerant, he says: 'Yes I do. The political system is very fair, very tolerant, and so are the media. There is a small element of the media that goes after these things for colour. People are caring, they are understanding, and they don't seek to use it ... I think for a person like me, that's something you appreciate very greatly.'

He agrees with the observation that he has very little interest in having personal wealth. 'I don't. I have a modest house and I feel lucky enough to have it. Obviously, I have commitments to my family that I have been very happy to contribute to. I have a modest house in a nice area, my own home area, and I am happy with that. People mightn't believe this but I have a very socialist view on life. I have it in my mind that I own the Phoenix Park, and I own the Botanic Gardens, I own Dublin Zoo. Because the State participates in these things, I am free to go in there whenever the opening hours are. And I don't feel I need to own any of these things. They are there.

'I don't feel I need to own a huge house with a huge glasshouse when I can go down the road 10 minutes and do it [visit the Botanic Gardens]. It's just the way I think about things. What is the best form of equality? It is the fact that the richest family in this area can go on a Sunday afternoon to the Bots, and the poorest family can too. And they can both share the same things. So I have fought for 15 years to improve the resources of things like that, the Phoenix Park, Dublin Zoo, and also things like sport.'

He acknowledges that this view of collective property rights is not one shared by many wealthy people and property owners, most of whom would like a few acres of their own in Dublin 4 and 6. 'I know that, but I can truthfully tell you that that isn't for me.'

He says he could have taken a job as chief executive of the Mater Private Hospital, which was offered to him after an interview in the 1970s. Or he could have set himself up as a tax consultant for hospital consultants, as he had been encouraged to do, but chose not to.

'If I had done those things I would be a very wealthy guy. But I opted not to do that. If I can go on my annual holidays to Kerry, get a few days sometimes, if I can get now and again to Old Trafford, if I have enough money for a few pints and if I can look after Miriam and the kids, I don't care a damn, I couldn't care. And tomorrow if I hadn't got very much it wouldn't matter. I'm well paid so I can't moan. But if I hadn't got that I wouldn't moan too much either. I have no desire to have a big house, no desire to have land. I'd consider it a nuisance, actually.'

He acknowledges that not many of the people hanging around the Fianna Fáil tent at the Galway Races would have this attitude to money and property. He says again he would like people who have been successful to give something back to society. But he insists that these people are the engines of the growth that is needed to help others.

'The only way we will ever succeed in helping the people in need is having a strong economy that generates the wealth so that we can redistribute the wealth. If there are not the guys at the Galway Races in the tent who are earning wealth, who are creating wealth, then I can't redistribute that. I can talk a lot about what we can do for the less well off in society, but I can't do anything for them.'

When it is put to him that Fianna Fáil is no longer the anti-Treaty party, or the party of the men and women of no property, he agrees to an extent. It is still 'a very Republican Party ... we still care, we care about the language, we care about things Irish'. And in relation to the fact that it has a lot of wealthy members and backers, he says: 'But we are a party of people who have come through the ranks. If you go through a lot of our people who are doing very well now, their fathers would have been very ordinary Joe Soaps. As Irish life has lifted they, having done absolutely nothing wrong, have achieved good success. Many of them are still prepared to go out and do their work on the ground and put work into the party.'

And there is no demand from party members and parliamentary party members for cuts in capital gains tax or increases in capital allowances. Rather, the priorities emerging from 'the hard core of Fianna Fáil people' concerned maximising increases for social welfare recipients, producing a good financial package to deal with disability and improving social housing.

'All our discussions have been about trying to help the less well off in society, the homeless, the Travelling community, so I think that the heart and soul of Fianna Fáil are still there.'

MONDAY, 15 NOVEMBER 2004

An Irishman's Diary

Godfrey Fitzsimons

How pleasurable to look back from this autumnal vantage-point to the piping days of summer! The endless sun-kissed afternoons. The glad cries of little children on the golden sands. Tarquin and Jocasta dancing on the terrace in the moonlight above a wine-dark sea.

The sights and smells and sensations of foreign climes. The hotel breakf ... Aaaaarrrgghhh! (Sorry, this is hard for me. Try again.) The ... hotel ... breakfast ... BUFFET! (Made it!)

Dr Charles Bird of RTÉ after receiving his honorary degree from University College, Dublin. Photograph: Bryan O'Brien.

Holiday apartment-renters (self-catering, ugh!) might not know of this pestilence, so pull up a chair, and I will explain. It used to be the ritzier hotels that offered this so-called facility, but like so many things these days it has suffered prole-drift and has moved downmarket in the hospitality industry.

Time was when you'd go into the dining-room of your modest hotel, and a waitress would come and take your breakfast order and serve it in the fullness of time. No more. Now, when you stagger in bleary-eyed, you're confronted by an array of assorted groceries on central tables, seductively displayed in baskets and glass jugs and on hot plates, and you're invited to help yourself.

The advantage of this arrangement for the hotel is that fewer staff are required; for the punters the selling point is that they can stuff their faces to bursting-point for a fixed price. But such seemingly democratic processes always have a downside, and in this instance it is that the prospect of open-ended morning grubstakes produces a startling transformation in people you might otherwise assume to be prosperous, delightfully middle-class, and therefore civilised.

Fat chance. Faced with this cornucopia of gastronomic riches these sophisticates turn into nothing short of ravening wolves. Get in the way of a Frenchwoman with orange skin bent on filling her cake-hole with scrambled egg or a stout Dutch burgher in a look-at-me-I'm-on-holiday shirt with his piggy eyes fixed on the cheese or cooked meats platter, and you risk being trampled into the deep-pile.

To make matters worse, you are suffering from the kind of acute disequilibrium that such infinite variety provokes in those of us who are happiest concentrating on one thing at a time. So, after a few minutes' orientation (bread rolls and toast nor'-nor'-east, cereals due south, juices north-by-north-west) you home in, to start assembling the components of your breakfast. Then, balancing your choice of comestibles in both hands, you beat against the current back to your table, avoiding that Italian woman with just the hint of a moustache making her second trip (or is it her third?) to the cheese table.

You sink with relief into your chair, quaff your juice and reach for the cereal spoon. There isn't one. The knife, fork and coffee spoon are all present and correct in their appointed place on the table, but the cereal spoon is AWOL. You furtively check neighbouring tables to see if they are similarly bereft, and indeed they are.

So back you track to the cereals table, and there they lurk, the little spoony rascals, a serried line of them peeping coyly from an enveloping linen cloth. Why this cutlery apartheid? Why won't the cereal spoon associate with the other implements in the place-setting, until it's made to? Funny, the milk-jug appears to be missing from the table, too. How can you eat muesli without milk? Oh, madame, s'il vous plaît! Comment? Oh, le milk-jug est sur la central table, is it? Of course it is! Silly me! Back you go …

After the muesli marathon the croissant melts deliciously in the hot coffee (oh, yes, indeed, dunking is absolutely de rigueur in even the most hoity-toity of Continental caravanserais). And there's your pert little pot of jam, just waiting to spread itself languorously on the crisp-crusted roll. But you forgot the butter. So back you track yet again …

With practice and hard experience all this morning misery can be conquered. Strategies can be devised to meet it head on. The real irritant of the buffet scenario is if you're a person of small matutinal appetite, as I am. Not for me the eggs, the bacon strips, the unclassifiable Continental sliced sausage with suspicious white bits in it, the holey cheese. Give me a glass of OJ, possibly but not necessarily a bowl of cereal, a croissant and a fresh-baked roll, and I'm as happy as a sandboy, whatever that is.

But what makes my gorge rise is that I'm still asked to pay the same as those gorgers of ham, sausage, eggs, cheese, bacon and more sausage ('I don't mind if I do!').

But I have found the answer. It consists of two short words: room service. Oh, I can already hear you tutting such words as 'unnecessary extravagance', 'shameful self-indulgence', 'lazy sod' and so on. Listen, for only a couple of euro extra, if you're a modest breakfaster like me, there's usually a Continental breakfast choice available in room service as well as the full Monty, unlike in the restaurant downstairs, and it's invariably cheaper. Also, if you're a cheapskate like me, you can squirrel some of the rolls, cheese and ham away in your bag to use as lunch later.

No, I will not apologise for being such a tightwad. I see it as a kind of virtuous vengeance on the hotel for trying to screw an exorbitant fee out of me for a breakfast I don't want. Yes, revenge can be sweet indeed, sweet as a breakfast croissant dunked in coffee. But dunked in my own room, far from that grunting, jostling, swigging piggery downstairs.

FRIDAY, 26 NOVEMBER 2004

Army Emerging as Key Wild Card in Struggle

Chris Stephen, in Kiev

Colonel Yuri Andreyivich Kasyanov ended his 32-year-career in the Ukrainian military yesterday morning. Shortly after breakfast he resigned his commission, donned his full green uniform with gold epaulettes, and went out on the freezing streets of the capital to throw his support behind the opposition demonstrators.

'I came to support them. I believe in democracy,' he told me, standing in his green army overcoat with bronze stars and peaked cap with gold braid across the front. 'I resigned from the army today so I can come and be here.'

Young demonstrators milling around him in their familiar garb of orange scarves and ribbons lined up to congratulate him, but the question on their lips was – will the rest of the army follow? In the ever more intense game of political poker played by government and opposition in recent days, the army is emerging as the key wild card.

Support from the armed forces will guarantee victory for either Prime Minister Viktor Yanukovich or opposition leader Viktor Yushchenko, each of whom insists he is the rightful president. For now the forces are staying out of it, with Defence Minister Oleksander Kuzmuk telling his troops to 'act in a measured way, and fulfil your constitutional duty in the respect of the law.' But if, as Yushchenko has warned, it is decided that the law was broken, by either government or opposition, the process will enter uncharted territory.

As the stakes get higher and the threat of violence between government and opposition increases, inaction may no longer be an option for Ukraine's armed forces.

Ukrainian police cadets show their support for the opposition leader Viktor Yushchenko. Photograph: Mykola Lazarenko/Reuters.

'Inside the army at all levels everyone is talking about this. It is hard to know what the conclusion will be,' said the colonel, formerly a lawyer with the army's internal security office. 'It is difficult to say what the final view will be.' But suppose push comes to shove and, for instance, Yushchenko demands army support to force his way into the presidential palace? 'I don't know, I don't know,' says the colonel. 'Right now, they would not obey. The high command would never obey that order. But many of the junior officers feel differently, many of them support this protest.'

Each day TV pictures show small handfuls of army and navy officers among the huge opposition crowds in Kiev, but the colonel said other officers are firmly supportive of Yanukovich's government. 'There are a lot of different opinions. Nobody knows what the army will finally decide,' he said.

In fact, the battle over who is the rightful president slices through the army's key doctrine, which is defence of the country. 'When you join the army you promise to defend Ukraine, and that is what the army will do. We will sacrifice our lives, that is our promise.' Yet Yushchenko has repeatedly warned that the country is on the brink of civil war, and the army may soon have to make a choice.

'I am finished with the army. I do not want to serve under the present government,' said Col Kasyanov. But if Yushchenko became president, and asked for commanders he could trust? 'I'd be back in the service immediately,' says the colonel with a smile. Complicating the problem still

A young Yushchenko supporter sporting the opposition's campaign colour orange at a rally in Independence Square in the capital, Kiev. Photograph: Darko Vojinovic/AP.

further is the need to restore prestige. Col Kasyanov spent the main part of his career with the Red Army of the former Soviet Union, when Ukraine was part of the USSR controlled from Moscow. At the time the army was powerful, its units disciplined and morale high.

Since independence budget cuts and low morale have become the norm, and the armed forces have endured a series of disastrous body blows to its prestige.

In 2001 a Ukrainian air defence missile fired in error during an exercise and shot down a Russian airliner over the Black Sea, killing all 64 on board. Two years ago a top-line SU-27 fighter jet crashed into crowds during an air show, killing 78 spectators in a fireball. And the decision to send 1,600 troops to join coalition forces in Iraq has also proved divisive at home, with many Ukrainians opposed to the war.

Yet the Ukrainian army can draw on powerful units, not least the Cossacks, who live in the southern plains and once provided some of the world's finest cavalry units.

For now, the army is keen to stay on the sidelines, but if the peaceful protests turn violent it will face an awkward choice between siding with the government or with the demonstrators. Making the right choice could see its past mistakes forgotten and its reputation soar. But the problem now confounding officers and conscripts in barrack rooms across the land is just what this choice should be.

SATURDAY, 27 NOVEMBER 2004

Israelis Troubled by Army's 'Culture of Impunity'

Nuala Haughey, in Rafah, southern Gaza

Iman Al-Hams's school is just around the corner from her southern Gaza home, but the teenager's daily journey took her past what is undoubtedly one of the most dangerous parts of the occupied Palestinian territories.

Her neighbourhood of Tel Sultan in Rafah abuts the Egyptian border and her school is overlooked by a heavily fortified Israeli army outpost perched on a not-too-distant sand ridge. The school building, like all the houses and shops along the street facing this border zone, is pockmarked from Israeli tank and gunfire. People living in houses facing the Girit outpost cover their windows and peel open their doors nervously to peer at the tall, skinny tower swathed in camouflage netting.

Iman (13) was making her way to school shortly before 7 a.m. on 5 October last when, for reasons which no one can explain, she strayed off course and into the lethal no-entry zone in the shadow of the Girit post. She was wearing her candy-striped school uniform and a white headscarf and was carrying her school satchel on her back.

Within minutes, Iman was gunned down by soldiers from the post, whose rules of engagement allow them to shoot to kill anyone who enters what is effectively a free-fire zone within 300 metres of the border posts. The soldiers said they suspected she was a terrorist carrying explosives. Her satchel merely contained her schoolbooks.

Iman would have quietly joined the ranks of hundreds of Palestinian minors killed in the territories but for the fact that some soldiers were so disturbed about the incident and concerned that it would be covered up that they contacted the Israeli press.

The soldiers alleged that a company commander, Captain R, left the post that morning to pursue Iman across the sand. He then emptied his automatic rifle into her at point-blank range as she lay, dead or possibly only wounded, in a 'confirmation of kill' operation. This is military jargon for firing at combatants to ensure they are dead. It is not an acknowledged procedure in the Israeli military's rules of engagement, which prefers the term 'neutralise the threat'.

One soldier told the Hebrew newspaper *Yedioth Ahronoth* that the commander 'charged toward her by himself. He shot two bullets at her ... and then gave her a burst of automatic fire. There is no logical reason for what he did ... This is the most sickening thing I have ever seen during my army service. It was a desecration of a body. That is not what we are taught to do in the army.'

Captain R denies these claims. He says he responded to Palestinian gunfire aimed at him by firing a volley of automatic fire into the ground, not into Iman's body. He also alleges that soldiers framed him because he wished to make changes in the company, where relations between him and some of his subordinates were strained.

Notwithstanding the soldiers' graphic testimonies, a swift internal army investigation cleared Captain R of acting unethically in shooting Iman. He was suspended for losing the confidence of his soldiers and a 'command failure'.

However, with sustained pressure from the soldiers' revelations, the military police launched a separate investigation into the incident which led to Captain R being charged this week on five counts, including illegal use of a weapon, obstruction of justice and unbecoming conduct. He is awaiting trial.

The story took another disturbing turn this week when Israeli television aired a shocking tape of military communications at the time of the incident in which Captain R stated that he had 'confirmed the kill'. After Iman was dead, he was heard telling his soldiers: 'This is commander, anything that's mobile, that moves in the zone, even if it's a three-year-old, needs to be killed. Over'. The tape also indicates that soldiers identified Iman as a frightened girl before she was killed, although the army maintains that this communication was not heard by soldiers in the Girit outpost.

Iman's father, Samir Darwish Al-Hams, has followed intensely the ongoing Israeli media revelations concerning his daughter's death. 'Iman was executed, not shot from far away. I heard that on the tape they played on television and the soldiers had been saying that as well,' he said. Samir (50) was sitting next to a gold-framed poster of Iman, who was claimed as a 'martyr' by the Hamas militant group, even though she clearly was not an operative. The photograph on the poster, taken two months before her death, shows a thin girl who had inherited her father's dark eyes and intense stare. As he spoke, the familiar rat-tat-tat of gunfire, some distant, some quite close, could be heard.

'The first thing is that this criminal officer should be punished. The second thing is, I want to show how this army is dealing with our children and to show that these soldiers are intentionally executing – by 20 bullets penetrating her body – this kind of innocent child,' said Samir.

'If an Arab killed an Israeli young girl in this way, how would the state deal with him and how much time would he be sentenced to? I hear that they are trying him for a maximum sentence of three years. This is a silly sentence. If somebody had stolen a chicken here they could face a three-year sentence.'

The revelations around Iman's killing in Israeli media have raised disturbing questions in a society where military service is compulsory and solidarity with the defence forces is almost an article of faith.

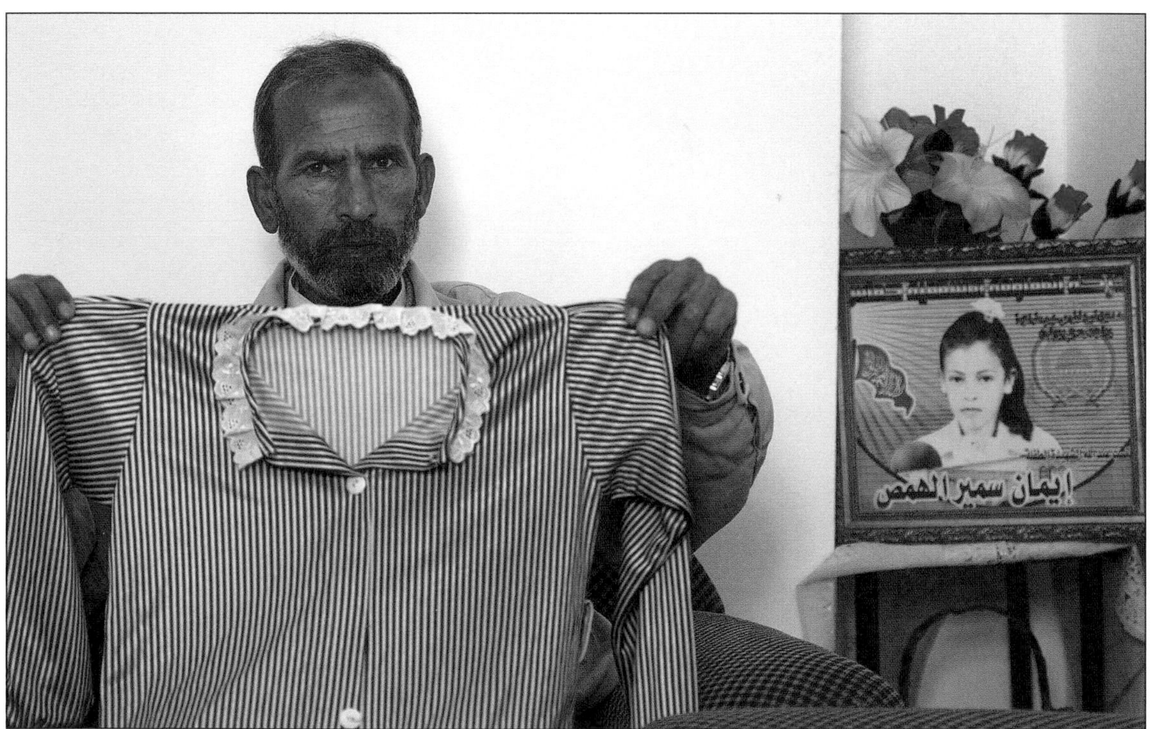

Samir Darwish al-Hams shows the school uniform of his 13-year-old daughter Iman who was shot dead by an Israeli soldier. Photograph: Nuala Haughey.

The Rafah controversy coincides with outrage over media allegations that Israeli soldiers abused the bodies of Palestinians killed during army operations, including a case in which soldiers posed for pictures with the severed head of a suicide bomber with a cigarette dangling from his mouth. These images, published last week in Yedioth Ahronoth, were reminiscent of the disturbing photographs of US soldiers placing Iraqi captives in degrading positions at Abu Ghraib prison near Baghdad.

A commentator in the right-wing Israeli newspaper *Maariv* this week blamed the corrupting effect of Israel's 37-year occupation of the Palestinian territories for making Israeli society 'sick'. 'Once upon a time, thousands of years ago, before we became an occupying people devoid of any inhibitions and one that holds the value of our enemies' lives in disdain, people here spoke seriously and whole-heartedly about the purity of arms,' wrote Mr Yael Paz-Melamed.

'In those days, which seem to have been elided from our collective psyche, there was not a commander in the army who would have given an order to kill in cold blood a 13-year-old girl ... on her way to school. And then go out, confirm the kill, and announce over the radio that the confirmation had been obtained.'

Soul-searching aside, the case also raises many practical questions about the rules of engagement of the army and, disturbingly, highlights the fact that such incidents are rarely investigated. Since the beginning of the four-year-long Israel-Palestinian hostilities, Israeli soldiers have killed at least 1,656 Palestinians who took no part in the fighting, according to the Israeli human rights group B'Tselem. Of these, 529 were children.

B'Tselem claims that these deaths take place amidst a 'climate of impunity' combined with rules of engagement that encourage a 'trigger-happy' attitude among soldiers. 'Over the past four years, the IDF conducted only 89 military police investigations into deaths and injuries of Palestinians. Of these investigations, only 22 resulted in indictments. To date, one soldier has been convicted of causing the death of a Palestinian. Thus in the vast majority of cases, no one is ever held accountable,' said B'Tselem spokeswoman Ms Sarit Michaeli.

An Israeli army spokeswoman, Maj Sharon Feingold, said the claim that a culture of impunity exits within the army is made out of context. 'War is an ugly thing and especially this kind of war that we are now fighting against Palestinian terrorism which uses civilian infrastructure to conduct military activity against soldiers and civilians. It is inevitable when civilian infrastructure is used that there will be civilian casualties,' she said. Maj Feingold added that youngsters were increasingly used as 'spotters' gathering information for terrorists, as bait to test the alertness of soldiers, or as attempted suicide bombers.

However, the nature of Israel's operations and incursions into neighbourhoods like Tel Sultan in operations to root out militants or uncover weapons means that Palestinian children are not safe anywhere.

Another bereaved family in Rafah's Tel Sultan neighbourhood is still awaiting any contact from the Israeli army six months after two of its members were shot in their heads on the rooftop of their home. Relatives of Asma Al Mughair (16) and her brother Ahmed (13) are convinced that the youngsters were killed by Israeli snipers during the siege of their neighbourhood as part of last May's massive Operation Rainbow in which the neighbourhood was pounded by Israeli munitions.

Then *The Irish Times* witnessed bloodstains on the rooftop where the children were killed and also discovered evidence that the roof of a house overlooking the site of the shooting had been used as an Israeli army snipers' lair. These included a loophole, spent bullet shells and an empty cardboard box of sniper ammunition. The Israeli army claimed the Al Mughair children were probably killed by a Palestinian explosive device in the area, but offered no explanation as to why such a device would be planted on a rooftop. Amnesty

International called for an independent investigation. The army conducted an internal inquiry and concluded that an investigation was not warranted.

'We are not able to determine that they were killed by Israeli fire or that there was any criminal intent,' explained Maj Feingold.

WEDNESDAY, 1 DECEMBER 2004

Nostalgia Tinged with a Little Hope as Bewley's Faithful Savour the Last Drop

Frank McNally

As befits a business founded by Quakers, Bewley's Cafés departed this world with a Quaker-style funeral. The mourners who queued outside the Grafton Street branch all day to pay their respects were determinedly sober.

Once inside, they drank nothing stronger than tea and coffee while celebrating the life of the dearly beloved in prose, poetry and song. And even as they said their goodbyes, many hoped the parting would be temporary. With the café doors closing behind him, the Lord Mayor updated supporters on the campaign to save 'the front room of the city' from permanent closure. It would require changes in both planning and rental law, Cllr Michael Conaghan said. But he added: 'We cannot allow a non-regulated rental market to drive every vestige of heritage off the streets of Dublin.'

Earlier, Michael James Ford of the Bewley's Theatre Group drew loud applause from customers in the Harry Clarke Room when he spoke of a 'glimmer of hope' that this was not the end. Dubliners still had a chance to decide whether the café remained as 'a monument to mahogany, stained glass and 1920s workmanship' or became 'a monument to mammon in a soulless age'.

Harry Clarke's stained glass window provides a colourful backdrop while customers have a morning coffee. Photo: Dara Mac Dónaill.

But the prevailing emotion in Grafton Street and Westmoreland Street yesterday was one of nostalgia for an era passing. Cameras flashed at the interiors all day as customers hedged their bets on whether they would be seen in this form again. A high number of buggies spoke of parents planning to tell children in times to come of the day they went to Bewley's.

The former *Irish Times* columnist, Sam McAughtry, who queued in Grafton Street with the artist Esmé Lewis, remembered arriving from Belfast in the 1970s and being welcomed in the café by three separate writers, Michael Hartnett, Benedict Kiely, and John B. Keane.

Staff at Bewley's Café on Grafton Street in Dublin hug each other on the last day of trading. Photograph: Dara Mac Dónaill.

Inside, nostalgia dominated the musical offerings. Managing director Cól Campbell danced with branch manager Deirdre Clarke as the theatre group performed the Carpenters' 'Yesterday Once More'. Hot-counter assistant Eugene O'Brien took a break from serving customers to deliver a magnificent version of 'Molly Malone' (an unfortunate precedent, in that she was a Dublin institution no one could save). Rathfarnham singer Ray McDonnell raised the rafters with 'Raglan Road'.

Campbell insisted that yesterday was not a sad day, but he admitted today would be as staff began new lives. Regretting that so much of the focus was on the cafés' physical structures, he compared the closures to the evacuation of the Blasket Islands. You could preserve the islands and the buildings on them, but today the community who lived and worked there would be gone, to be absorbed 'into the mainland'.

The daily specials blackboard in Grafton Street's balcony café became a multinational noticeboard yesterday as employees recorded the same message in umpteen languages: Au revoir, Adios, Ate mais, Zegnaj, Hejda, Auf Wiedersehen, Ciao, Slán, Goodbye.

SATURDAY, 4 DECEMBER 2004

They Won't be Home for Christmas

Róisín Ingle

On the 15th floor of a tower block in north London, an elderly Limerick woman tries to manoeuvre herself onto a chair using a walking stick and a Zimmer frame. Kathleen O'Connell (79) wants me to write a letter to a Co. Wicklow priest requesting a small prayer booklet entitled *A Shower Of Blessings*. She tells me where to find notepaper and an envelope and a first class stamp in her Abbey Road flat. The booklet only costs €1 but she wants to enclose £30 along with the letter. 'I'm not greedy,' she replies when I tell her what she already knows, that £30 is far too much.

She is, she says, like a monkey up a tree. 'I have high hopes,' she guffaws, laughter whooping out of her, hard and long and sad. There are the hopes that God will give her back the use of her legs so she will no longer be virtually housebound, relying on snatched conversations with a neighbour who brings shopping once a week. There are the hopes that someone will come and show an interest in her, someone kind to listen and laugh at her vast repertoire of jokes. There are the hopes that her remaining relatives in Ireland will visit more often. 'Who would bother with this life?' she sighs, buttering a slice of toast.

Kathleen is just one of hundreds of thousands of Irish people who were forced for economic reasons to emigrate in the 1950s and 1960s, the men destined for lives of hard labour and loneliness on building sites, on bridges, on tunnels, the women making money in factories and hotels. In 1961 alone the equivalent of €13.5m was sent back home in remittances.

For most of them there was no going back. Kathleen left Limerick in her early 20s to live with an aunt in London and worked in factories and hotels and 'didn't do too badly until now'. The man she married in England died when he was only 48 – they had no children – and she has lived in this flat alone for more than 20 years. The walls and most surfaces in her home are crowded with holy pictures. 'I've never seen such a religious flat before,' I say. 'Thank you,' she replies.

On the table is a box of Christmas cards she is planning to send. Would she go back to Ireland for Christmas if she could? 'No, I wouldn't want to see it at all, I don't want any part of it,' she says. 'There is no one there for me any more. I just want someone to keep me company here. I just don't want to be forgotten.' Of those living in post-boom Ireland she remarks: 'I don't think they know Irish people like me even exist. But here I am.'

We have all heard about the homeless Irish on the streets of London, the ones that reek of desperation and super-strength beer. We know about the ones queuing up at the soup kitchens, the ones that make it onto the lists of the wide variety of vital emigrant care organisations. We've heard stories about the Irish people who die on the streets and end up in the paupers' plots in Finchley, where coffins are made of cardboard and they dig deep so they can bury them twelve to a grave. Surveys carried out by the health service here show that Irish immigrants to England die younger and are at more risk of cancer, heart disease and mental illness than any other minority.

The recently announced 60 per cent increase in funding for the Unit for the Irish Abroad, part of the Department of Foreign Affairs, will go some way to help the visibly needy Irish in London, but it's becoming increasingly difficult to touch the lives of the invisible Irish, according to London Irish Centre Outreach worker Brian Boylan. 'The homeless Irish drunk on the street is a terrible reality but it's also a distraction from another less obvious problem,' he points out. It is certainly harder to help women like Kathleen O'Connell or Moira (not her real name) from Co. Waterford who sits in a tidy apartment in Kilburn every day with the radio on constantly, even as she sleeps. 'I'm not interested in the programmes – I just need to hear someone speaking to me,' she explains. 'Especially when I wake up. I don't know why but I do.'

Moira only came to the attention of Boylan when she went to ask advice about planning her funeral. 'She didn't want to cause anybody any fuss when she died,' he says.

The bell on Moira's flat is broken but that's grand, she says, because there aren't that many

Kathleen O'Connell. Photograph: David Bebber.

people who come to call. She arrived here from Waterford in 1942 as a 14-year-old, leaving the bed she shared with two sisters for a single bed in war-torn London. 'I wasn't forced to come but I don't remember anybody saying I shouldn't,' she says. She took a job in a make-up factory, sending most of her money home to Ireland every week and spending the rest on the cinema and sweets. She married at 16 to a man who drank and abused her for most of their marriage. 'I met him in the State cinema and I was in a state the rest of my life,' she says, managing a smile.

A girl, a boy and a set of twins she gave birth to all died as babies, and while she sees her two surviving children as often as she can, she doesn't make demands on their time. 'They have their own lives,' she says.

She turns 77 on December 20th. 'It has been a very lonely life,' she says. 'I helped my family in Ireland when they needed it, I sent parcels and money when they had nothing, but it isn't remembered now or spoken about. It's like it never happened.' She hasn't been home for Christmas in six years. If she did go home to Waterford she would have to stay in a B&B despite having family there.

'When I go back I don't feel good enough. When it comes to money and the clothes I wear I am different. The last time I went I got the feeling they didn't want me and I don't think I will be back there again. The Ireland that I knew doesn't exist anymore,' she says. 'It's great to see all the people spending money and having so much success and prosperity in Ireland. It came too late for me though.' Boylan recently arranged for her to be presented with a lifetime achievement award, a Cavan crystal trophy with her name etched on it that has pride of place in her cabinet. 'It's a lovely thing to be acknowledged,' she says.

After trawling through the electoral register, Boylan has collated a list of around 100 Irish-born people in the Kilburn and Cricklewood area who live in isolation, separated even from the Irish community, afraid to ask for help not only from the system but from their own. When he tried to fill tables for a dinner at the centre he had ten refusals for every acceptance of the free night out.

'We are talking about people who are too ashamed to be seen by the mainstream Irish community. They feel like failures and so just hide away,' he says. He goes to visit them but says it is impossible to give them all the attention they deserve. 'These on the list are only the ones I know about. There are 30 other boroughs in London filled with them,' he says. 'There used to be a saying, "the craic is good in Cricklewood". Ireland may be affluent now and the affluent Irish can be seen all over London, but the craic isn't good for many Irish people here and we need to start acknowledging that.'

Things have improved for some. After a year in hospital suffering from depression, John Donnelly (54) from Co. Meath finally has his own flat. He has been away from Ireland since he was 16. He tried going back once but ended up sleeping in hay sheds and barns, unable to get support from his community, and so left for London again. He spends most of his day in Paddy Power's bookies in Holloway; it's a social outlet but, with a new home to maintain, he is more careful now about keeping money safe for bills. He looks askance at the new Ireland and says going home for Christmas would be 'a waste of time. It's full of people trying to keep up with each other by getting further and further into debt,' he observes. 'If you are struggling they prefer you to go away so they don't have to look at you. I am proud of being Irish but if you are not self-sufficient there you better expect to be punished.' He is supportive of schemes which relocate emigrants to Ireland. 'I'd take them up on that if I ever got the chance but I never hear about those things,' he says.

Some of the long-term migrants manage to escape isolation despite their negative experiences, but they can never escape their often traumatic past completely. John Quinn (54) from Longford and Frank Costello (50) from Dundalk met in the London Irish Centre after coming over from Ireland as teenagers, and have lived together for 32, mostly wild, years during which gambling and alcohol nearly killed them both. John is Frank's carer – the younger man has suffered with depression – or he was until recently when John fell ill with a suspected heart attack; now both of them are on medication. Both say the other has kept them alive. They share a cosy, cluttered flat and a dog called Tommy in Holloway. While Frank is out doing volunteer work for the Islington Carers Forum, a group which does crucial work helping local carers, many of whom are Irish, John sips coffee and recalls why he left Ireland in the first place.

The sexual abuse began when he was nine and lasted until he was 14. He says a prominent man in Longford, now dead, would bring him to various houses in the town where he was systematically raped by local men and pictures were taken of him engaged in various sexual acts. 'They were naked and I was physically thrown in among them, forced to do things and then beaten. I got 10 shillings at the end of it. I could go to the cinema and I could buy whatever I wanted. He said if I ever told I would be taken to an asylum. When I left Longford I still had a fear that I was going to be taken away,' he says. A chronic dyslexic, when he went to England he carried a razor blade in his bag at all times so that if asked to fill out a form he could cut himself easily and use the injury as an excuse for someone to help him. 'I did that for a long time,' he says.

Years of counselling have helped but haven't healed all the wounds. He says he believed he was doing his family a favour by leaving and thought that by emigrating he wouldn't taint them with his shameful experiences. But while he is close to his

A Skellig Islands puffin captured by 16-year-old Amy Kelly of St Mary's College in Arklow, Co. Wicklow, winner of the Ireland.com Schools Photography Competition.

mother, when he goes home he says his family make him feel out of place, as though he doesn't belong and his sacrifice was for nothing. 'When I visited last year they said, when you come to Ireland we tell you what to do, you don't tell us,' he says. He has never spoken to them about the abuse.

Frank, who hasn't touched a drink for 17 years, was also sexually abused as a child in Ireland but says he is happy, for the moment, to stay in England, the place he now calls home. Devoutly religious, he goes to mass every day and says this has helped him to cherish his Irish identity. 'When I was a youngster playing in the fields of Dundalk I would hear the bells of the Angelus ringing out on a summer's day and that is Ireland to me. I didn't go to mass for years but now I have my faith back I feel I have my Irishness back too,' he says.

John and Frank know of many unseen Irish. People like Mr Brennan from Co. Kilkenny who sat in the flat upstairs for 20 years without electricity until the men found out and fixed it. He had been cooking on an oil stove with only the light from the street lamp outside his window.

People like Deirdre, a woman raped by her brothers in Ireland as a young girl, who, as an old woman, just wants them to acknowledge what they did, but is continually told when she tries to confront the issue with her family that she is mad. 'We have come through the worst of it. These are the people who really need help,' says John.

I met the two friends in the Archway Tavern, a landmark Irish watering hole in Holloway, where they introduced me to a man named Leo Cafolla. Fifty-eight-year-old Leo is from East Belfast and came to London in 1972 after his father's fish and

Sophia Loren on the arm of Italian designer Giorgio Armani at the first night of the refurbished Milan opera house, La Scala. Photograph: Stefano Rellandini/ Reuters.

chip shop was burnt down. He does the same thing every day. His first pint is drunk at 11 a.m. and he goes home for a nap at 4 p.m. His one daily meal is always the same – sausage, chips and beans in a local cafe. After dinner he goes back to the pub and sits drinking until closing time. He speaks softly but with urgency in a diluted Northern lilt, spilling out random facts about jobs he has had, people he has known, places he has seen. It's as though he might not get the chance to say these things to anyone again and he must make sure somebody knows. 'Thank you very much for the chat,' he says when we head off. 'Thank you very much,' he calls.

In a 15th-floor flat in north London, the day before I meet Leo, Kathleen O'Connell from Limerick realises that the person doing dishes in her home is a journalist and not, as she had thought, a home help 'sent from God to keep me company'. 'Will you be back again?' she asks, putting her hand to her head in anguish when I tell her that I don't know. I hug her and lock the door as I leave, pushing the key back through the letter-box.

The upcoming Streets of London concert in Dublin on Tuesday night will raise money for the valuable Aisling Return to Ireland Project, but it's obvious that any increased funding won't mean a thing if it doesn't raise awareness of people like Kathleen. Volunteers to visit people like her in their loneliest days are desperately needed, and imaginative moves must be urgently made to lessen their sense of separation from the country they still call home. Near the Abbey Road zebra crossing made famous by The Beatles, I post an envelope containing a letter and three crisp ten pound notes to a priest somewhere in Co. Wicklow. A Shower of Blessings. It's the least Kathleen O'Connell and the rest of the invisible Irish in Britain deserve.

WEDNESDAY, 8 DECEMBER 2004

Curtain Rises Again at Milan's La Scala

Paddy Agnew, in Milan

Punctually, at 6 p.m. local time, the world's greatest opera house got the show back on the road last night. After almost three years of closure for a €61 million renovation and restoration, La Scala was back in business with a re-opening performance of Antonio Salieri's *Europa Riconosciuta*, a 'show' that played to an audience of shakers and makers, glitterati and Milano Per Bene.

The refurbished La Scala. Photograph: Stefano Rellandini/Reuters.

As TV stars, models, sportsmen (ex-Formula One driver Jean Alesi), politicians, pop singers and royalty (Emmanuele Filiberto of the House of Savoy) made their entrance into a chaotic, crowded foyer, there was a lot of 'Who's she, then?' amongst the perplexed scrimmage of hacks and cameramen. When the indomitable Sophia Loren arrived, however, on the arm of designer Giorgio Armani, nobody needed to ask.

In the end, given that Prime Minister Silvio Berlusconi had opted to nutmeg the media by making a side-door entrance, it was left to 'La Loren' and 'Giorgio' to set the tone for the night. Both looked tanned and well, albeit not without the odd sign of kilometres on the clock. Smiling graciously, Loren stopped to tell us that media reports that this was a Scala début for her were untrue: 'This is my second opening night at the Scala and it's just wonderful,' said the 70-year-old grande dame.

On a night when the cool December airs did not prevent a number of the ladies showing much off-the-shoulder flesh, 'La Loren' was suitably elegant in full-length black evening gown complete with a transparent, glittery top. Standing beside her, Armani looked up in admiration – as well he might since he had designed her dress.

In the chaos of the opening night scrimmage, neither Loren nor Armani would have had time to notice the plaque on the wall above the foyer entrance where they stopped to pose for the cameras. That plaque recalls the last Scala restoration prior to this, namely a hurried, probably botched job carried out at the end of the second World War, leading to a May 1946 re-opening night under the baton of maestro Arturo Toscanini.

An hour and a half before curtain-up, the empty auditorium, complete with 20,000 fresh roses, looked utterly magnificent. Even though the

Michael Viney, the naturalist and Irish Times *columnist (left) with, left to right: Judith Chavasse, former Director of Nursing Studies at University College Dublin; Christina Noble, founder of the Noble Foundation; Evelyn Glennie, percussionist; and John Sutton, Professor of Economics at the London School of Economics, upon whom honorary degrees were conferred by Trinity College, Dublin. Photograph: Frank Miller.*

theatre had been 'gutted' so as to install state-of-the-art stage equipment and, even more importantly, to clear out second World War debris and replace it with a parquet, sprung floor, the external look of the new Scala is still gloriously, opulently red-velveted operatic magic.

As is now traditional on the opening night of La Scala, last night's performance was played off against a background of protest in the piazza in front of the theatre. Laid-off workers from the Alfa Romeo car plant at Arese near Milan and members of the CGIL trade union protesting health cuts were both making themselves heard, albeit at a respectable, police-cordoned distance:

'It is simply not right that Milan town council, the Milan region and the government should spend all that money on this restoration, nor that people pay up to €2,000 for a ticket tonight, when there are families all over the country that have difficulty making it to the end of the month,' union activist Roberto told *The Irish Times*. 'My monthly salary is just €1,000 after tax, half a ticket for tonight. That's just not right.'

Not that those objections appeared to spoil the fun for the La Scala faithful. At the end of the first act, they warmly applauded maestro Ricardo Muti and sopranos Désirée Rancatore and Diana Damrau whilst initial reactions in the foyer were largely very favourable.

Adding intrigue to an evening already loaded with historical significance was the choice of last night's opera. *Europa Riconosciuta* is by 18th century Italian composer Antonio Salieri, a contemporary of Mozart and composer in residence at the

Hapsburg court in Vienna. Salieri would have long since passed into oblivion were it not for the (historically false) accusation that he poisoned his great rival, an accusation brought to cinema screens by Milos Forman's *Amadeus*.

Back in 1778, Salieri was commissioned to write a work for the opening night of the new Teatro Regio Ducal, which soon became better known as the Teatro alla Scala. Dedicated to 'His Most Serene Archduke Ferdinand, Royal Prince of Hungary and Bohemia, Archduke of Austria', and given a lavish production, *Europa Riconosciuta* was a total flop which, until last night, had gone the intervening period without once being performed again anywhere. Every dog has its day, even 226 years later.

THURSDAY, 9 DECEMBER 2004

Not so Much *Groundhog Day* again as *Waiting for Godot*

Gerry Moriatry, in Belfast

People often compare the Northern political process to the film *Groundhog Day*, where the characters are condemned to relive the same day over and over. But they are wrong. The process is like *Waiting for Godot*.

For those few *Irish Times* readers unfamiliar with the play, Samuel Beckett's characters Vladimir and Estragon are still waiting. And so are we. And we will wait for a while longer before there is a comprehensive political agreement in Northern Ireland. Good old Vlad and Estragon: they generally travel in hope, occasionally losing faith, but always prepared to face the night in the possibility of a bright dawn, of Godot wandering on to the stage. So it was with the Taoiseach, Mr Ahern, and the British Prime Minister in the Waterfront Hall in Belfast yesterday.

Mr Ahern said this final issue of pictures could be resolved before Christmas. Later, though, he conceded that a pre-Christmas solution was perhaps 'aspirational'. But like Beckett's men, both the Taoiseach and Prime Minister hold to their duty of hope.

Nine days ago the question was asked here: would Gerry Adams see the chance of a deal wasted over a picture of a redundant AK47? Would Ian Paisley sacrifice all that the DUP gained for a photograph of a redundant rocket launcher? We got our answer yesterday: yes, and yes again.

We are now into the blame game, a more popular past-time than PlayStation 2 up here. At the DUP press conference in east Belfast yesterday, the Rev Ian Paisley blamed republicans for the crash of this agreement. Over in west Belfast, the Sinn Féin president, Mr Gerry Adams, said it was all the DUP's responsibility.

No surprises there. The tendency at such times is for culpability to break down along sectarian lines. It's simple: nationalists blame unionists and unionists blame nationalists. It's already shaping up for that pattern of fault-finding, but there could be some variations on that game this time.

The reasonable question being asked yesterday was, What was the point in Mr Ahern and Mr Blair coming to Belfast without a deal? Wasn't that an abject admission of yet another failure in this process? To try to understand the governments' reasoning one must also understand that in recent weeks the consistent line from Dublin and London was that they hoped that the IRA might make some compromises on photographs.

Mr Adams and Mr Martin McGuinness in the negotiations during and since Leeds Castle in September didn't say yes to pictures, and they didn't say no, we were told. The governments drew hope from this absence of a definitive response that the IRA might live with pictures being perhaps shown to Dr Paisley, and even possibly being published.

But, as Mr Blair acknowledged yesterday, it is not a 'sensible' negotiating tactic to try to humiliate your opponent. Yet that's what Dr Paisley with great gusto and zeal did over the past week and more. Even yesterday, he said if republicans couldn't tolerate sack cloth then they should try a 'hairshirt'.

Objectively, there's a reasonable point here. As Dr Paisley said, republicans have many acts to be repentant for. Maybe he has some himself? But in the face of the most sensitive negotiations and only inches away from the 'deal of all deals', why lash out in such manner? People around him tried to prevent him flailing away in his predictably unpredictable manner, and for several weeks they succeeded. But in the end they just couldn't keep the rein on him – the preacher man took over from the politician.

There are several logical reasons why the IRA should have produced pictures. After all, as several DUP people have stated, unionists had to see the destruction of the RUC, the toppling of watchtowers, IRA killers walking free early – why couldn't the Provos take a little grief for the overall good? That point can't be gainsaid. But equally, and most people wish it were otherwise, the majority of informed observers in their gut, based on their experience and intuition, feared the game was up when Dr Paisley launched into rant mode last Saturday week in Ballymena.

Perhaps republicans would have baulked at pictures even if Dr Paisley had remained temperate in his language. But the fact remains that short of the line the governments felt there was a possibility the photographic issue could be finessed, and that would have required compromise from Mr Adams.

The Sinn Féin president probably was being genuine when he portrayed Dr Paisley's onslaught on republicans as the deal breaker. Certainly republicans now have an excuse for not producing pictures that most nationalists in Northern Ireland, at least, will accept.

Dr Paisley is confident that he won't take any hits in the blame game. Again based on experience he is probably correct. But there are some unionists who are angered that Northern Ireland has lost

Ian Paisley after meeting General John de Chastelain to hear about the IRA's latest 'offer' on decommissioning. Photograph: Paul Faith/PA.

a deal that the governments say involved the IRA retiring, decommissioning, Sinn Féin signing up to policing (perhaps the biggest prize of all), a power-sharing government, and Dr Paisley as first minister. Couldn't the DUP leader have bit his lip just a little bit longer to test at least whether all that was attainable?

Alan McBride who lost his wife and father-in-law in the IRA Shankill bombing was clearly upset and frustrated when he spoke on BBC Radio Ulster's Talkback programme yesterday. Dr Paisley should be wearing 'sack cloth and ashes' for robbing Northern Ireland of such a powerful deal, he said. That may not be a typical unionist response but quite a number would have similar views.

Tony Blair (left) and Bertie Ahern at a press conference in the Waterfront Hall in Belfast. Photograph: Cathal McNaughton/PA.

So, like Vladimir and Estragon, will we be waiting forever for a deal? Mr Ahern and Mr Blair will meet on the margins of an EU meeting next week to see if there is a way forward. The Northern Secretary Paul Murphy and Minister for Foreign Affairs Dermot Ahern will meet the parties next week. Mr Murphy told *The Irish Times* last night, 'Yes, we are disappointed, but we are not despairing.' Like Beckett's characters.

There really is just one issue left to resolve; not guns, not Semtex, not policing, not even whether there would be independent observation of IRA decommissioning in addition to Gen de Chastelain – but photographs.

Mr Blair, when advising Dr Paisley against humiliating his opponents, also said it wasn't sensible to overreact to such talk. Somewhere in that comment lies the solution: a little more restraint from the Doc, a thicker skin, just a little more give from republicans. How long we must wait for that to happen is hard to call. But if Northern Ireland politicians have any competence, it shouldn't be as long as Vladimir and Estragon have to wait.

MONDAY, 13 DECEMBER 2004

The Violent and Terrifying World of Insurgency

Jack Fairweather, in Mosul

There's a body lying by the side of the street. Behind the corpse, zipped up in a body bag, is a cargo truck with its windscreen dotted with bullet holes.

The man was shot by B company, Deuce-4 battalion as they were ambushed uncovering explosives by the side of the road on the western edge of Mosul. They think he was just a truck-driver, but they're not sure. Another soldier's shouting that he can see Iraqis running for cover. Somewhere between the residential houses gun shots ring out. The ambushers are still out there.

There is a war being fought in Mosul. It's not the pitched-battle seen last month in Fallujah when insurgents stood, fought and were soundly beaten. This is the violent and terrifying world of Iraq's insurgency, where the enemy fades in and out of the local population, untraceable until they strike. It shows no signs of abating. 'What they're dealing with now is an insurgency gone to ground, reorganising, and looking for its next base of operations,' said a senior American diplomat in Baghdad.

The US military believes hundreds of insurgents fled Fallujah, most before the fighting began. They include Abu Musab al-Zarqawi, terrorist ringleader, America's most wanted, who US intelligence reports indicate came to the Mosul area of northern Iraq with the fighting still raging in Fallujah. His influence, and that of other escaped insurgents, was devastating.

On November 23rd teams of insurgents stormed five police stations in the city, torching them, before handing them over to looters. A recently completed Iraqi army base to the south of the city was left a gutted wreck in a further attack. US army units were rushed northwards to contain the violence, but most of the damage had been done.

For the past month the Iraqi police force has refused to go back to work. Many Iraqi contractors have stopped work on American contracts for the city's meagre reconstruction projects. For a city, Iraq's third largest, that once prided itself on its ethnic mix of Sunni Arabs, Christians and Kurds, there have been worrying attacks on churches and Kurdish political offices.

The US military now has a 5,000-strong force in Mosul, the largest since the war, and is the *de facto* government in the city where many Iraqi leaders have disappeared from view. The military says its focus is to prepare the city for elections next month by recreating confidence in civic leadership, but much of its time is spent countering the daily assaults of the insurgents.

'We know that elections are our ticket out of here. But first we've got to bring security to the area,' said one senior officer.

US officers are confident, despite the increased insurgency, they can do this in time. 'To break this insurgency what we need is intelligence, and to get that we need to win the trust of the Iraqi people,' said Lt Col Eric Kurilla, commander of the 8,000-strong Deuce-4 battalion, which bears the brunt of the attacks in western Mosul, the Sunni Arab Yarmuk district.

Lt Col Kurilla embodies the American fight against the insurgency, and its inherent contradictions: brilliant in attack, but unable to convince locals that the US presence and elections will make their lives better.

He is a great bear of a man, loved by his soldiers and spends most of his day touring the battle space 'looking for a fight' as he puts it – the tried and trusted method for weeding out insurgents. Visiting 'B company' a few hours after they were ambushed, he trotted eagerly around the pitted streets. 'Scusi,' he shouted at an Iraqi girl standing on a balcony, before asking his translator to ask 'Where are the insurgents?' Two miles down the road he found them.

His team of five 'strykers', an eight-wheeled armoured personal carrier, had stopped to search an area of wasteland and concrete houses, the scene of an ambush the day before. It didn't take long to find stashes of artillery shells, sniper bullets and RPGs hidden among broken masonry and old scrap along the side of the road.

From a distance a crowd of residents watched. 'Now that's a goddam complicit population,' fumed Kurilla. 'I know they're scared to act against the insurgents,' he added.

Most of Kurilla's men were loading up into the 'strykers' when the suicide bomber struck, ramming the slowly closing ramp door of one of the vehicles. A fireball sucked up air, and a body part landed on the ground.

Soldiers began racing over to the vehicle. There were casualties. Sgt Shannon Kay, who had managed to set off three shots at the vehicle as it approached, had blood pouring down one side of his face. He climbed into the rear shooting hatch of one of the 'strykers', as a mortar landed 30 metres away. 'You should get down, you're hurt,' said the officer in charge. Sgt Shannon Kay leaned back into the vehicle. 'I'm going to finish this thing.' Sgt Victor Brazfield (23) said, 'He's fine. He's just f***ing mad.' An F-18 flew over the building from which insurgents had been firing with small arms. A guided missile hit on the ground outside.

Back at the headquarters of Deuce-4, Lt Col Kurilla tucked into a plate of pasta. It was the second such attack in as many days. Six US soldiers had been injured. 'We got seven of the bad guys,' he said. 'There's an end in sight. Pretty soon the people of Mosul are going to see that the insurgents want nothing but destruction and we want to rebuild the place.'

TUESDAY, 14 DECEMBER 2004

Stop the Sleigh – I Want to Get Off

Fionola Meredith

It's a secret, almost inadmissible fantasy that steals over many of us at this time of year. You know the scene. You're standing in a long queue for the check-out with your arms full of garish, multi-coloured tinsel, a bumper pack of novelty Homer Simpson boxer shorts, and a mini fibre-optic Christmas tree your kids persuaded you to buy. It's hot and stuffy, Slade's 'Merry Christmas Everybody' is making a determined assault on your jangled nerves, and the woman behind you in the queue is pressing her shopping trolley with pernicious insistence into the backs of your thighs.

Just as you're meditating on the universal truth of Jean-Paul Sartre's insight that 'hell is other people', the naughty fantasy creeps enticingly into your tired brain. I know, you think, why not just opt out of Christmas this year? Of course, most of us dismiss this idea at once. The children would be outraged and besides, what would we do all day if we weren't opening presents, eating turkey and fighting with the in-laws over the remote control?

But some people are so desperate to avoid the enforced jollity of the festive season, they'll do anything to escape. A few years ago, Colin Wood, a 30-year-old financial services worker, hit the headlines. He paid €320 to spend two weeks alone in a decommissioned nuclear bunker in Essex over the Christmas period. Retreating underground behind blast-proof doors and 10-foot-thick concrete, he survived on Spam, baked beans and tap water. Wood was one of 50 would-be bunker dwellers who bid at an Internet auction site to hire the bunker, billed as 'the site where even Santa is unlikely to venture'.

Although his tactics were extreme, Wood's escape is part of a tradition of festive dissent. Irish dramatist and intellectual George Bernard Shaw was a notorious anti-Christmas ascetic. The playwright was keen to do a normal day's work on December 25th; he steadfastly avoided festive revellers and observed his usual vegetarian, alcohol-free diet. Others with reclusive tendencies adopt similar tactics, using everyone else's complete immersion in Christmas-related activities as an opportunity to withdraw quietly from the populist melée.

Philip Hammond is a composer living in Belfast. He says: 'I use the Christmas season for composing because I can have several days unencumbered by phone or people and can therefore get into the compositional context, which is "withdraw from the world and suffer"! Everyone else is doing the "family thing" and as I don't have a family it is the perfect time to be hermit-like and

A boy passing a window of Saks Fifth Avenue department store in New York. Photograph: Mike Segar/Reuters.

avoid humanity. Also, not being a Christian, I have no hang-ups about being involved in doing social conscience things such as being nice to people (and their children too) or going to endless carol services and seasonal activities which mean nothing to me.

'But I will admit to the odd little touch of nostalgia which inevitably creeps in when I hear a really good choir singing a really good piece of Christmas music – but definitely not Messiah.'

Another way to do Christmas differently is to simply cherry-pick the bits you like and ditch the bits you don't. Dick Spicer is ceremonial co-ordinator of the Humanist Association of Ireland. While humanists emphatically deny the underpinning Christian elements of Christmas, Spicer says: 'we're perfectly happy to have a bit of fun; it doesn't bother us to go along with the celebrations. We believe that since we have only one life to live, we have a duty to try and enjoy it. So I think there's a kind of logic in participating in the festive season, even though we reject religious dogma.

'The ancient Greek ideal of the Golden Mean teaches us that moderation is the source of pleasure, and we certainly don't believe in abstinence for its own sake. We're not puritans by any means. So we simply secularise Christmas. Actually, the myth of Santa Claus provides very good humanist training in religious scepticism for children – it's the story of a kindly old man who doesn't exist!'

Barbara Smoker, former president of the National Secular Society, argues that secularists can join in the festive feast boldly without losing face, since 'if anyone ought to abstain from the seasonal celebrations of the fourth week of December on grounds of credal consistency it is the believing Christian. The pantomime, the Christmas tree, candles, mistletoe, holly, feasting on special kinds of meat, the mince pies and the flaming sun-shaped

Residents of the Beaufort Day Care Centre in Glasthule, Co. Dublin, watch TV as finance minister Brian Cowen reads his first budget. Photograph: Brenda Fitzsimons.

Christmas pudding – all were pagan in origin and symbolism, and all were anathema to the Fathers of the Church.'

The undeniably pre-Christian roots of the celebrations are indeed anathema to some Christians today. Jehovah's Witnesses find this 'pagan inheritance' repugnant, refusing to participate in Christmas in any way – including gift-giving and feasting. Ewen Watt, a spokesperson for the Jehovah's Witnesses in Ireland, says: 'Christmas is un-Christian. It's against the spirit of what Christ stood for, and we certainly wouldn't get involved in it. It's as offensive to us as taking Hitler's birthday and making it into a huge celebration would be to the Jewish community. For us, the most sacred day in the religious calendar is Easter. We prefer to commemorate that.'

But it's pagans themselves who really feel disenfranchised at this time of year. Many pagans see the Christian usurpation of the pagan midwinter festival of Yule as an expression of the privileged position of institutionalised Christianity in the Western world. Yule, which takes place around December 21st, is one of the traditional Celtic fire festivals, marking the return of the light after the longest night of the year.

Pat Boston, who works as a life model for art students, is a practising pagan who detests the 'month-long panic' known as Christmas. Boston thinks that the long, drawn-out preparations for Christmas are symptomatic of our disconnection with the natural rhythms of the earth: 'As pagans, we worship the earth as the main giver, marking the turning of the seasons, the cycle of life and death. Everything must be in its own place and time, and it's wrong to falsify that natural order for monetary greed. It leads to spiritual turmoil. Pagans believe that following the cycle of the year helps us maintain who we are, reminds us that we are all part of a never-ending cycle.'

Pat is especially uncomfortable with the 'forced festivity' of Christmas. 'Within paganism, you are allowed a dark side – the side of your being which is raging, or sad, or lonely. Pagans honour that dark side – without it, you can't be a whole person. The short, dark days when everything is underground are a reflective time which enables us to withdraw, to dig deep within ourselves.' Although other pagans meet to enact the ceremonial 'battle of the oak and the holly' (representing summer and winter) with drums and chanting, Pat observes Yule at home with her daughter: 'We celebrate the birth of the Sun, not the Son. We gather holly and ivy to decorate the house and we exchange small gifts. Often we'll have a meal of all our favourite foods to celebrate life. It's a quiet, contemplative time to be together.'

Swimming against the torrent of seasonal jollity isn't easy. But for those who 'don't do Christmas', it's the only way to ensure that December 25th is just one more unremarkable day in the year.

Newgrange, Co. Meath, dawn 21 December 2004. Photograph: Alan Betson.

WEDNESDAY, 22 DECEMBER 2004

Slow Farewell to Winter after a Dazzling Solstice

Eileen Battersby, in Newgrange

Fingers of pink began to disperse the stars as the longest night of the year slowly surrendered to dawn. Honouring a late 20th-century practice, created by ancient man long before modern archaeologists had studied the calculated alignment of science and nature, Newgrange watchers gathered at the majestic Late Stone Age monument in Co. Meath yesterday. Drawn by the hope of watching the rising sun herald the decline of winter, both the ticket-holding elite and the onlookers standing outside were magnificently rewarded.

For many pilgrims, attendance at Brú Na Boinne is part of an annual ritual marking the start of Christmas. For others, arriving with expressions of anticipation, and some uncertainty, it was a new experience. 'Will Santa be here?' asked one little boy, who quickly answered his own question, 'I know, he's still really busy at the North Pole.' Other watchers looked to the sky and smiled knowingly.

Multi-coloured woollen hats and other seasonal headwear did suggest the morning was far colder than it was. Despite the icy roads, the temperature

Newgrange, Co. Meath, dawn 21 December 2004. Photograph: Alan Betson.

was no sharper than brisk. There was no wind. A filigree of cloud maintained a respectful distance. So clear had the brightening sky become by 8.30 that the large crowd collectively relaxed, confident of sharing a glory devised by nature and brilliantly recognised by early man.

A young woman draped in a rainbow muffler arrived solemn faced and carrying a yellow lantern. She stood at the outside wall of the monument, looking east. A small white dog pattered about, sat and prepared to groom herself as if in preparation for the coming spectacle. Two men in business suits surveyed the scene. 'There's no druids,' said one of them. His companion took another look before announcing: 'I think they tend to be based at Tara.' Below the local horizon, topped by its tree-lined ridge, the River Boyne emerging from the light mist was a motionless silver ribbon. Outside the monument, a triumph of science and spirituality, there was no tension, no anxious whispers. No black clouds arrived to threaten the outcome. Sunrise, during the five mornings of the mid-winter solstice, enjoys a far greater significance than throughout the rest of the year. On no other morning, bar Easter Day, is the sun as symbolic.

Across the valley, a yellow light began to rise as if from behind the ridge. The crowd chatted on. The light became brighter, even more yellow. At 8.52, a slim golden blister appeared. On cue, the onlookers cheered. As the glow increased, the hill-side retreated into shadow. By 8.55 the sun was moving faster, climbing higher. Its powerful beam had found its heart, the roofbox of the monument built by the ancients in honour of their dead.

Meanwhile, the great boulder-like standing stones that seem to guard the entrance, basked in the light. Ironically, the pilgrims, having turned their backs to the sun, now looked towards the long, narrow passageway about to be illuminated. Cameras were hoisted. Members of the Gardaí smiled benignly.

Inside the chamber, darkness began to yield to the golden beam that proceeded up the sanded floor of the passage. On dull mornings the party inside the chamber discuss other solstices, years in which the sun made a triumphant appearance. Yesterday was perfection. In the flood of warm honey light mere words became redundant. Tom Parlon, Minister of State for the Office of Public Works exited the passageway as if he had seen a vision, a rare experience for any politician. The emerging photographers looked so smug, those standing outside could only squeeze their camera in silent frustration.

The same little dog who had groomed herself now dashed towards the passageway in search of fame, or at least a photo. She was apprehended by her embarrassed owner. 'I didn't want her to spoil the sacred moment.' She didn't. No one could have.

Later a much smaller group of solstice pilgrims gathered at Dowth, another of the Boyne Valley ceremonial mounds. After a day of beautiful skies, a fine sunset was expected. The clouds decided otherwise. A startled bat fluttered about the chamber.

Light faded. Even so, Winter had now begun its slow farewell.

FRIDAY, 31 DECEMBER 2004

This Gorgeous Island Now Turned into a Hell...

Clifford Coonan, in Phuket

There is no way on earth of preparing for the visions of hell in City Hall in Phuket Town, where an emergency relief centre has been set up to help the victims of the St Stephen's Day tsunami which devastated the resort of Phuket in southern Thailand.

This was supposed to be paradise.

Walking through the tents, you come to a wall of photographs of the missing, a catalogue of horror similar to the one outside the World Trade Centre after September 11th. So many children are in the photographs – beautiful Swedish babies and German toddlers and cheeky young British boys – it's heartbreaking. Wedding photos, beach photos taken just hours before the tsunami, graduation pictures.

Driving from the airport to the town, the scattering of beach furniture all over what used to be a bustling resort shows just how powerful was the tsunami which tore up the western coast of Phuket Island. Everyone on Phuket is traumatised in some way by what they just call 'the Wave'. In parts it looks like a giant hand scooped up chunks of the shoreline and carelessly tossed them at the landscape behind. You remember how often the word 'paradise' appears in advertising blurbs for Phuket – and it is paradise. The ironies are just too cruel to bear when you see this gorgeous island turned into a hell.

One wall of photographs in the centre features a horrifying tableau of photographs of unidentified dead, young and old. Local officials, fearful of an epidemic, want to bury the rapidly-decomposing bodies quickly, while foreign governments want to make sure they don't get buried before they have been identified.

Hundreds of people mill around, looking for information, particularly about those on the outlying islands. The embassies of many countries have desks set up, including one manned by Ireland's Ambassador to Thailand and Malaysia, Mr Dan Mulhall, and his team.

As we drive along the seafront near Karala, we pass mountains of detritus, benches, tables, even cars. One green Mazda looks like it has been picked up by the same giant hand and dropped, nose down, from a huge height. In one place where there used to be beach bungalows in a development called Karala CoCo Hut, there is

Among photographs of the dead at Ban Muan temple, a Thai woman searches for members of her family on Phuket island, Thailand. Photograph: Adrees Latif/Reuters.

nothing left but sticks. In a small lake opposite, they are dredging for more bodies, which keep appearing.

A soldier, wearing a mask against the stench, tells us they've only turned up a few cars so far and a lot of palm trees, but no bodies have yet been found.

By night, there are few lights on the street other than the big ones illuminating the teams cleaning up the mess. But the hazy glow picks out a single Birkenstock sandal outside the Delphine foot massage shop. And a shamrock dangling from what was once an Irish bar.

FRIDAY, 31 DECEMBER 2004

Resort Still Reeling from the Day 'the Wave' Hit

Clifford Coonan, in Phuket

Warawadee Hemaratna, who runs an upmarket furniture shop in Phuket, was supposed to go and hang out with friends on the beach on the morning of what those in the area now call 'the wave'. But she felt lazy and slept in, before calling at the shop to pick up some things. 'We were in the shop and people said "run". We'd heard about the earthquake and the rumours were flying. Two waves, then three waves and everyone was running for higher ground,' she tells me.

With her excellent English, she has been working in the hospital, helping the families of tourists who outnumber the local dead by three to one, by some reckonings. 'There are lots of people volunteering, students. There was nothing we could do initially but we've been helping people, looking for their missing family and friends,' says Warawadee, who goes by the nickname Nurh and who comes from Bangkok. She moved here a month ago to help get the new shop going.

Phuket is an island made prosperous by tourism and looks like a resort in Spain or Italy in many ways. The beach is so central to life on the island, for both locals and tourists, that almost everyone who emerged unscathed from the tsunamis which lashed the southern resorts has got a lucky escape story. Everyone goes to the beach all the time, to swim, to relax and read a book and watch the sun go down, to jet-ski, for the kids to play in the sand.

NTR Emergency Radio is issuing guidelines in English, Italian, Chinese, German, French, many languages, on where people can get information about their missing loved ones and on how to help with the rescue effort. 'They need clothing,' says

Two German tourists, Carsten Simms (left) and Hans Sirries (right) searching for five members of the Mintzel family missing from Khao Lak. Photograph: Adrees Latif/Reuters.

an Australian DJ. 'We've got enough shoes for a while. We need razors and sanitary napkins, things to keep people clean.' His message is repeated in Italian and German.

'It used to be very beautiful around here,' Nurh says as we cross a tricky patch of beachfront road demolished by the Wave.

A busy bar area in Patong, centred on a statue of Buddha, has been turned into a disaster area. The golden statue has been cleaned and garlanded with puangmalai flowers.

Paul Clark works at the British embassy in Mumbai but was snorkelling in Thailand when the Wave hit and he stayed to do what he can. 'We're all trying to get a database together. There are a lot of lists and some of them are getting duplicated. It's getting complicated, though the Thai PM said he would try to centralise things,' he says. In one case, Paul was talking to someone on the phone about a missing person on Phi Phi island. Another man overheard the conversation, thought he sounded familiar and tapped him on the shoulder. A mystery solved, though scores remain. 'We are getting some good news stuff, which is a boon amid all this bad news. But it's getting less,' he says.

Panic is in the air in Phuket – people were running around wildly when the power went down at one stage yesterday. Fears that sea-quake aftershocks were sending more tsunami towards southern Thailand sent thousands of people running through the streets of Patong on Phuket again in a grim echo of the horror of the St Stephens' Day disaster.

Regulars and visitors at Lek Murphy's Irish Pub on Soi Sansabei sit and compare experiences of the day everything went wrong.

'This wave blasted ATMs out of the wall, there were cars in swimming pools,' says co-owner Tony Waters, from Cork, gesturing towards the seafront of the town, where he came four years ago on holiday and never went back. 'They are still taking the bodies out of the shopping plaza down there. Everyone ran into the basement when it hit. Terrible. A lot of our Thai friends are dead.

'We just saw people running up the street, scattering. We were a bit higher up, but we saw a lot of people trampled on. At the same time we had no idea how bad it was. We were worried about Anthony here because he lives above the pub and we had no way of contacting him,' he says. He points to his business partner, Anthony Ronayne, also from Cork, who says the bar has become a focal point for the expatriate community in the crisis.

There is an atmosphere of a community facing adversity in the bar, which was untouched by the tsunami but is just metres away from horrific devastation. The contrast is profound. 'We get people asking us about people but we've no contact with a lot of the guys who come through here – they come here and have a few drinks and then are gone on somewhere else the next day,' he says. 'There would be some fellows using this as a staging post for getting to Australia.'

Jocky Neville, yet another Cork man, who works in purchasing and planning in the IT industry, says the day was 'absolutely frightening'. 'It's frightening to look at the destruction. You almost can't appreciate what this thing has done here,' Jocky says. 'There was a car jammed in Ocean Plaza. They were lined up on top of each other, the cars. And all the bodies they were taking out.'

Richard Harrington, a Kinsale man living in Dublin, who is on a six-week holiday in Patong, reckons that over-imbibing in Lek Murphy's probably saved his life. 'I go for a walk at 9.30 every morning on the beach. On Christmas night I had a late one here so I missed it,' he says, shaking his head at the irony. 'I opened my door and there were three feet of water in the courtyard, with fridges, deckchairs, everything in it. I watched 15 bodies being taken out of a supermarket,' says the engineer.

Jocky Neville is defiant and says he has booked to return to Patong Beach in July. 'People are asking me: am I coming home? I am not, I'm staying here to show support. This is a time to stand by our Thai friends,' he says. Everyone nods agreement.

Anthony Ronayne thinks business will definitely fall off after the shock sets in and he is not optimistic. But he is defiant nonetheless. 'It'll probably take years, I don't know, we've had SARS, chicken flu and Bali [bombing], and we survived that. Who knows?'

Rattling along in a jeep by the shoreline at sunset, it's a picture straight out of the brochures, a red sky over gently lapping waves on the beach.

Then I and my companion have to go by foot through the beachfront part of Patong, which until a few days ago was full of open-fronted pubs with bar girls and boozing expatriates. The Wave has played hell with the sex industry in Phuket – many of the very superstitious young bar girls have fled the scene, worried about meeting too many ghosts.

Narong Chaidum, who lost his travel agency and another tourist shop to the Wave, guides me through the streets, which feel post-nuclear. 'They are clearing away the debris of my shop, then I will just have to start rebuilding again. But whether the tourists will come is another thing. I don't know, but I have to do this. I live from tourism,' says Narong.

And yet, not all normal life is gone. Just around the corner you hear the sound of a Thai band playing the opening chords of The Eagles' 'Hotel California', a candidate for Asia's national anthem if ever there was one. The Wave is gone. People are coming back to the fleshpots of Phuket. But everyone is asking: can it ever be the same again?

THURSDAY, 6 JANUARY 2005

Where the Ocean Now Sleeps like a Baby

Kathy Sheridan, in Sainthamaruthu, Sri Lanka

The smell is unmistakable. Mohamed Assim Jameel is standing on the remnants of his house on the beach. His grief and despair are evident in his exhausted body and his bloodshot eyes. His legs and arms are heavily bandaged but that hasn't stopped him returning repeatedly to sift and sit among the rubble.

He believes that his wife and two little boys, one aged six, the other eight months, are under the smashed masonry. The smell today confirms it. He last saw them on December 26th after he spotted sea-water 'bubbling from the bottom of the sea'. He grabbed one of his children and started to run. His wife – five months pregnant – was behind running with their two other children. 'I looked back and they were there. But I never saw them again,' he says, his eyes filling up as he gestures towards the ruin beneath him. 'All I have left is this sarong and a shirt loaned to me by a neighbour.'

A composed little gathering of five or six stand around him. There is no hysteria or demands that something must be done. There is too much despair. For the 1,300 families of this densely populated 1½-km long beachfront of Sainthamaruthu, already with 2,500 confirmed dead and another 500 bodies awaiting discovery in one tiny area, this has become routine.

Thirty minutes before, a group cleaning the stinking debris from a house found the body of a child. They believe it was a child, a boy of around seven or so, from the size.

But his grotesquely decomposing body allowed for no formalities or final goodbyes. He was immediately wrapped in a sheet, taken to the burial ground less than 100 yards away on the beach, where a five-foot hole was dug in the sand and within half an hour, the anonymous little body was buried. Other small mounds in the sand signify a similar fate for many others buried without ceremony. 'Many fathers are looking for their children,' shrugs a weary local man. 'One of them thinks it is his son. But how can we know?' In this small patch of hell, intolerable smells permeate through the bricks and masonry. The detritus of everyday family life lies scattered around – a tiny shoe, a beautiful blue sari, a schoolbook lying open on a rock, a damp, torn Koran.

Identity cards and bank cards belonging to people missing in the tsunami in Thailand put on display by police in Phuket. Among them is the AIB card belonging to Dublin woman Eilis Finnegan. Photograph: Kin Cheung/Reuters.

Behind the mosque, a gentle, courteous member of its board of trustees, shakes the strangers' hands and thanks them for coming. He is sitting among what looks like numerous piles of sandy clay.

They turn out to be mass graves, each containing about 50 bodies, some 400 in all, hurriedly buried. He still looks bemused when he remembers December 26th. 'I saw all the people running, and shouting "the sea is coming, the sea is coming". I thought, how could the sea be coming? And then I saw it too.' A few yards away, less than 100 metres from the magnificent shoreline, a smashed hulk of a building is recognisable as a hospital by the ambulance lying crushed and battered against a collapsed water tower. The building was a sitting target for the brunt of the waves.

The children's ward, with its barred windows, held 42 children that day. Only four survived. The room where the water crashed in and reached well above the windows is now a ghostly place of twisted bedsteads, a child's potty, a single small high-heeled sandal, IV needles and saline drops.

There are no cellophaned bunches of flowers, no grieving relatives to make a shrine of this place of loss. The silence is profound, with only the rhythmic sound of the ocean – 'now sleeping like a baby', in the words of a local – to serve as a requiem. The school alongside is almost destroyed. The one piece of luck these people had is that disaster visited on a Sunday.

The other piece of good cheer relates to a man who identifies himself as S.M.A. Madeed. He was taken to the mosque as a dead body but suddenly rose up and walked. When he got back to his substantial house on the beach with its adjoining grocery shop, however, he found he had lost his 22-year-old daughter and two grandchildren. His shop, worth 300,000 rupees (about $30,000), has simply disappeared. Both his sons are fishermen whose livelihoods have been destroyed.

Men who suddenly look old stand bewildered among the wreckage of their homes and trawlers.

Boats, driven by the ferocity of 30-foot waves, are stuck in houses more than half a km from the beach. Three hundred of them were scattered like matchsticks across the village. Nets lie tangled and useless near the bridge that crossed the little harbour to continue the Beach Road. The bridge was swatted out of existence. The road is gone. The pretty little harbour has been seriously damaged. The view is that the first task of any agency is to re-energise the fishermen.

But while undiscovered, decaying bodies lie so close and the streets remained filled with the debris and muck being cleared from the houses, it is difficult to see how they can move on. GOAL workers, who see this as a priority, yesterday hired two JCBs and 12 tractors to start the clearing process on the Hospital Road.

With a sense that something was needed to kick-start a new phase for the village, Paul Jowar hit on the idea of getting the president of the mosque to formally launch the project. He floated the idea as a joke initially, but yesterday the mosque president duly turned up at 10.30, when he and Peter Nuttall, GOAL's team leader, cut a blue ribbon, flanked by the JCBs and a 12-strong convoy of tractors, washed and shining for the momentous occasion.

Nuttall made a speech, a short one, on the basis that 'the biggest need is for action' and Paul Kelly, whose day job involves working as an engineer for Louth County Council, saw them off. There was a palpable air of achievement and no small neglect of health and safety requirements as people crowded around to see the first load of debris loaded into the first trailer.

Then, amid enormous good will, a reception was laid on in the mosque, with Nice biscuits, spicy delicacies and tea, followed by discussions about latrine design for the refugee camps. The plan is to have 30 tractors working on site within days.

But this little area has a long way to go. The immediate priority is caring for those who have left, either through losing their homes, through trauma, or simple fear of the sea. How such a small community can cope with so much loss is for another day – but a day that must assuredly be faced up to sooner rather than later.

SATURDAY, 8 JANUARY 2005

Race against Time

Lynne O'Donnell, in Meulaboh, Sumatra

Crammed into what once served as the government headquarters for the stricken city of Meulaboh, on the west coast of Aceh, thousands of people crouching in family groups on rattan mats laid out on a hard, cold, white-tiled floor received an esteemed visitor yesterday when United Nations Secretary-General Kofi Annan dropped in to see how they were.

Annan wandered around the building, talked to some of the still-dazed people who wander in and out with a glassy-eyed disorientation, chatted with some of the few military and aid people who have made it this far south, and climbed back into his chopper to head north for Banda Aceh, the provincial capital.

His descriptions of the damage wrought by the massive tidal wave that devastated swathes of South Asia have already entered the historical annals: the worst blight on mankind since the end of the second World War, the biggest relief effort in the history of the world.

And the enormous sums donated by people all over the world, touched by the images of devastation that have defied a collective global imagination, keep hitting jaw-dropping heights.

Banda Aceh in Indonesia after the tsunami. Photograph: Romeo Ranoco/Reuters.

But Annan might have just stopped by one of the large green tents standing on the grass opposite the front door of City Hall and asked Dr Denny Irwansyah how things are in Indonesia, where the death toll stands at just over 100,000, with at least the same number injured. If he had, Denny would have told him: 'It's like a ground-zero situation here' – no government officials or administrative infrastructure, no doctors or nurses or professionals of any sort, no shops or food outlets. If the Indonesian army had not arrived on December 28th, the region would have plunged into anarchy.

'Everyone had to run,' says Denny, who deployed to Meulobah nine days ago with the First Medical Battalion Field Hospital of the Indonesian army, a rapid emergency response group. 'Most people in need from the area come here, and we have been concentrating on treating disease – bronchitis and chest infections, pneumonia, neglected wounds and, of course, we have been doing amputations.'

Two weeks after the giant wall of water triggered by an underwater earthquake in the early hours of St Stephen's Day slammed into a vast circle of coastal communities in South Asia, it's a race against time to prevent many thousands of the survivors joining the death toll. The devastation caused by the tsunamis shocked even Colin Powell, veteran soldier and the world's highest ranking diplomat, who was overcome by what he saw during a three-hour helicopter tour of the Indonesian coastline early this week.

'I have been in war and I have been through a number of hurricanes, tornadoes and other relief operations, but I have never seen anything like this,' said the Vietnam and Gulf War veteran after a swift helicopter ride over Banda Aceh.

Like other leaders from across the world, Powell has pledged unconditional help to South Asia in its recovery, and appeared willing to mend the rift between the US administration and the

United Nations in order to ensure that aid is swiftly and effectively targeted at those in greatest need. The special summit held in Jakarta this week heard promises that the US Secretary of State summed up in a single sentence: 'We will do everything we can to contribute.'

Those pledges so far add up to billions of dollars, and will involve tens of thousands of international troops and relief personnel, many of whom are already working around the clock, in scorched-earth conditions, to put into effect the expectations of people from Dublin to Durban, Melbourne to Mexico, eager to share what they have with those hundreds of thousands in Asia who now have nothing.

As people all over Aceh's coastline slowly make their way to field hospitals in relief hubs such as Meulobah and Banda Aceh, their wounds, already rendered septic by the filthy water, are festering in the humidity and heat. Many people die before they can be helped, many are having limbs amputated. The most unfortunate survivors of the tsunami carnage die of blood poisoning and blood loss after their infected limbs have been removed.

'We have enough drugs and food,' says Denny, thanks to the early American aid drops. 'What we really need is fresh water and sanitation facilities like latrines, for the refugees.' Local water resources were swamped by the seawater, which mixed with waste and sewage to become a toxic cocktail that has made the landscape look more like a ferocious fire has swept through, burning everything to brown.

The aid effort here on the remote coast, up to 300 kilometres south of Banda Aceh, is hampered by the wreckage. Roads that disappeared under the water have been further damaged by aftershocks,

An Achenese woman and child survey the devastation of their neighbourhood after the tsunami hit it. Photograph: Kimimasa Mayama/Reuters.

such as the one on Thursday, which measured 6.0 on the Richter scale. Even passable roads south of Meulobah are seriously fissured by quake damage. Ships cannot enter Meulobah because the harbour two kilometres away has been wrecked. Supplies from ships moored on the coast have to be brought in, laboriously, on smaller boats.

Added to the difficulties in bringing help to those most in need, Annan would also have heard that in west Aceh alone, about 100,000 people are homeless and receiving daily deliveries of rice, dried fish, wheat biscuits and other staples that keep them alive.

Add that to the figures, still being collated, for the country as a whole – the most recent estimates are 102,000 dead and more than half a million homeless – and it is easy to understand why this disaster has elicited such an outpouring of sympathy across the world.

While hundreds of Indonesian volunteers are arriving in stricken regions from the Indonesian capital, Jakarta, few foreign aid organisations have made it to Meulobah. Those that have – mostly Red Cross and medical teams from Singapore and Japan – are sorely needed and warmly welcomed.

The spirit of giving appears to have inspired a global unity, with disparate cultures, fractious nations and seemingly intractable opponents coming together for a common goal. However, some cynical commentators have suggested that the Bush administration's motive in offering help is to improve its international image after two years of opprobrium over the war in Iraq.

There is anecdotal evidence to support the claim that some US aid lifts have been staged for the television cameras, but there is little doubt that any other nation could have mobilised such a massive military relief effort within 10 days and distributed such enormous quantities of food and medicine to some of the poorest and most remote places on earth.

Other commentators have attributed the western outpouring of sympathy to the fact that many people from rich countries take cheap holidays in some of the devastated regions, notably Thailand and Sri Lanka, and that it is only in this way that they can identify with the extent of their loss.

The suggestion from Tony Blair, the British Prime Minister, that stricken nations should be relieved of their debt burden was not greeted with enthusiasm everywhere. Australian Prime Minister John Howard echoed opinions expressed by people standing on a Phuket beach surveying the wreckage of their lives when he said that cancelling debt would give no guarantees that money needed for relief and reconstruction will meet its intended destination.

Many of the tsunami-hit countries are notoriously corrupt, with the rich/poor divide obscene, and aid and loan funds often disappearing into the pockets of the rich. Donations to non-government organisations and through national treasuries at least have a good chance of being funnelled to those in real need.

The total debt of the affected countries – India, Sri Lanka, Somalia, Burma, Thailand, the Maldives, Malaysia and Indonesia – is, according to *The Times* of London, £192,407,000,000. For some of the countries that are doing well in the development stakes, wiping out their debt burden would damage their international credit standing, not something a sensible government wants to do.

But Barbara Stocking, director of Oxfam, says: 'The tsunami crisis has proved that people can and do care about others on the other side of the globe.' Writing in the *International Herald Tribune* this week, she said that parents anywhere could feel the pain of parents in the blighted areas who had lost their children in the deadly waters. 'The tsunami may go down in the history books as one of the world's most tragic natural disasters, but the global wave of compassion and solidarity that followed it could be equally historic,' she wrote.

Her optimism that the global grief could lead to a global awareness 'that abject poverty and suffering do not have to – and must not – exist' may be naïve. But in the weeks since the tsunamis, both Stocking and Kofi Annan have focused on the idea that humanity is united in its similarities and need not be divided by differences of culture, politics or socio-economic categorisation.

SATURDAY, 8 JANUARY 2005

Tough Terrain almost Inaccessible in Places

Barry Roche, in Midleton

To most Corkonians, east Cork is as flat as a snooker table, but this week's search for missing Midleton boy Robert Holohan has introduced the public to another east Cork: rough gnarled terrain riven with nooks and gullies – a searcher's nightmare.

Yesterday at 1 p.m., Sgt Seán Leahy led a group of over 80 volunteers out on their second search of the day for Robert, concentrating this time on an area south of Leamlara village including parts of the Leamlara river. The group was transported in a convoy of police vans, ambulances and four-wheel drives, which snaked its way along main roads and boreens to the search area.

In other times, the Leamlara river would undoubtedly be scenic – a beautiful deciduous wood flanking either side of a steep v-shaped valley tapering down to the river. But yesterday it was far from hospitable as the rain sheeted down.

The volunteer nature of the searchers was reflected in the huge array of implements they brought with them to beat back briars and gorse as they arrived at the rendezvous point at Knockakeen bridge. Sticks, pieces of piping, golf clubs, walking sticks and hurleys were all employed in the battle with briars and furze and the difficulty of crossing over barbed wire and electric fences. Once briefed by Sgt Leahy, they began their search, breaking through gaps in the ditch to spread out and sift through the earmarked fields.

It was not the fields but the scrubland that posed the biggest problems. Tangles of briars, forests of furze and screens of alder saplings down by the riverside made the task all the more difficult, with its impenetrable stretches of terrain that were almost impossible to search.

Inevitably, searchers had to detour, as there were pockets that could not be penetrated. Searchers consoled themselves with the thought that if they couldn't get in there, then hopefully no one else could have either.

John Moore, from Edenderry in Co Offaly, was on his second day of searching. A student at UCC, he decided to join the search on Wednesday. 'I was sitting at home watching it the first night and I was thinking this was desperate. But it's one thing just to sit there and think how desperate it is – it's another to get up and do something about it. So I came down to help out.'

Ruth Flood, a Dubliner who lives at nearby Ballinacurra, decided to join because of her son Adam, who is about the same age. 'Adam knows him [Robert] from the hurling and Adam will be 11 next week, so that touched home. It really hits you when you're putting them to bed at night to think about him out in this.

'It really is every parent's worst nightmare.'

(On January 17, a neighbour, Wayne O'Donoghue, was charged with killing Robert.)

SATURDAY, 8 JANUARY 2005

Does the IRA Take us for Fools?

Editorial

Do they take us democrats, North and South of the Border, for complete fools? What a con-trick they tried to perpetrate on us all, nationalists as well as unionists on the island.

The considered view of the Chief Constable of the Police Service of Northern Ireland, Mr Hugh Orde, that the IRA was responsible for the Northern Bank robbery is a most serious development that may not end the peace process but inflicts fatal damage on the political process as we have known it. We have been conned, those of us North and South of the island, who were urging Sinn Féin and the IRA to do the deal of deals with the Democratic Unionist Party in order to bring about final acts of completion on decommissioning, demilitarisation, policing, the restoration of the Northern institutions and an accommodation between the DUP and Sinn Féin in government.

This the darkest hour in the political process in Northern Ireland where there is no immediate means of reconciling the monumental breach of faith. The Northern Bank robbery has demonstrated that we are more than a photograph away from a restored Executive now.

The offer by the IRA in its New Year message to move into a new mode is meaningless. Especially as it failed to provide clarification sought by the governments that, in such a situation, its members would not 'endanger anyone's personal rights and safety'.

The idea that the IRA would be planning the Northern Bank robbery at the same time that the president of Sinn Féin, Mr Gerry Adams, and the proposed Deputy First Minister, Mr Martin McGuinness, would be negotiating final acts of completion with the two governments just beggars belief.

The IRA initially denied any involvement. But the latest, formal statement from the IRA leadership does not do so. Instead, it speaks vaguely of attempts to criminalise its volunteers but does not refer directly to the robbery. There are echoes here of the mendacious statements made after the murder of Det Garda Jerry McCabe, after the importation of arms and ammunition, and following the arrests of the three men in Colombia. It will not do. Republicans have been allowed to wrap themselves in the mantle of victimhood far too frequently in order to deflect public concerns.

Mr Ahern, and Mr Blair, have accepted Mr Orde's view on IRA involvement. Mr Ahern has expressed disappointment that while he was negotiating in good faith with Sinn Féin, the IRA leadership was planning the robbery. But there was no sense of outrage, of a determination to lock up the criminals. Mr Ahern spoke, instead, of previous disappointments and of 'keeping at it'. That mindset cannot last.

The breach of trust with the democratic community is so serious this time that both governments have to take stock of the peace process.

FRIDAY, 21 JANUARY 2005

'Why Did they Shoot Us? . . . We were Just Going Home'

Chris Hondros, in Tal Afar, Iraq

It was a routine foot patrol in Iraq: a dozen or so men from a platoon, carefully walking the dusky streets of Tal Afar just after sundown. Usually little more happens than finding someone out after curfew, patting him down and then sending him home. On daylight patrols, troops sometimes stop to briefly play with children or even drink tea. On evening patrols – past curfew – no one is on the streets, and the men are extra-vigilant and professional.

Tal Afar is an ethnically-mixed town, primarily Turkoman, and had only days before been the scene of a gun battle between US forces and local insurgents.

On the evening of January 18th, as we made our way up a broad boulevard, I could see a car making its way towards us. As a defence against potential car-bombs, it is now standard practice for foot patrols to stop oncoming vehicles, particularly after dark.

A blood-spattered Iraqi girl after US troops shot dead her parents. She and four siblings were in the rear of a car driven by her father, accompanied by his wife, when US soldiers fired at it at dusk in the town of Tal Afar. Photograph: Chris Hondros/Reuters.

'We have a car coming,' someone called out as we entered an intersection. We could see the car about 100 metres away. The car continued coming. I could not see it any more from my perch, but could hear its engine now, a high whine which sounded more like acceleration than slowing down. It was maybe 50 yards away now.

'Stop that car!' someone shouted out, seemingly simultaneously with someone firing what sounded like warning shots – a staccato, measured burst. The car continued coming. Then, perhaps less than a second later, there was a cacophony of fire – shots rattling off in a chaotic, overlapping din. The car entered the intersection on its own momentum, and still shots were penetrating it and slicing into it. Finally, the shooting stopped, the car drifted listlessly, clearly no longer being steered, and came to a halt on a curb. Soldiers began to approach it warily.

The sound of children crying came from the car. I walked up to it and a teenaged girl with her head covered emerged from the back, wailing and gesturing wildly. After her came a boy, tumbling on to the ground from the seat, already trailing a pool of blood. 'Civilians!' someone shouted, and soldiers ran up. More children – it ended up being six, all told – began to emerge, crying, their faces mottled with streaks of blood. The soldiers carried them to the nearby pavement.

It was by now almost completely dark. Working only with the aid of lights mounted on the ends of rifles, an army medic began assessing the children's injuries, running his hands up and down their bodies, looking for wounds. Incredibly,

Phyllis Spillane (left) and Nancy Glavin from Togher in Cork enjoy a cup of tea as John and Gabrielle McCarthy Lynch take to the floor at the Dance for the Young at Heart in Cork's City Hall. Photograph: Bryan O'Brien.

the only injuries were a girl with a cut hand and a boy with a superficial gash in the small of his back which was bleeding heavily but was not life-threatening. The medic immediately began to bind it while the boy crouched against a wall.

From the pavement, I could see into the bullet-riddled windscreen more clearly. The driver of the car, a man, had been penetrated by so many bullets that his skull had collapsed, leaving his body grotesquely disfigured. A woman also lay dead in the front, still covered in her Muslim clothing and harder to see.

Meanwhile, the children continued to wail and scream, huddled against a wall, sandwiched between soldiers either binding their cuts or trying to comfort them. The army's translator later told me that this was a Turkoman family and that the teenaged girl kept shouting: 'Why did they shoot us? We have no weapons! We were just going home!'

There was a small delay in getting the armoured vehicles lined up and ready, but soon the convoy moved to the main Tal Afar hospital. This was fairly large and surprisingly well equipped, with sober-looking doctors in white coats ambling about its sea-green halls.

The young children were carried in by soldiers and by their teenaged sister. Only the boy with the gash on his back needed any further medical attention, and the army medic and an Iraqi doctor quickly chatted over his prognosis, deciding that his wound would be easy to treat.

The US army informed me that it would be holding a full investigation into the shooting.

SATURDAY, 22 JANUARY 2005

The Death Machine

Daniel McLaughlin

The Holocaust entered thousands of lives with a postman's light tap on the door. In Hungary and Greece, it came as a postcard from relatives, with entreaties to follow them quickly to a wonderful place in the north. In Germany, it arrived as a written order to tidy homes, pack some things and prepare for 'resettlement'. For Jewish women in Vienna, it came wrapped in a small parcel with the request: 'To pay, 150 marks, for the cremation of your husband – ashes enclosed from Dachau.'

The Third Reich excelled in bureaucracy as it excelled in killing, and fashioned a Europe-wide murder industry with a cold eye for efficiency.

Early in Hitler's campaign to annihilate the Jews, mass murder was a bloody business. Refined officers who loudly cherished the classics of German art and culture began to demur at placing bullets in Jewish bodies and shovelling them into mass graves. Gypsies, homosexuals and political prisoners proved no cleaner to kill.

It was not enough to open a special hospital department to deal with SS men whose minds had collapsed under the weight of their crimes. A system was required not only to make mass murder as impersonal as possible, but also to accelerate the obliteration of a race that was seen to be poisoning Germany's lifeblood, a parasite enfeebling its increasingly futile efforts against the Allies.

The alternative, according to the logic of Hitler and his deputies, was inevitable defeat by a Jewish-led cabal of capitalists and Slav communists, who would wreak hideous revenge on Germany's sons and daughters before enslaving them for centuries. The shame and misery that engulfed Germany after the first World War would be repeated tenfold, and Aryan mastery over the globe would be postponed indefinitely, humanity's golden dawn obliterated by a dark Semitic cloud of racial and moral mediocrity.

'This is not the second World War. This is the great racial war. In the final analysis, it is about whether the German and Aryan prevails here, or whether the Jew rules the world, and that is what we are fighting for out there.' So wrote Hermann Goering, the Gestapo chief whose vanity was almost as intense as his loathing for the Jews. It was this self-proclaimed 'last Renaissance man' and lover of archaic German hunting dress who had ordered the seizure of all Jewish property after the Kristallnacht pogrom of November 1938, an orgy of violence that prompted him to predict 'a final reckoning with the Jews' should foreign powers dare to challenge Nazi expansion.

While feeding Hitler's appetite for acquiring territory from the hated Slavs, the push into eastern Europe and the Soviet Union also lumbered him with millions more Jews, whom Germany was already struggling to put to use making weapons, digging stone for bombastic building projects and in deadly labour camps such as Dachau.

When Reinhard Heydrich offered, at Wannsee in January 1942, to ensure that all Jews in German-controlled territory were worked to death or exterminated, it was nothing new to the attendant Nazi officers. Back in 1939, Hitler had vowed that a world war would bring about 'the annihilation of the Jewish race in Europe'. What Heydrich did was slide the Nazi killing machine into a higher gear. Jews were violently evicted from most of the remaining city ghettos and fed into a vast system designed to sweep people hundreds or thousands of miles to their deaths, with as little fuss and expense as possible. Poland – sparsely populated and with a good rail network – was at the dark heart of Hitler's Final Solution for Europe's Jews.

The country played unwilling host to almost 6,000 prison camps of various sizes and regimes, including notorious names such as Treblinka, Belzec, Majdanek and Sobibor, where up to two million people, almost all of them Jews, perished.

Railway tracks leading into Auschwitz, the former Nazi extermination camp for Jews and others, set alight during ceremonies to mark the 60th anniversary of its liberation. Photograph: Katarina Stoltz/Reuters.

Auschwitz – revelling grimly in the lie that welcomed its victims in iron letters: 'Work Brings Freedom' – was the most deadly of the lot. Originally a prison camp for Poles and Soviets, the mass killing began in September 1941, when 850 inmates were crammed into a sealed room and blue pellets of Zyklon B – a gas used in low doses to kill insects and rats – were poured inside.

Auschwitz commandant Rudolf Höss recalled how 'the gassing set my mind at rest, for the mass extermination of the Jews was to start soon, and I was not certain as to how these mass killings would be carried out. Now we had the gas, and we had established a procedure'.

The camp, near Krakow, was extended to neighbouring Birkenau in 1942, where a complex of gas chambers and crematoria was built to deal with the thousands of new prisoners who arrived in filthy cattle-trucks from across eastern Europe every day.

'No one will get out of here alive,' the guards told Alfons Walkiewicz when, as a captured 18-year old fighter from the Polish resistance, his packed wagon clanked into Auschwitz in October 1942. 'The Germans warned us when we arrived: in this place, no one will hold out for more than 100 days,' Walkiewicz recalls. 'All our personal belongings were taken from us. We had to strip naked, keeping only our belts to hold up our trousers.

'They shaved us, not only our heads but also under the arms and the genital region. Then they dunked us in disinfectant, gave us a cold shower, and only then was I given a pair of trousers, a jacket and a striped cap, and shoes with wooden soles. We stopped being human beings. I became a number – 73,526.'

Perhaps 1.5 million people had an Auschwitz number crudely tattooed on to their wrists. Few survived to show their scar to the outside world. The pace of killing, at all the extermination camps, quickened as the war rolled on, and US involvement and the Soviet counter-attack turned the tide against Germany.

Some survived the relentless 'selections' that spared those who were still strong enough to work, but most of the women, children and elderly were taken immediately from their train wagon to the gas chambers, and kept docile by the promise of a shower, food and rest. Anyone heard to warn new arrivals of their fate was hurled alive into the crematorium. The Nazis liked their enemies to die quickly, cleanly and quietly.

A few people, such as Sophia Litwinska, survived to tell the tale of the gas chamber: 'There were towels hanging round, and sprays, even mirrors. People were in tears; people were shouting at each other; people were hitting each other. Suddenly I saw fumes coming in through a very small window at the top. I had to cough violently, tears streaming from my eyes, and I had a sort of feeling in my throat as if I would be asphyxiated.'

Litwinska was dragged unconscious from the chamber and, when relating her story after the war, still seemed unsure why she had been spared. Not many were so fortunate as the Final Solution gained momentum.

Dr Charles Bendel, a Romanian Jewish doctor, was ordered to work at the Auschwitz crematorium in August 1944. By then, the ovens were not able to burn bodies quickly enough to keep up with the efficiency of the gas chambers, which could kill 2,000 people at a time. So a set of canals was dug in the earth nearby, 'through which the human fat or grease should seep so that the work could be continued in a quicker way,' Dr Bendel recalled.

'The capacity of these trenches was almost fantastic. Crematorium number four was able to burn 1,000 people during the day, but this system of trenches was able to deal with the same number in one hour.'

Dr Bendel worked with Dr Josef Mengele, the notorious Nazi doctor who experimented on scores of Auschwitz inmates before killing them with a lethal injection. His involvement at the camp, and that of medical colleagues at several others, belied the macabre scientific interest the Nazis took in their 'sub-Aryan' victims.

The gas chambers of the Polish extermination camps were descended from the shower rooms in the extermination centres set up around Germany in the late 1930s, where some 70,000 mentally and physically handicapped people were executed. There, carbon monoxide rather than Zyklon-B was the preferred poison. This 'euthanasia' project, T4, tempered a hard core of scientists and killers for the later work of exterminating the Jews.

Hitler argued that modern society was dulling the effects of natural selection by keeping alive the handicapped and the elderly, and so wasting resources that could be devoted to strong, healthy – and above all, Aryan – citizens. In economically depressed post-war Germany, the Nazis portrayed the elimination of the sick, the elderly and the Jews – as well as 'anti-social elements' such as the gypsies – as a quick way to cut welfare costs and allow a hike in military spending. Empty hospital beds were also needed for the war-wounded, while Jewish forced labour freed up German men to join the military, and their empty houses were snapped up by Germans 'repatriated' from eastern Europe.

The Nazis co-opted economic ideas and twisted evolutionary theories to create a hatefully poisonous ideology of race, mingling extreme prejudice and expedience to seduce a nation that was poor, demoralised and hungry for a scapegoat for its suffering.

'They [the Jews] had to be treated like a tuberculosis bacillus, with which a healthy body may become infected,' Hitler told Hungary's wavering wartime leader in 1943. 'This was not cruel, if one remembers that even innocent creatures, such as hares and deer, have to be killed, so that no harm is caused by them. Why should the beasts who wanted to bring us Bolshevism be spared more? Nations that did not rid themselves of Jews perished.'

As the Allies got the upper hand, Hitler began to fear that Hungary could go over to their side, and ordered the immediate occupation of the country in March 1944. Despite the efforts of Raoul Wallenberg and Carl Lutz, Swedish and Swiss diplomats who issued thousands of life-saving visas to Budapest's Jews, more than 400,000 of them were deported to Auschwitz. Before being killed, they were forced to sign postcards urging their relatives to quickly join them in lovely 'Waldsee'.

The Red Army arrived at the camp on January 27th, 1945. The SS had already abandoned the place where more than a million people had been murdered. The Final Solution had come up short – about five million of Europe's 11 million Jews escaped its maw.

'Among the inmates, you could not distinguish the men from the women, the young from the old. They were wide-eyed human beings with translucent skin,' recalls Genry Koptev, now aged 80, who was part of the Soviet 322nd division that liberated the camp. 'They were laughing and crying all at once, and telling us about their lives in all possible languages. Then I saw a whole alley bordered with two-metre high bonfires, from which human bodies emerged. The alley was leading to the camp's crematorium. I also saw a room where human hair was stockpiled, and another where there were only spectacles. Then I went into the shower room, whose walls were covered in dark blue tiles. But only after the Nuremberg trial did I learn how they were used. I could never understand how a human mind could conceive of this.'

Neither, quite, could Primo Levi, the Italian chemist and writer who was one of the few men to walk away from Auschwitz. In *If This is a Man*, Levi's account of the year he spent in the camp, he recalls being perused by a curious Nazi doctor:

'If I had known how completely to explain the nature of that look, which came as if across the glass window of an aquarium between two beings who live in different worlds, I would also have explained the essence of the great insanity of the third Germany.'

TUESDAY, 25 JANUARY 2005

Only a Trembling Hand Betrayed his Feelings as he was Led Away

Frank McNally

The great legal motto 'Let justice be done though the heavens fall' has never been fully tested in the courts, and yesterday was no exception.

As a former minister for justice was done – on two counts of tax fraud – the heavens stayed exactly where they were, yet again. But if something did fall on a momentous day, it was the idea that anybody is above the law. The writing was on the wall for Ray Burke from about halfway through the sentencing speech. Yet even at the end he seemed to have trouble seeing it.

For several seconds after the judge declared him a prisoner, the former politician stared straight ahead, unblinking. Then he reached for his overcoat, and only a trembling hand betrayed his feelings as he was led away. His demeanour in court was a condensed version of the manner in which his political career ended in 1997.

For the second time in a month, he found himself surrounded by petty criminals, some released from handcuffs only long enough to step forward and plead guilty. But dressed in a smart suit, Mr Burke again stood out from the crowd, and at first looked calm and even confident. He stood out literally too. Well before he was called, he moved from the back of the court and took a prominent position in the aisle near the front. When Judge Hogan began reciting the facts of the case, Mr Burke stood with hands clasped behind his back, looking almost as assured as when he was still a minister.

It was just after the judge emphasised the role of the Oireachtas in defining tax fraud as a serious crime that the bearing of the former Oireachtas member changed slightly. Now for the first time the defendant looked defensive: clasping his hands in front of him, like a footballer facing a free kick. The defensive posture was fully justified by the turn the speech had taken. Judge Hogan was now talking about breach of public trust, about abuse of 'a special position', and about the 'impact of the offence on the body politic'.

Ray Burke stepping into a prison van to be taken to jail after being sentenced to six months imprisonment for tax crimes. Photograph: Frank Miller.

The impact of the speech on the body of the former politician was becoming clear. He folded his arms across his chest, staring straight at – or maybe through – the man on the bench, as he was told he had been guilty of 'a premeditated act of commission, not one of omission'. By the end of the half-hour summary, the judge's words were sounding like a drum-roll. Only an act of contrition would do Mr Burke now, and that wouldn't save him from his penance.

Seven years ago, he answered questions for 90 minutes in the Dáil and claimed he had drawn 'a line in the sand'. Unfortunately for him, it was quicksand, and he was to face a lot more questions, from the tribunals and finally the Criminal Assets Bureau. So when he finally went to jail, he had nothing left to say.

The consensus among journalists before the hearing was that the defendant would 'walk' afterwards. He did, but only the short distance to the white Garda van that would take him to prison.

A reporter shouted: 'Have you anything to say, Mr Burke?' But Mr Burke went quietly.

WEDNESDAY, 26 JANUARY 2005

What's in a Number? If it's 53, Murder, Suicide and Ruin

Rome Letter: Paddy Agnew

Franco Grassi sounds the sort of person who liked to tie up loose ends. Last Sunday week he took the family dog down the road to a local kennel club, close to his home in Signa, outside Florence, asking them to look after it for him for a while. On that same Sunday night, after his wife, Patricia, and their 27-year-old son, Giacomo, had both gone to bed, he unplugged the house phone and took the batteries out of all the family mobile phones. Then, notwithstanding the late hour, he unlocked the door of the house, leaving it ajar.

His preparations concluded, 56-year-old Franco then took out his 44 Magnum Smith and Wesson and shot his wife, then his son and finally himself. The triple deaths were discovered only last Wednesday when colleagues, worried that Giacomo had failed to turn up for work for three days and unable to contact him, had gone round to his house. Franco Grassi and his family are but the latest known victims of Fever 53, a betting epidemic that has seen hundreds of thousands of Italians bet on the possibility of the number 53 coming up in Lotto, the national lottery.

Lotto has a twice-weekly draw of five numbers (1-90) linked to 10 Italian cities (Bari, Cagliari, Florence, Genoa, Milan, Naples, Palermo, Roma, Turin and Verona). As luck, or ill-luck, would have it, the number 53 last came up in the Venice draw of May 2003, or 178 draws ago.

That statistic alone has seen 53 become so popular a bet that €3.2 billion has been wagered (and lost) on it in the last 18 months. The longer 53 fails to show up, the more frenetic becomes the urge to bet on it, based on the statistically questionable belief that, sooner or later, it has to come up again.

Just five days before the Grassi family tragedy, Fever 53 had struck in Carrara on the Tuscan coast. That Tuesday morning 58-year-old housewife Maria had taken the bus to the end of the line at Marinella, close to the beach. There she took off her overcoat, leaving it hanging on a winter-abandoned deck chair, and walked into the sea. She was still wearing her high heels. Her body was discovered later that day. When Maria's husband came home from work, he found the morning's shopping in a plastic supermarket bag on the kitchen table. There was also a note from his wife: 'Forgive me. I can't take it any more, I'm destroyed by remorse, I've run up so many debts at the Lotto'.

Lotto receipts showed that Maria, like Franco Grassi, had gambled (and lost) consistently on 53. Gambling fever has had a less tragic but still potentially devastating effect on many other Italian families.

In the last week Italian media have been full of stories of how families have been ruined by the obsessive gambling habit of one family member. There was the housewife from Frosinone who wagered a total of €53,000 on 53 and then had to resort to loan sharks to get herself and her family out of trouble. There was the woman from Rossignano Solvay, near Livorno, who gambled €50,000 on 53, using two dud cheques, and had to leave town in a hurry.

Or there was the bank clerk from Oltrepo Pavese who got the sack last week after it was discovered that he had 'borrowed' nearly €1 million from clients' current accounts, all of it to bet on the accursed 53.

The epidemic has become so serious that last week the consumer group Codacons called on the government to throw 'water on the fire' and block bets on 53. Thus far the government has not moved either to block the 53 or in some other way limit gambling on Lotto. The government's reluctance is understandable given that the state-run Lotto on average pays out only 43 per cent of its introits. Understandable, too, when you consider that in the first 11 months of last year Italians spent a total of €23 billion on betting games (Lotto, Superenalotto, Tris, Totip et al), of which Lotto is by far the most popular. €23 billion, too, represents not only a remarkable 2 per cent of Italian GDP but also a 38 per cent increase on the same period in 2003.

Even the authoratitive figure of Cardinal Ennio Antonelli of Florence has called for moderation, arguing that people should 'not exacerbate the obsession with gambling'. Yet, neither Church nor government can seriously hope to curb a habit that has been around in these parts for some while given that a Genoa version of Lotto dates back to 1576. Maybe the cursed 53 could do us all a favour and just turn up.

MONDAY, 31 JANUARY 2005

Tensions Finally Lifted as Baghdadis Turn Out

Jack Fairweather, in Baghdad

The mood of foreboding finally lifted from Baghdad yesterday as Iraqis turned out to vote in their thousands. For weeks Baghdad has had the feel of a city under siege, with daily car bombings, assassinations and threats driving election workers and candidates undercover.

But yesterday even the intermittent sound of explosions and gunfire could not stop Iraqis from

Patrick Collison (16) from Castletroy College in Limerick steps forward to receive the Esat/Young Scientist of the Year award at the Royal Dublin Society in Dublin. Photograph: Joe St Leger.

casting their ballots. Some were nervous, others excited. Most said they were voting to reject the terrorism that has come to dominate their lives and which few have been able to protest against. 'The Iraqi people have been silent for too long. I want to show the terrorists that I am not afraid. This is my country, and they must now stop destroying it,' said Mr Hussein Hadi, a 33-year-old minibus driver.

Across Baghdad, residents made their way to polling stations on foot, an unprecedented security operation having locked down the city. Traffic was banned and streets sealed off with barbed wire, with dozens of Iraqi policemen manning each polling station. American forces on the ground stayed largely in the background. At times, the scene was reminiscent of the days after the war, when residents emerged from the bombing to eagerly discuss their future.

On Abu Nawass street, one of Baghdad's main thoroughfares, US helicopters flew overhead, Iraqi policemen at checkpoints confiscated cigarette lighters and pens, and families promenaded down the centre of the street on their way to vote.

'Don't worry, don't worry,' said one Iraqi man, smiling, as the sound of an explosion ricocheted off surrounding buildings. 'This is our day, a special day for all Iraqis to savour freedom,' said the man. 'But now I must go and vote.'

At polling station 6504, in a middle-class Shia district, the crowds began arriving shortly after 7 a.m. The building, a temporarily converted school, was surrounded by three cordons of barbed wire and a large hand-drawn poster for the main Shia list, an indication of who many would be voting for. Iraqi policemen, most of whom had spent the night at the station, frisked voters as they approached, directing women to a nearby tent. By 10 a.m., a queue had formed at the entrance to the polling station, men and women forming separate lines.

Inside, following directions on a blackboard, voters registered their names in one of four rooms set aside for voting in the two-storey concrete school. They then took two A3-size voting papers, for national and district elections, to a voting booth constructed from two cardboard boxes, before placing them into ballot boxes.

Mr Sayada Abid, a 65-year-old female voter, burst into tears as she recalled how Saddam Hussein's regime had executed her son for praying outside a mosque. 'God willing we will now have a proper government running this country, and Saddam Hussein will rot in hell,' she said, dipping her finger in a pot of indelible ink to prove she had voted.

Outside the room, polling centre manager and headmaster of the school, Mr Talib Ibrahim, fielded questions from worried voters. 'I insist on my right to vote,' said one man who could not find his name on a voter list. Last week Mr Ibrahim had received a letter containing a death threat. But like many yesterday, he was undeterred. 'This is the first step in one thousand miles towards freedom and stability,' he said. 'We want to send a message that in spite of the violence, in spite of the three wars Saddam put us through, we are an advanced people.' By 5 p.m., Mr Ibrahim said, almost 75 per cent of registered voters had cast their ballots.

At another polling station in Ameriya, a predominantly Sunni part of Baghdad, polling officials estimated that 50 per cent had cast their votes. Officials said that figures had been kept down by a brief exchange of gunfire between policemen and insurgents, a reminder of the intensity of anti-election activity in Sunni areas which had threatened to keep turn-out down to a minimum. In some parts of the city, like the Baathist-dominated Aadamiya district, voters did stay away.

'We're still surprised by the number of people who have turned up today,' said the polling station manager in Ameriya, Mr Raed Jamal. 'It is clear to me that Sunnis as well as Shias want to have a part in this election. We all want to shape the future of our country,' said Mr Jamal. He said he had been expecting four or five people to show up. Instead there were 8,500.

Tweenie, a boxer pup from Monkstown, Co. Dublin, gets a wash at the new special dog wash facility at a local petrol station. Photograph: Bryan O'Brien.

As darkness fell and gunfire echoed around the city, polling wound down and Mr Jamal and his officials settled down to begin counting the votes. To the sound of fighting outside he shrugged, and said: 'The terrorists are too late. This city has spoken.'

MONDAY, 7 FEBRUARY 2005

From Lad to Dad in just Nine Months

Shane Hegarty

For men like me, facing parenthood for the first time, there are plenty of books. Most, though, are written by women and assume that the man is an appendage to the process, there to pick up things around the house and be yelled at in the delivery suite. Recently, however, there has been a glut of books by men, for men. Their angle: the man is an appendage to the process, there to pick up things around the house and be yelled at in the delivery suite – but here's how to do it well.

They have such titles as *From Lad to Dad* and *The Bloke's Guide to Pregnancy*, based very much on the idea that fatherhood drags men from a happy life of watching football in the pub and drops them into an alien land called Responsibility (following a stopover at Maturity). They are written in mates-down-the-pub language. If women's books can be earthy, men's tend to veer toward the crude. How does Stephen Giles, author of *From Lad to Dad*, react to the prospect of being a father? 'I'm shitting myself,' he admits. Telling people the good news, though, was 'a piece of piss'. He mentions his genitals a lot. He recommends reading basic pregnancy books because, if nothing else, they are full of pictures of naked women.

While books for pregnant women are very much manuals for a changing body, men don't have to deal as much with the medical stuff, so the books go down the personal route. It means that they are a mix of helpful information and man/child angst.

Perhaps books for men used to be so rare because it was believed that they didn't really get involved with their offspring between conception and somewhere around the teenage years. Now books are written by and for New Men, but based on the assumption that their readers have been enjoying the advantages of being Old Man for a while.

One thing comes across immediately: the men really hadn't thought about babies before. That was the woman's job. So, each book takes a standard route: She's pregnant. Oh God! I've to change my lifestyle. Oh God! She's in labour. Oh God! I'm a father. Oh God! It's nine months of constant surprise. Overall, men are advised to tippy-toe through the term, nodding where appropriate. A supportive man is one who accepts that he will never fully understand his partner's experience, who gets used to his new role as domestic slave and who doesn't complain about her unavoidable flatulence. What else, though, can a pregnant man learn about impending fatherhood from these books?

The pregnancy

Learning that your partner is pregnant is the scariest thing that can happen to a man. Ever. It is so scary for men because (cue apocalyptic music) it means having to 'grow up'. In *Fatherhood: The Truth,* Marcus Berkmann is somewhat more forthright than is necessary. 'Coming to terms with impending fatherhood has much in common with the process of bereavement,' he writes, melodramatically. 'First you feel anger (it's not mine, you bitch), then denial (whose is it then, you bitch?), then despair (oh f--k, oh f--k, my life is over), then bargaining (well, you never know it might not be too bad), then finally acceptance (will you marry me?).'

There are quite long sections on money, most pithily summed up by *The Bloke's Guide to Pregnancy* through the title of a section: 'Me, hunter-gatherer'. Men lie awake worrying about supporting the family, although each book is quite broad-minded about the idea of becoming a house-husband. Sure, you'll get some funny looks, but if you want to go for it, then why not? The coffee mornings are good.

Men wish to avoid being like their dads, and they fear the worst. 'Will I be able to restrain myself from imposing my views on the poor kid?' wonders *From Lad to Dad*. 'Will I make them support my team and follow my uncertain footsteps or will I force the little soul to become a lawyer or a doctor, or something else "worthwhile"? Will I be a pushy dad or a laid-back dad? Will I be like my own dad or the complete opposite?'

The Bloke's Guide says that most men want a boy, and that the idea of having a girl is intimidating to fathers. Girls get pregnant as teenagers, boys score winning goals in FA Cup finals. It's a straightforward choice. But when asked what they want, a man should reply, like a mantra, that he 'really doesn't mind either way'.

The partner

Women have hormones. The exact detail of these hormones is not important; their unpredictable effects are all that matter. These books reflect the general bafflement with which men greet women's mood swings. It is, as *The Bloke's Guide* calls it, 'pregnancy venom' and it gives men a temporary partner in place of the woman they used to know. It can be cute though, as women suddenly cry at the slightest thing such as a bad movie, baby clothes or 'a two-for-one deal in Iceland'.

Each book advises that the reader does not get angered by these emotional swings, especially given

Shane Hegarty boning up on being a Dad. Photograph: Bryan O'Brien.

that a man cannot blame his hormones. Some of the tips seem quite straightforward. 'Don't tell her that her bum is getting bigger,' for instance, is sound advice. Some of it, though, seems oddly suicidal. *The Bloke's Guide* suggests that if her transformation from object of lust to mother puts you off sex, then just explain this to her. Great advice, as long as you have prepared the spare room in advance.

The bedroom

In many of the women's books, sex is dealt with in a no-nonsense way. In Dr Miriam Stoppard's *Pregnancy and Birth Book*, for instance, pencil sketches of hippies in sexual congress are included without the slightest snigger. In the men's pregnancy books, though, a lot of the information is laced with a bit of Hugh Grant-esque awkwardness and embarrassed talk about 'bits'.

The Bloke's Guide is actually very honest and open on this topic, but it makes sure to soften it up with a bit of lad-speak about being a 'shag monster' and the opportunities that are presented when the pregnant woman gets a visit from 'the Breast Fairy'. Its section about the possibility of sexual frustration arrives with the sensitive euphemism, 'Pamela and Her Five Sisters'.

Oddly, it also feels the need to warn readers that even if there is a lack of action at home it is not wise to have a drunken fling with another woman. There are men who need this advice? Good luck to their partners.

The labour

The man's job is to bring a camera, have enough change for the parking meter, make sure the birth plan is adhered to, and be shouted at without ever shouting back. And by the way, the birth is messy. Very messy. When mother and child are in hospital recovering, then this is the last chance for some time that a man will have to get very drunk. He should take it.

The baby

Fatherhood: *The Truth* covers both pregnancy and the early months of being a dad. Finally, after nine months of feeling slightly disconnected and ineffectual, the man can look forward to ... well, several more months of feeling slightly disconnected and ineffectual. A new father can also expect, like the author, to be 'Competitive Dad': 'If you told me that you had an ugly baby, I would probably say that mine was uglier.'

There are plenty of books on actually being a dad, although too many are American ones written like corporate self-improvement books. *The One-Minute Dad*, for example, is from the people behind *The One-Minute Manager* and applies business techniques to being a parent. Sounds like fun.

Another American book, *Come On Dad: 75 Things for Fathers and Sons to Do Together*, is for fathers who want to either a) bond with their son or b) exclude their daughters. It is filled with advice that is both practical and pushy. For instance, why not set up a lemonade stand with your son? ('He'll learn the rudiments of setting up a business and earn a few dollars as well.') It also suggests ways to make each activity harder: 'Explain that in real business, the key to success is selling the product for more than it cost to acquire and produce.'

To be honest, I'll wait until I actually have the child before I start attracting the attention of the anti-child labour laws, but thanks for all the advice.

THURSDAY, 10 FEBRUARY 2005

I, Keano in the Olympia Theatre, Dublin

Fintan O'Toole

The dancing has all the grace of a chorus of drunken uncles practising *The Chicken Song* in a bog. Some of the singing wouldn't make the grade on the terraces at Tolka Park on a wet Wednesday night. The songs are both good and original, but the original ones aren't good and the good ones aren't original. It has all the subtlety of a head-butt and all the sophistication of a late-night phone-in show on Yob FM. And …

I, Keano is a scream. At its best, the self-styled 'musical epic' on the clash between Roy Keane and Mick McCarthy on Saipan before the 2002 World Cup is sublimely ridiculous.

It is not, of course, the first dramatisation of the story. Sophocles got there first in 409 BC, with his play Philoctetes, in which the Greek army's preparations for the world mass-murder championships at Troy come to grief on a remote island when its greatest archer goes into a huff and refuses to take part in the coming battles. The writers of *I, Keano* – Arthur Mathews, Michael Nugent and Paul Woodfull – have taken their cue, however, from another classic, Stephen Sondheim's *A Funny Thing Happened on the Way to the Forum*. It is a smart choice. The mock-heroic, cod-Roman setting captures perfectly the inflated egos and delusions of grandeur that saturate contemporary soccer. And given that the Saipan episode was already a mock-heroic episode in which an essentially trivial affair was given epic importance, it makes sense that *I, Keano* is a parody of a parody.

This doesn't mean that it could not be much better than it is. It draws together much of the best comic talent from Irish broadcasting: Mathews, co-writer of *Father Ted*; Gary Cooke and Risteárd Cooper from Après Match; Mario Rosenstock from Today FM's *Gift Grub*; and Joe Taylor from numerous RTÉ shows. Radio and TV comedy demand brilliant moments and there are many of them here.

But the architecture of a musical – even a musical parody – is very different. *I, Keano* suffers from problems of structure that even Peter Sheridan's adept production can't solve. Most obviously, the writers fail to deal with the problem that almost all the drama lies in the build-up to Keane's explosive outburst against McCarthy and that the rest is anti-climax. Thus, we get a seriously unbalanced show, with most of the hilarity packed into a joyous first half and the second act moving forward with a slow puncture.

Paul Woodfull's songs will also come as a bit of a let-down to fans of his savagely accomplished Wolfe Tones parody, Ding Dong Denny O'Reilly. There are some inspired moments here, where musical parody chimes perfectly with the broader caricatures: Cooper's Niall Quinn as a soppy Michael Jackson singing of his love for all the children of the world, or Paul McGlinchey's Packie Bonner as a saccharine Daniel O'Donnell sing-alike. But too many of the tunes are just Broadway boilerplate that remind us that the best send-ups come from people who really know the stuff they're setting out to parody.

All of this matters much less than it ought to, however. The atmosphere of *I, Keano* is a bit like that among the home crowd at a football match. If your team pops up from time to time to score a great goal, who cares that there are passages of scrappy football in between? There are enough goals scored here to keep a partisan crowd happy. Cooper and Tara Flynn as Surfia, wife of the saintly Quinness, engage in unmercifully entertaining slagging that reminds us how no good deed goes unpunished. Cooke adds a very funny piss-take of Alex Ferguson (here conceived as Fergi the Dolphin God) to his familiar caricature of Eamon Dunphy. Dessie Gallagher's Macartacus manages to be both an uncannily accurate depiction and a wild send-up of the hapless manager.

And, in a clear case of art imitating life, it is Keano who takes a talented but limited outfit and drags it towards moments of greatness. Rosenstock is the show's midfield general, taking it by the scruff of the neck and driving it forward. He is so funny here because he is so serious, his fixed gaze, furrowed brow and simmering intensity clashing with his clownish surroundings to hysterical effect. The way he sings Keane's famously foul-mouthed tirade against McCarthy is itself worth the price of admission.

The pin that bursts a balloon doesn't need to be especially sharp. Crude though it may be.

I, Keano tears a mighty hole in the nation's ridiculous over-hyping of the Keane/McCarthy wars, and lets the bad air escape in the form of a laughter directed more at ourselves than at the protagonists in that over-inflated drama.

Mario Rosenstock, Keano in I, Keano, *striding forth to do his thing in the Olympia Theatre, Dublin. Photograph: Bryan O'Brien.*

Braving the elements on Dublin's Clanbrassil Street. Photograph: Bryan O'Brien.

THURSDAY, 10 FEBRUARY 2005

The Terror of Anyone Finding out that I was 'Illegitimate'

Kitty Holland

I was six. I remember asking my father when his and my mother's wedding anniversary was. He told me they had never married. Thrown by this piece of information, I asked why not. 'We didn't feel there was any need. We love each other and we love you and your brother, and a wedding is an awful lot of fuss to organise,' he told me.

It should have been a sufficient answer. But, in 1977, I was horrified at the implications. I doubt I had heard the word 'bastard' but on some childish level I understood that to have parents who were unmarried was something to be ashamed of. It did not matter that my mother and father had been partners for almost a decade, and would continue to be for almost another. What shamed and embarrassed me was that they had had my brother, and me, and had not had a wedding beforehand.

I went to a liberal, Protestant national school in Rathmines, where no one spoke much of sinning. There was some Bible-reading but religion was not high on the agenda – morals were rooted in the promotion of tolerance, behaving decently and being good to people. Words like 'nigger' and 'wog' were banned, with discussions about all humans being God's children. And despite all of this, I remember clearly my terror of it being found out that my parents were not married, that I was 'illegitimate'.

I remember one lunch-break when I was about 10, sitting with my heart in my mouth, as two friends, Lisa and Karen, argued about what a

Glendalough. Photograph: Eric Luke.

'bastard' was. My stomach was clenched with terror as I sat in silence, hoping I would not be called upon to contribute in case I was caught.

I had not thought as far as to wonder what would happen if they found out I was indeed the personification of all these evils. They might have disowned me as a friend. They might have asked me what it was like to be such an exotic bird. They might not have cared. All I remember at the time was the terror that I might be caught, and the relief when I wasn't. And I remember carrying that low-level terror with me for perhaps another two years until I realised in fact that three of my friends too were 'illegitimate', and two of them were living with their single mums. I rarely see them now, but I recall them fondly as happy, kind, fun, intelligent, beautiful girls, loved and nurtured by their parents.

The sense of shame, I must stress, was not all-consuming by any means. Being 'illegitimate' did not impinge enormously on my thoughts as a child. It was not a day-to-day concern. But it was there, always in the background, an issue I did not want to hear being discussed. And in my child's world the word 'bastard' gave rise, quite simply, to a painful sense that I wished I was not one. As a child, questions of morality are always black and white, right and wrong, with no scope for shades of grey. Choices are simple to a child. The things you do are either good or bad.

Life experience, one hopes, teaches us to understand the frailty of the human condition, to realise that the choices we make might not be simple, that life can disappoint and hurt. And even our infallible parents, who may have embarked on a path together full of hope and optimism, can make mistakes. They may have had an unplanned pregnancy. Or may, as loving, unmarried partners, have planned one.

Which is why an offensive term like 'bastard' is so obscene when applied to a child. The simplicity with which that child views the world can easily be lost sight of. Legally, technically and linguistically, 'bastard' may be the correct term for a baby born to two unmarried people. But it implies a difference, a morally degenerate difference. And to a child who sees only right and wrong, only good and bad, the ifs and the whys are irrelevant. The only thing a beautiful, optimistic, full of potential child knows is that to be a 'bastard' is to be shameful. Six-year-old optimists can too easily be confused and hurt, if society tells them they are bastards.

My sense of embarrassment was, of course, nothing to that poisonous shame inflicted on the thousands of women forced into Magdalen laundries throughout the last century. It was nothing compared to the agony inflicted on 15-year-old Anne Lovett, whose shame of being unmarried and pregnant forced her into a Co. Longford graveyard to give birth and die, alone, just over 20 years ago.

Nor was it anything comparable to the torture Joanne Hayes endured giving birth to her baby in Kerry in the early 1980s. Nor again does it come close to the torment that the children of some of those Magdalen women have since gone through trying to find their mothers years after they had been given up.

The word 'bastard', however, resonated for the same reasons with them as it did, in a small way, with me. Language is never neutral. Language is a reflection of the way we interpret our society and by extension how we treat its members. Kevin Myers is an intelligent man who well knows this. To use the word 'bastard' in reference to children is to legitimise the connotations around it. To make the use of the word bastard permissible about children is to make once again permissible the victimisation, discrimination, shame and hurt inflicted on thousands of children and their parents. It is to inflict confusion and shame on children. It is an incitement to – at best – think less of children 'disadvantaged' by circumstances over which they had no control.

The label 'bastard' is not just a word. And the hurt it has given rise to is too close to argue otherwise.

SATURDAY, 12 FEBRUARY 2005

One Up for the Cardigans

Maeve Binchy

The news programme announces the engagement in the little mini-market where people are doing their morning shopping. The younger people ignore it, as they continue to root around looking for extra complimentary CDs among the magazines or to lick bits of frozen yogurt from the outside of the cartons …

The older people are more interested. 'That will be a relief to her majesty,' says the woman with a basket full of lentils for herself and choice cuts for her cat. 'Her poor majesty was exhausted trying to turn the other way; now it will all be above board.'

'A lot of bloody nonsense,' says the man in the cloth cap with the north of England accent, who buys tins of pilchards and oven chips and nothing else. 'Pair of them were perfectly all right living over the brush like half the country; he's only marrying her because they're asking questions about how much of our money he spends on her anyway.' And the large comfortable woman who sits like a wise old bird at the checkout is very pleased. 'It's one up for the cardigans,' she says. 'I knew the day would come when a woman as shabby as myself would marry a prince.'

I lived here in these London streets in 1981 when Charles was getting married for the first time, and the atmosphere was electric. The playboy prince was going to settle down, and he had found a nice virgin girl to marry. Yet, at his engagement press conference, when asked was he in love, he had said rather ominously: 'Yes, whatever that means.' But the country had gone mad with an innocent pleasure. It was July 1981, and there was a huge fireworks display in Hyde Park the night before the wedding. There were street parties, and I was almost afraid to tell people I was talking to on the tube to St Paul's that I had an invitation to the do in my handbag. They might have killed for it. And I say 'the people that I talked to' because for a day or two London forgot its introversion and everyone spoke to everyone else. It was like the day the Pope had come to Dublin two years previously.

It was something that was of its time and will never happen in the same way again. There's no excitement about Charles and Camilla in the streets of west London this time around. No spontaneous flags and bunting, no lump in the throat empathising with the happy event. The past 24 years have seen too much murky water flow under too many bridges. The little virgin bride shed all her shyness and puppy fat and became one of the world's most beautiful women, and Charles, who had never loved her remotely, behaved as badly as any pantomime

Britain's Prince Charles and his new wife, HRH the Duchess of Cornwall, the former Camilla Parker Bowles, after opening a playground while on honeymoon in Scotland in April 2005, the first official engagement since their marriage. Photograph: Jeff Mitchell/Reuters.

villain. The disastrous royal marriage was lived out in public, with other parties briefing the media about the rights and wrongs of the situation. The couple's two little boys struggled on, surrounded by butlers, nannies and non-speaking relatives.

Princess Diana, who at one stage held all the cards because she was nice to people and full of charm, lost out in the end in every possible way. Charles, who became more arrogant and mutinous with every passing year, made little attempt to hide his relationship and now seems, oddly, to have won. It looks now as if he is being rewarded: he is getting the marriage he should have had 35 years ago when Camilla was certainly up for it but when he dithered and couldn't make a decision. It's not a love story that immediately sets the bells ringing or promises to get to the heart of the nation. But never underestimate the power of the media.

About 20 minutes after the usual messed-up announcement from Clarence House, a statement that left so many questions unanswered and showed a complete lack of planning and preparation, all the television channels had wheeled in the ageing royal-watchers. They were brought out of mothballs and dusted down and wound up to go. I know what I'm talking about; I was one of them.

Queen Elizabeth II has four children. I was at three of their weddings and I didn't bring any of them much luck. Only Prince Edward's first marriage has survived, and Princess Anne's second marriage. I am sure Charles and Camilla, who have had each other out on approval for some time, will make a go of it. And truly, most people of goodwill will wish them happiness, as you would to anyone who has had a troubled journey in romance. But it's such a different scene this time around. I wonder whether Charles, in his very narrow world, knows this.

Models adjusting the straps on their Paul Costello shoes at the Irish Tatler *Design Showcase fashion show in Dublin Castle. Photograph: Fran Veale.*

It's hard for any of us to know what other people think and how they live and what their values are. But it must be harder for the Prince of Wales, surrounded as he is by sycophants and by people who grew up in the same strange enclosed world as himself, where journalists are called 'reptiles' and where there are the People Who Matter and then the rest of the world, which doesn't matter a bit. He must think he is a scream, because I have seen the awful, fawning, servile press, really worse than reptiles, laughing hysterically if he makes a stupid joke. Why would he not think that his forthcoming wedding should be on the same scale as the last one? He has no loving family to lean on.

His parents never went to visit him when he was at that terrible school, Gordonstoun. Do you know anyone who was never visited at boarding school by their parents? He was completely out of touch with the life his first bride wanted to live, and there was nobody to advise him, except in the ways of protocol, history and tradition, which could be summed up as 'wives must learn'. He was singularly unlucky in that his wife never did.

His polo-playing friends told him that Diana was a loony tune and that his best bet was to invite Camilla to their house-parties. Then, somewhere along the line, somebody taped his intimate conversation with Camilla years ago and broadcast it to the world. That was the only day I felt really sorry for Charles. I could have wept for his sheer embarrassment as I saw him on television straightening his cuffs and going to see his mother, who was after all the queen of the country that was rocking to his bizarre sexual fantasies. Strange as they were, they were his and Camilla's own business.

So the man who will presumably one day be king may not have a clue how his future subjects think of him and his wedding.

For a start, most of the broadcasts and breaking news and interviews focused on the issue of what poor Camilla would be called. She would not dare to call herself Princess of Wales, would she? She couldn't ever be queen, could she? And eventually, two hours later, Charles's expensive spin doctors and PR people issued a statement defining what the woman would or would not be called.

Then there were hours of debate about whether a civil ceremony would be a proper marriage for a head of the church, or whether a church wedding would be worse. Then they debated whether Charles was only marrying Camilla now because the House of Commons Public Accounts Committee might uncover something too damaging about what he had spent on the lady. Or because the results of the second inquest into Princess Diana's death were to be published, possibly throwing up even more bad publicity about the royal family. Or because the Archbishop of Canterbury said that they should regularise their situation. And as if all this wasn't bad enough for a couple planning their wedding, it was said that the Labour party was incandescent with rage because Charles and Camilla's plans were messing up the timing of the next election.

I am basically a big custard-heart. I don't know these people at all. I've watched them for three decades, notebook in hand, but I don't know them or know anybody who knows them. But I am interested in their love story.

I think Charles is arrogant and selfish, but the roots of that lie in his upbringing.

I think Camilla is basically a decent and horsey cardigan who loves Charles and is prepared to go through all this (like she has gone through so much already) from the sheer accident of falling in love with him. And really, I don't think she cares what she is called. She isn't even trying to be 'queen of hearts', and it must be painful and hurtful when she is compared to her beautiful, warm, but deeply unhappy predecessor.

The young have no interest in the affairs and doings of such elderly people. The Diana activists may feel that somehow Camilla triumphed in the end, and perhaps they will dislike her for that. I can't be the only person in the world who doesn't think hereditary monarchy is a good idea but who still does genuinely wish these two confused middle-aged people a great wedding day and a good time together.

FRIDAY, 18 FEBRUARY 2005

Name That Loon

Anna Carey

'What's in a name?' a petulant Juliet once asked her new boyfriend. Four hundred years later, plenty of celebrities might answer, 'not much.' Mariah Carey, who recently announced her desire to be publicly known by her 'personal nickname', Mimi, is just the latest in a long line of stars who suddenly change names mid-stream.

Performers have always changed their boring birth names to something more glamorous and exciting. But those who've established a career under one moniker rarely change it – unless there's some sort of crisis or profound spiritual awakening going on.

Ms Carey, whose name rarely appears in print without the word 'troubled' attached to it, says that her decision to go by Mimi is an attempt to connect with her fans. 'Mimi is a very personal nickname only used by those closest to me. By naming [her forthcoming] album *The Emancipation of Mimi*, I am letting my guard down and inviting my fans to be that much closer to me.' One might think her fans have already been close enough, considering her slightly deranged appearances on MTV's Cribs. But no, Mariah has something to prove. 'I now feel I can honestly say "this is me, the real me, take it or leave it".'

Trying to force your nickname on the world doesn't always work (Janet Jackson is never going to be known by the tabloids as 'Danita Jo', no matter how hard she tries), but sometimes it does. When Jennifer Lopez first started calling herself J-Lo, it seemed like just another annoying affectation, especially when Lopez kept insisting that the name had been bestowed upon her by her fans. And then, horribly, the name caught on. Soon the diva was being referred to as J-Lo by tabloids and glossy magazines alike, and her nickname has well and truly stuck.

Religious faith is perhaps a more traditional reason for changing one's name. Cassius Clay and Cat Stevens both changed their names after converting to Islam. Clay was already an Olympic gold medalist when he changed his name to Muhammad Ali, but he went on to become the most famous boxer in the world. Stevens, on the other hand, had more or less retired from the spotlight when he became Yusuf Islam.

Young Jim McGuinn was just starting out his musical career in the Byrds when Indonesian guru Muhammad Subuh Sumohadiwidjojo, founder of the Subud faith, advised him to change his name to something beginning with 'R' because it would 'vibrate better' in the cosmos. McGuinn – who now admits that he actually prefers the name Jim but feels it's too late to go back – considered Rocket and Ramjet before settling for the more prosaic Roger.

And then there's Madonna. A prominent practitioner of Kabballah, Madonna announced in November that she'd changed her name to Esther. But the formerly material girl insisted that her change wasn't just influenced by her religious beliefs. 'My mother died when she was very young, of cancer, and I wanted to attach myself to another name,' Madonna said. 'This is in no way a negation of who my mother was. I wanted to attach myself to the energy of a different name.' Canny Madonna, however, isn't going so far as to use her new name in her career; the Madonna brand remains intact.

Some stars go back and forth between names. At the age of four, Joaquin Phoenix decided that he wanted to be called Leaf. He was using that name when he got his first film roles, before changing it

A young girl gives her verdict on Britain's prime minister, Tony Blair. Photograph: Jeff Mitchell/Reuters.

back to Joaquin in his late teens. Late hip-hop star Ol' Dirty Bastard went by a variety of names, including Big Baby Jesus. But the most celebrated indecisive name-chooser has to be Prince. So proud was Prince Nelson Rogers of his regal name that he devoted a whole song to it. 'My name is Prince!' he cried in 1992. 'And I am funky!' Just a year later, he may still have been funky, but he was no longer Prince. Instead, in a gesture intended to symbolise his disaffection with his record contract, he changed his name to a mysterious squiggle and was subsequently known as the Artist Formerly Known as Prince, and then simply the Artist. And then, four years ago, he decided to go back to Prince. Prince claims this change is final, but you never know with him.

But perhaps the star with the most cavalier attitude to name changing is Portia de Rossi, the Australian actress currently starring in the hit sitcom *Arrested Development*. Born Amanda Rodgers, de Rossi made up her stage name aged 14 when she was trying to get into a club. She liked it so much that she legally changed her moniker, and thinks that changing one's name is a positive thing. 'It's the most self-expressive thing a person can do. People that don't change their names are weird,' de Rossi told *Entertainment Weekly*. In fact, she doesn't even know how long her current name will last.

'I may change it again,' she said. 'I may change it right now.'

FRIDAY, 18 FEBRUARY 2005

Seven Held in Crackdown on Money-Laundering Operation

Mark Brennock, Conor Lally and Barry Roche

The Provisional republican movement was last night facing its biggest political crisis since the beginning of the peace process, following the apparent exposure of a major money-laundering operation and the arrest of people associated with Sinn Féin.

Garda raids were continuing last night in Louth, Meath and Westmeath after euro and sterling notes worth a total of €3.6 million were seized in Dublin and Cork. Seven people were arrested, including a Sinn Féin general election candidate from 2002 and another figure associated with the party. One of these acted in an official capacity for the party in the 2004 European Parliament elections. As the raids continued, there was speculation that further arrests would be made. Gardaí strongly believe that some or all of the cash seized was part of the haul from the raid on the Northern Bank in Belfast before Christmas.

The home of a close relative of a man working in a key position for the Government was among the premises raided in Co. Louth, although he was not arrested. A Cork businessman is also among those arrested. Last night a man walked into Anglesea Street Garda station in Cork and handed Gardaí more than £200,000 in cash. He is believed to have been given the money to hide by one of those arrested.

There was no comment last night from the Taoiseach or the Minister for Justice on the dramatic developments. The Minister for Defence, Mr O'Dea, said that the scale of the operation had been 'quite staggering' but said he would not comment on the political implications until at least somebody had been charged. Other ministers were said to be delighted at the turn of events, which they believe vindicates their new tough approach to Sinn Féin on IRA criminal activity.

The Opposition demanded an explanation from Sinn Féin, with the Fine Gael leader, Mr Enda Kenny, saying the arrests raised 'grave questions' for the party. The Labour Party leader, Mr Pat Rabbitte, said the cash seizures and arrests were 'an astonishing development', while the Green Party leader, Mr Trevor Sargent, demanded that Sinn Féin 'come clean on their involvement with criminal activity'. The Sinn Féin leader, Mr Gerry Adams, would only say 'I never comment on speculation' when questioned by reporters in Barcelona where he is promoting his latest book. In Dublin, a Sinn Féin spokesman urged against a 'rush to judgment … We would urge people to exercise caution on this occasion and allow the truth to come out,' he said.

However, the Provisional movement now finds itself in its most difficult position since the peace process began. Sinn Féin is under intense pressure to cut itself off from IRA activity; it faces pressure from within its own community in the wake of the Robert McCartney murder; and the IRA faces a new Garda onslaught on its criminal activities.

The latest arrests and seizures come after the pre-Christmas conviction and jailing of Niall Binéad, a Sinn Féin activist and associate of Mr Aengus Ó Snodaigh TD; the Northern Bank robbery, widely believed to have been carried out by the IRA; and the murder of Mr McCartney, believed to have been carried out by IRA members who subsequently intimidated witnesses.

There was speculation in political circles last night that further Garda operations against IRA activity may be planned. The legislation used by the Criminal Assets Bureau was strengthened by the signing into law by the President last week of the Proceeds of Crime (Amendment) Act 2005. The Taoiseach told the Dáil on Tuesday that this would 'allow criminality outside the jurisdiction to

Garret FitzGerald watching a Leinster Junior Cup rugby match between Blackrock College and Gonzaga College, which is attended by his grandson, Garret, a member of the school's team. Photograph: Eric Luke.

be taken into account and allow the bureau to work more closely with the Assets Recovery Agency in Northern Ireland. These changes will help the CAB to examine assets with a paramilitary origin.'

In this latest money-laundering investigation, two men were arrested in Cork on Wednesday night – one in Douglas and one in Passage West – and around £60,000 in Northern Bank notes was recovered. The same night in Dublin, three men – one from Cork and two from Northern Ireland – were arrested close to Heuston Station. More than €94,000 was seized. Yesterday morning, a man and a woman were arrested in the Farran area close to Cork city and over £2 million in cash was seized.

The four arrested in Co. Cork are being held under Section 30 of the Offences against the State Act at Garda stations in Cork city. The three men held in Dublin are being detained under the same Act in various Garda stations. All seven can be held for 48 hours from their arrest until they have to be charged or released.

Senior investigators from specialist Garda units – including CAB, Crime & Security and the Garda Bureau of Fraud Investigation – will meet their counterparts from the PSNI at a special security summit at Garda Headquarters in Dublin's Phoenix Park today. They will discuss the sensational developments of yesterday and Wednesday and plan how both forces will work to advance the investigation.

FRIDAY, 18 FEBRUARY 2005

Seeking Justice for a Brother

David Adams

It must have been the sisters that got to me: with their instinctive protectiveness towards a brother. Faces etched with pain and voices buckling under the weight of sudden and almost unbearable loss are commonplace here in Northern Ireland, so it couldn't only have been that.

Neither is courageous dignity on the part of bereaved relatives particularly novel. No, it must have been the sisterly love that breached my defences. Perhaps recalling my own two sisters' fiercely protective attitude to each of their crowd of eight younger brothers.

Whatever the spark, the pleas of the McCartney sisters for proper justice following the brutal murder of their brother, Robert (33), outside a Belfast bar three weeks ago, touched a chord with me, and with many others as well. Decent, ordinary people, determined to hold fast to their decency, they were at pains to make clear it is only proper justice they are interested in, not the 'summary' kind. Normally, in this part of the world, after making the right noises and quietly thanking God it wasn't us or ours, we cross to the other side of the street and move quickly on our way, emotions barely ruffled. But the McCartney sisters jolted us out of our protective lethargy and dragged back to the surface again a basic humanity that has been too long submerged beneath tragedy heaped upon tragedy.

That this casual butchery happened in Belfast is, on its own, of little significance; it could just as

Paula McCartney with a picture of her murdered brother, Robert (holding his son Brandon), stabbed to death by IRA members outside a Belfast bar following an argument inside the pub that was witnessed by leading members of Sinn Féin. Photograph: Alan Lewis/Photopress.

easily have happened in virtually any town or village in Northern Ireland. And, outside the political ramifications, neither is it of particular import that it was off-duty republican paramilitaries who were responsible: it could have been paramilitaries of any stripe. Locality determines which paramilitary group's members are beating you to death or to a pulp, not any recognisable difference in standards of morality or behaviour.

It's estimated that at least 70 people were present in Magennis's bar when Robert McCartney and his friend, Brendan Devine, were attacked. At time of writing, not one witness has come forward to the police to make a formal statement identifying the killers. Afterwards, as the two men lay bleeding (and, in Robert's case, dying) outside on the street, before being noticed by a passing police patrol, no one bothered to call an ambulance. So, can we take it from that, that everyone who witnessed the vicious attack and murder, was either supportive of the attackers or simply didn't care? No, even in Northern Ireland basic humanity has not yet been submerged deep enough to be able to ignore such butchery at close quarters.

Instead, it clearly illustrates the extent to which paramilitaries wield almost total power and control over those they live and socialise amongst. A control based not on support, loyalty or admiration, but on an acquiescence bred from abject and well-founded fear. Where there is power without any measure of accountability, and particularly where it rests in the hands of those least qualified to hold it, it is wielded endlessly and, progressively, with more and more brutality.

In Northern Ireland, as the untouchables luxuriate in their invincibility, the local communities become ever quieter. How else to explain the silence of 70-odd witnesses to the brutal murder of Robert McCartney? How else to explain, in recent times, the communal silence that followed a senior paramilitary attempting to rape an underage girl; or another using a steam iron to burn the breasts of a young woman; or a 'volunteer' throwing his girlfriend from a balcony while on holiday in Spain? All the above, and God knows what else, involved people living within a mile of Magennis's bar.

The same things are happening in communities all over the North, and, as in Belfast, people are too terrified to speak out. In a display of helpless naïvety, some of Robert McCartney's neighbours, in strictly off-the-record interviews of course, were quoted as saying: 'If only the leadership knew what was happening here.' It was chillingly reminiscent of the plaintive cries of Soviet and German citizens, who just couldn't bring themselves to believe that Uncle Joe or their beloved Führer had any idea what was happening in their localities.

But, like Stalin and Hitler, the leaderships in the North know only too well what happens in the areas under their control. They publicly distance themselves from the actions of their 'volunteers' only when it becomes impossible for them not to do so – which isn't very often. Pious-sounding statements from leaders are invariably driven by opportunism or damage limitation: not any sense of what is right or wrong. When you are in control, you decide what is right and what is wrong.

Robert McCartney's sisters have broken from the crowd to demand justice for their brother, and I hope they are successful. I hope, too, that more people follow their example and the walls of silence begin to crumble. For while the silence remains, the untouchables continue to wallow in their invincibility, and we pay a terrible price.

SATURDAY, 19 FEBRUARY 2005

Is the Party Over?

Mark Brennock

Gerry Adams flew home from Bilbao yesterday afternoon into the biggest crisis facing what he calls the republican movement. Minister for Justice Michael McDowell calls it the provisional movement, not wanting to surrender the title of republican to Adams's organisation. The crisis for Adams is that when McDowell called this movement a 'colossal crime machine' on radio yesterday, he will have been believed by more people than ever before.

The Government has led a two-month rhetorical onslaught on Adams's movement for its refusal to leave violence and criminality behind, seven years after the signing of the Belfast Agreement. In parallel, the IRA has carried out a series of actions that could not have been better planned or timed to prove the Government's point. Adams arrived home from his book promotion tour yesterday to a leadership floundering as it attempts to come to terms with a political environment that has changed utterly in just two months. It faces pressure from above and below.

The Government – aided ably by the IRA itself – has severely damaged the veneer of political respectability that Sinn Féin has so carefully created over the past decade. Meanwhile, in Belfast, IRA members killed a party supporter Robert McCartney in an act of murderous thuggery, before threatening witnesses to shut them up. The anger from within its own community has shaken the republican movement severely.

The sudden crisis has caught the movement by surprise. After all, since the peace process began, IRA killings, beatings, shootings, robberies and money-laundering have continued in parallel with political developments and nobody has seemed to mind all that much. Last December Sinn Féin was on the verge of yet another 'historic' deal, this time one that would have put it in government with Ian Paisley's DUP and would have put its members on police boards. Nobody in the Government was denouncing it as a criminal mob then.

But now there is no way back into normal political discourse until the question of IRA activity has been resolved. Until recently, Sinn Féin had hoped that its candidate, Joe Reilly, could challenge for a Dáil seat in the forthcoming Meath by-election. Now it must fear a demoralising slump in support in the wake of its worst period of publicity in a decade. The same concerns apply in relation to the British general election in May. For years there has been a sense that Sinn Féin would destroy the SDLP electorally. Now, within the SDLP, there is some hope that the attention being paid to the ongoing IRA criminal activity will remind nationalist voters why a large majority of them voted SDLP rather than Sinn Féin before the peace process began.

As he prepared to leave Bilbao yesterday, there was a suggestion in Adams's remarks that we are at a major watershed in the history of the peace process. He said he was 'coming home to deal with the situation'. He had asked for a full report to be ready for him. Asked on RTÉ's *News at One* yesterday what would happen if evidence emerged that the IRA had, after all, carried out the Northern Bank raid, he said this would 'take very serious reflection by me and others who are in the leadership of Sinn Féin'. He said he did not want to be tainted with criminality: 'I don't want anybody near me who is involved in criminality. I will face up to all of these issues if and when they emerge.'

Asked whether that meant he would walk away from 'certain people' if presented with proof of an IRA connection with the Northern Bank robbery he said: 'We will weather the storm and I will not walk away from any challenge which presents itself in the time ahead. If Sinn Féin has issues to deal with, we will deal with those issues.' This, of course, could mean something or nothing. At most it could mean he recognises that Sinn Féin must 'deal with' its relationship with violence and criminality once and for all, possibly breaking ranks with those who want to continue with such activity. At its least, it could simply mean that Adams was seeking to say something that sounded interesting but was essentially meaningless in response to a tricky question.

McDowell made it clear yesterday that he believed it was the latter. Don't be fooled by talk of splits and divisions, he said. The movement is

Republicans in paramilitary dress march through Strabane in Co. Tyrone in memory of dead IRA colleagues. Photograph: Trevor McBride.

coherent and united under a single leadership.

The new situation is so shocking for the republican – or provisional – movement because it was completely unexpected. It is behaving more or less according to the same pattern as it has done since the peace process began. The ceasefires saw an end to the killings of police, soldiers and others seen as 'legitimate targets', and the bombing campaign in the North and Britain in the struggle against the British occupation. But other activity – robberies, extortion, 'punishment' attacks and murders of alleged petty criminals and internal dissenters continued. Such occurrences were much less frequent than before the ceasefires, but they were regular. However, those who wrote about such activity and drew attention to it were denounced as peace process saboteurs.

In July 1998, just three months after the Belfast Agreement was signed, the RUC said the IRA had shot dead Andy Kearney in Belfast. The following year the FBI disrupted an IRA gun-running operation in Florida, and three men were subsequently jailed. The then Northern Secretary, Mo Mowlam, said she accepted security advice that the IRA shot dead Charles Bennett in July 1999. The killings of Belfast drug dealer Edmund McCoy in May 2000 and of Joe O'Connor in October 2000 were blamed on the IRA. In August 2001 came the arrest of the Colombia Three. In October 2002 Daniel McBrearty was shot dead in Derry – another killing blamed on the IRA.

On and on it went, with talks that made breakthroughs and talks that broke down. The executive was formed, suspended, re-formed and suspended again. Acts of weapons decommissioning took place out of public view. The sense was of a political process inching forward slowly but going in the right direction. While nasty incidents took place regularly in different parts of Northern Ireland, these were tolerated as inevitable blips during what was believed to be a total transition of an armed and violent organisation with a political wing into a political party which had left behind its violent history. In the meantime, the Government made little fuss about the regular IRA actions. The policy was one of 'constructive ambiguity' in which the parallel lives of the movement were tolerated in the hope that this was simply a transitional phase on the road to a total end to violence and criminality.

Sometimes, the illegal and legal elements of the movement's activity cohabited in the same building. In November 2002, the PSNI uncovered an IRA spying operation at Stormont. In May 2003 it said Armagh man Gareth O'Connor, who had been abducted and disappeared, was an IRA victim. The PSNI Chief Constable, Hugh Orde, reported some intimidation of members of District Policing Partnerships later that year. In December, 2003, the Garda and the PSNI said the hijack of a truck, carrying cigarettes worth about €1.6 million, had all the hallmarks of an IRA operation.

On it went into last year. Orde said the IRA was responsible for an alleged abduction of dissident republican Bobby Tohill (47) in Belfast city centre and for punishment beatings. In November, as hopes remained for a historic power-sharing deal involving Sinn Féin and the DUP, the Independent Monitoring Commission reported that the IRA was making millions of pounds from robberies and smuggling in the North.

The commission relies heavily on information from the security forces both sides of the Border, and this information is in turn provided to the two governments. It blamed the IRA for a multimillion pound robbery of goods from the Makro store in Dunmurray in May 2004. Up to the end of September 2003 republicans were blamed for 52 'punishment' shootings; to the end of last September republicans were accused of 22 such shootings. A political associate of Aengus Ó Snodaigh TD, Niall Binéad, was convicted of IRA membership late last year and evidence was heard of a spying operation on politicians in the Republic.

In short, the IRA has been carrying on like this for years. But in December, the Government's tolerance ran out. The Government was both disappointed and angry at the failure to reach a comprehensive deal before Christmas. Until close to the end of negotiations, those talks were believed to be foundering on the sole issue of whether IRA decommissioning should be photographed or filmed. Indeed, when Michael McDowell announced there was a second issue – the IRA's failure to sign up to a pledge not to engage in criminal activity – there was initial scepticism over whether this was as big an issue as he was making out.

This marked the start of the Government's turn against the republicans, and the end of the policy of constructive ambiguity. Displaying an impressive grasp of republican theology, McDowell announced to a surprised public that the IRA did not believe any of its actions were capable of being seen as criminal, because it was the IRA and therefore the legitimate government of the Republic. The scepticism did not last long, however. Adams indicated on television that this was indeed the position. Then McDowell got Mitchel McLaughlin to admit on television that he did not see the revolting killing in 1972 of Jean McConville, mother of 10, as a crime.

No sooner had the talks on the decommissioning and crime issues broken down in December than the IRA lifted £26.5 million from the Northern Bank in Belfast. The persistence with which the Taoiseach asserted that the Sinn Féin leadership knew about this robbery in advance, and had therefore behaved duplicitously during the failed talks, deeply angered Adams and Martin McGuinness.

Then came the stabbing to death of Robert McCartney in a Belfast bar, believed to have been done by IRA members. The dead man's family, Sinn Féin supporters all, laid into the IRA for allegedly intimidating witnesses and said those with information should go to the PSNI. Pitted against the family of a man killed by IRA members, Sinn Féin backed off its usual line of refusing to say people should cooperate with the police. If people saw the PSNI as a 'respectable' body, they could go to it, said Adams.

And now comes this major money-laundering operation, apparently with Sinn Féin members' fingerprints – perhaps literally – all over it. All that is required to complete the linkage between Sinn Féin, the IRA and the Northern Bank robbery – and to make liars or fools of the Sinn Féin leaders who insisted they believed IRA denials – is confirmation that some or all of the money seized over the past three days was stolen from the Northern Bank.

There is no going back to the twin-track strategy now. Sinn Féin has five TDs and three MEPs, and it is the largest nationalist party in the North. A refusal to end IRA activity might not cause huge electoral damage in the North. It hasn't damaged it in the Republic in recent years, but it would almost certainly do so now.

The extraordinary recent events promise to leave no doubt that Sinn Féin and the IRA are, as the Taoiseach says, 'two sides of the same coin'. They will show that the movement, whatever you choose to call it, is involved in major criminal activity and has no plans to stop. It must be likely that in time, at least one of the 20 people involved in the Northern Bank robbery will be caught and IRA involvement will be established. And continuing money-laundering investigation will surely lead to the doorsteps of prominent figures in the IRA and Sinn Féin.

It will not then be credible for Sinn Féin to deny involvement in various criminal acts, or to

Sergeant Major Willy Scott keeping his guard of honour in line at Collins Barracks in Cork. Photograph: Daragh MacSweeney/Provision.

dismiss those acts as isolated or unauthorised incidents carried out by rogue elements. At that point, if it is to have a political future, the republican, or provisional, movement will have to have something new to say.

SATURDAY, 19 FEBRUARY 2005

Marriage Still the Best Place to Rear Children

Breda O'Brien

I have come to the conclusion that there are two types of opinion columnists. There are those who are fired with a missionary spirit and the need to point out to the world on a regular basis where it is going wrong. Such controversy as this generates, except when it gets out of hand, is to be welcomed, and indeed is taken as evidence that the message is getting through. Then there are the other columnists like me, a natural-born coward, who wakes regularly in the night wondering glumly how she ever got herself into the position of writing columns that are going to bring opprobrium on her head yet again.

Such wakeful moments become even more frequent when the genial Fianna Fáiler with whom you have been chatting amiably, and with whom you are about to go on a programme, asks where the right-wing Catholic is, who will probably agree with everything Kevin Myers says about lone parents. He has been told that such a person has been booked for the programme, and he wants to know where she is. I stare helplessly at him, wondering how to explain that, while I disagree with everything that Kevin Myers said about lone parents, I probably am the person about whom he has been warned. Luckily, at that moment another panellist arrives and saves me.

For the record, as an alleged right-winger, I believe in generous social welfare, redistribution of wealth and the notion of putting people before profit. That is one reason why I feel the issue of social welfare and lone parents is completely the wrong one to focus on.

There has been a nasty sub-text to the lone-parent debate, which is that I should not be required to fund someone else's decision to become pregnant or carry a child to term. What seems to be forgotten is that we are talking about children, and if we wish to cherish all the children of the nation equally, surely we want to ensure that children are not reared in even worse poverty than they are at the moment?

However, I know one reason for my right-wing reputation, and it is not from my use of the b-word, but the frequency with which I use the m-word. If some commentators have their way, the m-word will become as obsolete as the b-word, or at least will be confined to the privacy of people's homes, with no impact on public policy. I refer, of course, to marriage. You will get politicians to assent cautiously to the notion of having two parents actively involved in a child's life. Ah, but mention the m-word, and it is then that you will smell the burning rubber as politicians skid away from the issue. Part of it is a kind of native decency that does not want to stand in judgment on other people. Part of it is sheer cowardice. However, when it comes to the welfare of children, running for cover is not very laudable.

Can someone explain to me why people who say that, on balance, marriage is the best place to rear children are said to be in denial of reality? Yet one is not permitted to describe ignoring mountains of research which back that assertion as any form of denial of reality at all? Over the past week I have grown tired of hearing that there are no Irish longitudinal studies that show the beneficial effects of marriage as a family form for children. That is true, but there is a huge amount of easily accessed research from other countries showing that, all things considered, children do best in stable married families. Even when you control for poverty, there is evidence that family form matters.

Brian O'Driscoll on his way to scoring Ireland's crucial try in their 19-13 victory over England at Lansdowne Road. Photograph: Alan Betson.

The immediate riposte is that British, or American, or Australian research cannot be taken to indicate the same outcomes for Irish children. If that is true, why are the same people blue in the face citing the wonders of the Scandinavian model, as evidenced by research? Are people seriously trying to tell us we have more in common with the upright, cradle-to-the-grave welfare-providing Swedes than with the Brits or the Yanks?

Also, some Irish research is being used for purposes for which it was not intended. For instance, the Ceifin study which found that family form had little impact on happiness, and that it was the quality of relationships that mattered, is widely cited.

However, the Ceifin study is a snapshot and makes no attempt to predict outcomes for children in different family forms. In fact the author, Kieran McKeown, has said that, far from his research proving that marriage does not matter, it does now more than ever.

None of this should be used to stigmatise children of lone parents, or to draw the deeply offensive conclusion that all children of lone parents are automatically headed for delinquency. But will anyone engage with the question I have been plaintively attempting to ask, which is: how do we encourage more people to have children within marriage, without stigmatising those whose lives do not conform to that pattern? My genial Fianna Fáiler was certain it could not be done.

If such defeatism were a characteristic of everyone in his party, we would still have plastic bags waving merrily from every whin bush and be inhaling smoke along with our alcohol. The welfare of children is surely more important than either of those issues, and deserving of more than instant dismissal.

Lone parents rightly ask for societal and State support because they face a difficult task. We should give such support with a heart and a half.

However, do we have to say that one person can do as easily what two can do, while at the same time offering support because it is hard on the person who has to do it alone? Do we have to accept that poverty is the only problem, while ignoring the fact that part of the poverty may result from only having the resources of one person, both financial and emotional, rather than two? Does sensible recognition of diversity have to go so far as to deny all differences between family types?

FRIDAY, 25 FEBRUARY 2005

Murphy Family Hurriedly Leave the Court after Verdicts

Conor Lally

Within seconds of the Court of Criminal Appeal setting aside Dermot Laide's manslaughter conviction and Desmond Ryan's conviction for violent disorder, Brian Murphy's parents, Denis and Mary, had left the court without pausing to make any comment to waiting journalists. So sudden was their departure that only those members of the media who had failed to get into the packed courtroom, presided over by Mr Justice McCracken, saw them leave.

Mr and Ms Murphy have made several public comments in their quest to bring their son's killers to justice. But yesterday, immediately following the court's ruling, they were clearly in no mood for conversation. Behind them the scene was somewhat different.

As the two men before the court sat on benches listening to the verdicts being handed down they stared blankly ahead. Outside the court their subdued demeanour melted away as they were showered with congratulatory handshakes, kisses and hugs from their large group of family and friends. Most of this group lingered in the corridors anxious to share in the men's relief at the ruling. Dermot Laide's father, Brian, had just heard the court set aside his son's manslaughter conviction and half his prison term from four years to two. He did what most fathers would do under those circumstances and cried.

Before he was taken to the holding cells and being whisked back to the Midlands Prison, Portlaoise, to serve the remainder of his two-year sentence for violent disorder, Dermot Laide was given some time with his family and supporters, which included Father Aidan Troy. Sitting on a bench in an alcove in the corridor off the Four Courts round hall, he sat flicking through a copy of the 51-page judgment. His sister sat beside him, and both allowed themselves small smiles as they chatted. Other well-wishers followed, including a group of around six young men of his own age. He was finally joined and comforted by his girlfriend, Cecilia, who has been at his side during his many court appearances of the last 12 months. The pair sat for a while, at times kissing, apparently oblivious to the prison officer chained to Laide's right arm.

After around 20 minutes Laide was taken from the courthouse and into the cold morning rain. Journalists' microphones where thrust in his direction as he was brought to the holding cells. He had nothing to say and kept his eyes fixed on the ground as photographers' flashes and the lights from television cameras illuminated the scene.

Back inside, Desmond Ryan's father smiled and shook hands with some of his son's legal team. Ryan himself looked relieved and was hugged by a smiling female companion. The verdict setting aside his conviction and not directing a retrial means he is cleared of any part in the events which cost Brian Murphy his life.

When he was first convicted along with his co-accused – Laide and Seán Mackey – and sentenced to nine months' imprisonment last March, Ryan was granted a request that his prison term not start until after he finished his university exams. Upon lodging his appeal the court agreed that the prison sentence would not start until after the appeal. It means Mr Ryan has never spent a day in prison. Now that he faces no further charges he will never join his former Blackrock College schoolmates in prison.

MONDAY, 7 MARCH 2005

A New Golden Age of Athletics

Ian O'Riordan, in Madrid

First Europe, now comes the world. It's going to be hard to stop these Irish conquistadors. Winning a European Indoor title is one small step towards total domination, but what happened in Madrid this weekend marks one giant leap for David Gillick and Alistair Cragg. They'll head home later today with the jingle-jangle of gold medals, still in celebratory mood and already planning their next mission. There's a World Championships in Helsinki next August with far more precious metal on offer, and that could be only the beginning of another golden era for Irish athletics.

For a while on Saturday, though, neither Gillick nor Cragg really cared what happens next. They'll always have the memories of their first major title, and the slightly more vague memories of a great night. Together they spoiled Spain's two main gold medal hopes, and with that transferred the best fiesta of the weekend to an Irish bar in the heart of Madrid.

Only three other Irish men have won European Indoor titles: Noel Carroll, Eamonn Coghlan and Mark Carroll. No Irish man has yet won a European outdoor title, and for Gillick and Cragg that event in Gothenburg next year can't come around quick enough.

For Cragg, though, there is a far more immediate assignment at the World Cross Country in France in two weeks. Saturday's 3,000 metres

David Gillick celebrates winning the men's 400-metre final at the European Indoor Athletics Championships in Madrid. Photograph: Jasper Juinen/AP.

Barry Geraghty stands in the saddle on Kicking King after they won the Cheltenham Gold Cup in Gloucestershire, England. Photograph: Brendan Moran/Sportsfile.

victory was practically ideal preparation for the 4km short-course race, and even the presence of the ruling east Africans won't lesson his ambition of claiming another title.

Gillick's attention now turns from Madrid to Helsinki, where the new European Indoor 400-metre champion will bring his new-found fame on to the world stage for the first time. That too means taking on the American ruling class, but he hardly needs reminding that their Olympic champion is a skinny-looking white kid just like himself.

Some sight it was on Saturday, though, with Gillick standing aloft the medal podium just as Cragg went on his victory lap. Cragg was back inside the arena yesterday evening for his medal ceremony, and it seemed a little unfair to be asking him straight afterwards if he could win another one at the World Cross Country.

'Well, I think I can,' he said with his typically cool composure. 'And that's my goal. I wouldn't be going there if I didn't think it. I went there last year after running some good times indoors and didn't have a great race. But I'm different runner now, and am running more off strength.'

So he'll head back to his US base at Arkansas for some rest and recuperation, though he's clearly not intent on resting at all on his laurels: 'Hopefully all the excitement of this weekend won't get the better of me. I know I'm not going to get any better in the next two weeks, but I'll get sharp and focused again and try to come back for another good one. I've always been a little more motivated about indoor running than cross country, because you have the clock to tell you how good you are. But I'm definitely geared up for that 4km race. I still think a medal at the World Cross Country is one of the hardest ones to get in distance running. And I know European indoor running does not equal

World Cross Country. The Africans that specialise in 4km cross country aren't like Reyes Estevez.'

Estevez was the man who felt the full brunt of Cragg's 3,000-metre victory, and the Spaniard's ambition of coming back to win the 1,500 metres last night ended in similar fashion, with another bronze medal behind Ukraine's Ivan Heshko. After the most competitive European indoor event in a while Ireland ended up fourth on the gold medal count – safe in the knowledge that both were squeaky clean.

In fact, Gillick and Cragg represent all that's still good about athletics, that talent when combined with hard, hard work can take you anywhere. Gillick's moment of victory in the 400 metres should prove particularly inspiring to the next generation. 'Crossing that line with the arms raised and going on a lap of honour, that's something you dream about as a kid,' he admitted. 'You really do. So you'd live for a moment like that again. And I suppose that's my ambition now. That's the motivation.'

The confidence of both performances was particularly breathtaking. Cragg had watched Gillick's victory from his warm-up area and realised this was an athlete he could straight away relate to: 'You could see his confidence. And that's all it takes. I know other Irish athletes aren't that far off. I'm no professor of the sport, but you need to have that confidence to compete.'

Like Gillick, that sort of confidence can only start to rub off. Just like our old school athletes really.

WEDNESDAY, 9 MARCH 2005

Shooting Itself in the Foot

Editorial

Clearly the IRA hasn't gone away. The latest statement from the Provisional IRA on the murder in Belfast of Robert McCartney by some of its former members is a breach of its ceasefire, in intent if not in action. It shows just how detached from political reality and democratic values that organisation has become. It underlines the imperative for the Sinn Féin leadership to convince the IRA that the greatest contribution it can make to the peace process is to decommission all weapons, end all criminal and paramilitary activities and disband now. Is this goal deliverable by Gerry Adams and Martin McGuinness?

There is little doubt this detailed statement about the killing of Mr McCartney, issued in the name of P. O'Neill, is designed to provide a breathing space for an organisation that is under enormous internal and external pressure. It is aimed primarily at the republican community in Northern Ireland where a perverted form of law and IRA order has been in operation for many years. It is attempting to resist the growing demand by ordinary people in those areas for justice, normal policing and the rule of law. The most chilling aspect of this extraordinary statement concerns the offer made to the McCartney family to shoot four of the people directly involved in the murder. The statement did not specify whether those reprisals would involve IRA 'executions' or merely 'punishment shootings'.

But the brutal nature of the offer – represented as a gesture of goodwill to the family and an indication of the IRA's good faith to the community – will act as a wake-up call to democrats on both sides of the Border. It exposes a mindset that should have withered many years ago if the IRA was truly committed to the peace process and to the principles of consent, equality and democracy. The family has rejected the gruesome offer. The McCartney sisters demanded the people responsible for the murder should be tried in a court of law. With tremendous courage and perseverance, they have challenged the IRA – and Sinn Féin – within their own community and outside it, insisting that the only way forward is through due process through the Police Service of Northern Ireland and the courts.

We were treated to some theatricals at the Sinn Féin ardfheis in Dublin last weekend. The McCartney sisters were invited to attend as guests of honour. They heard soothing words from the Sinn Féin leaders who condemned the killing and said those responsible should be tried in a court of law.

Did Mr Adams and Mr McGuinness know about the latest IRA statement? After everything that has been said by them, do they agree with the IRA reserving the right to impose summary justice, summary shooting, perhaps summary execution? And to join a government and assume responsibility for policing? Something has to give. Sinn Féin and the IRA cannot proceed with the peace process, inside and outside democracy.

THURSDAY, 10 MARCH 2005

Department Failed to Deal for 30 Years with Illegal Charges

Eithne Donnellan, Health Correspondent

The Department of Health failed at the highest levels for almost 30 years to deal effectively with the illegal nursing home charges issue, the Travers report has found. It makes it clear the department was 'well aware' of legal concerns around charging medical card holders for care in public nursing homes as far back as 1976.

The report sets out in detail the numerous times when legal opinions provided to the department over the years cast doubt on the legality of the practice but nothing was done. This ranged from the advice provided by its own legal team in 1977, the Eastern Health Board which got the advice of senior counsel Thomas McCann and Ronan Keane in April 1978 and forwarded it the department, and legal advice obtained by the South Eastern Health Board in 2002 which was also forwarded to the department in late 2002 or early in 2003.

Mr Travers said the failure to take effective action at any time over the years was 'somewhat surprising'. 'The only reasonable conclusion, at this time, is one of overall systemic corporate responsibility and failure within the Department of Heath and Children at the highest levels over more than 28 years,' he said.

His report deals in detail with a meeting held in December 2003 at which the legal advice to the South Eastern Health Board was considered. The meeting was attended, among others, by secretary general of the Department of Health Michael Kelly and by former health minister Micheál Martin and his two junior ministers, Ivor Callely and Tim O'Malley. It was decided at the meeting to seek the advice of the Attorney General on the issue. Minutes of the meeting showed Mr Callely said he would speak with the Taoiseach and with Mr Martin about it. However, he didn't raise it with Mr Martin as Mr Martin arrived at the meeting himself later and his (Mr Martin's) advisers were present for the discussion.

Mr Callely told Mr Travers 'he briefly mentioned the eligibility issue of long-stay care of the over-70s medical card holders in the course of a Dáil vote on an unrelated matter to An Taoiseach in December 2003'.

There are conflicting accounts in the Travers report on whether Mr Martin was told there had been a discussion on the legality of nursing home charges at the December 2003 meeting. The meeting was at the Gresham Hotel, Dublin, and Mr Kelly said he left the meeting for about 10 minutes to meet Mr Martin at the hotel entrance when he arrived. He claims in the report that he told him there had been a discussion on the issue. Mr Martin claims in his statement to Mr Travers that he was not told this.

Furthermore, the report states that when it was decided at the meeting to seek the advice of the Attorney General on the legality of the nursing

Michael Kelly, former Secretary General of the Department of Health. Photograph: David Sleator.

home charges, a background file and draft letter to be sent to the Attorney General was prepared for Mr Kelly. Mr Kelly recollected reading the submission and draft letter at the end of January or early February 2004 but the letter was never sent and the file has, the report states, 'disappeared'. Mr Kelly told Mr Travers it was not his practice to hold folders or files in his office and he normally cleared items submitted to him within 24 to 48 hours. 'I did not retain the folder and my firm belief is that I referred it elsewhere in the department … given its potential consequences, my belief is that I would have brought it to the attention of the minister [Mr Martin] in advance of issuing the letter,' he said. But he could not recollect doing this.

But he said he had a 'clear recollection of a subsequent discussion with the minister on what the best solution might be, if it proved necessary on the basis of legal advice to introduce amending legislation'. He believed this discussion took place on March 10th, 2004. Mr Kelly also stated that a folder containing the January 2004 submission 'was observed by another official of the department (who would have recognised it and was aware of its significance) in the outer office of the minister's office at some point in early 2004'. He believed, had the folder been returned to him, it would have prompted 'the appropriate response' on his part.

Mr Martin, however, said he never got the file and there was no discussion on this issue when he met Mr Kelly on March 10th. 'It is difficult to understand what purpose would have been served by referring such a file to my office as I was not being requested to sign the proposed letter or to contribute to the matter,' Mr Martin told the Travers inquiry. He added: 'At no time did I shy away from sensitive issues because they might have cost implications or because they might reflect badly on governments ... the fact is that this was not drawn to my attention either formally or informally at any time.' Mr Travers observed that the failure of the department to seek the advice of the Attorney General following the December 2003 meeting was 'highly deficient' and 'inexplicable'.

'That failure rests primarily with the management of the department. Absolutely no documentation was made available to me to demonstrate or to indicate that the minister had been fully and adequately briefed by the department on the serious nature of the issues arising, which the management of the department acknowledged carried significant potential legal, financial and political consequences. The special advisers to the minister might have been expected to be more active in examining and probing the underlying issues.'

Mr Travers concluded there was no single reason for the almost 30-year delay by the department in seeking the Attorney General's advice. 'The explanation lies in a constellation of reasons. These included a strong desire to protect what was regarded as an important source of own income by the health boards, a failure to attach due weight to the legal concerns because of a somewhat unfounded belief that there was a defensible legal case for the practice, an undue concern about political sensitivity, the embedding of the practice over time appeared to have weakened any inclination by the Department of Health to question it.'

Health Minister Micheál Martin. Photograph: Bryan O'Brien.

Other reasons included weaknesses of the risk assessment procedures in the department and 'ultimately, poor overall corporate judgment in the Department of Health and Children in relation to the operational, legal, financial and political significance of the issues surrounding the practice of charge for long-stay care in health board institutions'.

In summary, the report said, the fundamental reason for the long delay 'lies in long-term systemic corporate failure'. 'That failure is principally a failure of public administration which, essentially, failed to identify, recognise and acknowledge the difference between actions and practices widely regarded as fair and reasonable and supportive of the development and protection of essential public health services and actions and practices that were legally valid. The failure of administration was compounded by the fact that the solution to the dichotomy ... was readily amenable to remedy through the introduction of a simple legislative amendment.'

The failure was further compounded by ignoring for many years a range of legal advice which was left to one side in the persistent belief that the practices at issue were at least defensible in a legal sense, the report stated.

SATURDAY, 12 MARCH 2005

Every Parent's Worst Fear

Carl O'Brien, Social Affairs Correspondent

All Mikala Gourney could hear when she picked up the phone was a shrieking voice and a jumble of words. 'It was Mary. She was hysterical. She could barely speak. All I could hear her saying was, "they're taking my children away". One of the kids crying in the background. There was this ferocious banging noise, which turned out to be the gardaí knocking on the doors and windows. I've never had such a distressing phonecall in my life.'

At that moment social workers and gardaí were outside the small bungalow of Pádraig and Mary O'Hara in Kells, Co. Meath. They had a care order seeking to commit the couple's five children – four of whom have autism – into health board care. In a panic Mary began to phone her friends to try to get whatever help she could.

The couple had been giving media interviews a few days earlier about their battle for therapeutic services for their children. Later in the week, without the couple's prior knowledge, health authorities arrived at their house with a care order seeking to commit their children to health board care. Friends, including Mikala – who is also the mother of two special needs children – arrived at the house. Following talks between the O'Hara solicitor and the health authority, they voluntarily decided to hand over their children to health authorities. The couple grabbed the children's toys and clothes, and prepared some food for them. The five children, aged between four and 16, clambered into the car and prepared to say goodbye.

'Mary was saying to them that they were just going away for a little holiday and they'd be back soon,' says Mikala. 'As they got into the car, Blaine [nine] gave Mary a Mother's Day card he had made. That's when it really hit. She had tried to hold herself together, but we all just hugged then. I can't begin to say how traumatic the whole thing was.'

It is a week since the O'Haras handed their children into care. Yet many say the fear provoked by the State's response on that Friday night is still resonating among parents of autistic children. The speed at which health authorities acted, followed by official silence surrounding the case, has only added to the sense of foreboding. Parents, many of whom already feel ignored by a system where battling for basic services seems to be taken for granted, say they are fearful of the consequences of speaking out about how difficult it can be to cope. More than 100 parents and campaigners this week gathered outside the local headquarters of the Health Service Executive in Kells to protest at the

State's treatment of the O'Haras. Conversations among the group were filled with different versions of one question: will the same thing happen to us?

'People are literally scared stiff,' says Séamus Greene, the chairman of the National Parents and Siblings Alliance, one of the groups involved in the protest. 'I just got a phone call from a woman who lives in a fortress at home, where her son has major behavioural problems. She was ringing to say she was afraid her son would be taken from her. But someone like her needs all the help and support she can get from the State. Yet now she's afraid to even ask for it.' He adds: 'What worries me most is that the O'Haras are articulate, middle-class people, surrounded by supporters. So what happens to the people who aren't as articulate and don't have the support network that they do?'

Pádraig and Mary O'Hara. Photograph: Fran Caffrey/ Newsfile.ie.

The Health Service Executive (North Eastern Area) has declined to comment on the case except to say that care orders are taken out in the interests of the welfare and safety of children. While the precise reasons for the local health authority's actions have not been publicised, campaigners are quick to point to the lack of health or educational services for autistic children as playing a central role in the series of events that led to the O'Hara children being taken into State care. Two of the O'Haras' youngest children don't have a school placement, while they have to pay privately for speech and language therapies and other services. The Co. Meath couple, who say they are forced to survive on a few snatched hours of sleep a night, say their battle to secure services for their children has turned into a blur of correspondence with officials, searches for therapists and assessments which don't result in needs being met.

There are many families in a similar situation to the O'Haras. The number of parents seeking appropriate education services and therapies for their autistic children has grown dramatically in recent years due largely to increasing awareness that, with early intervention, many children can be rescued from the worst effects of the condition or can have their diagnosis changed. Most schools or home programmes which provide one-to-one education for autistic children have been established largely due to lobbying by parents or High Court proceedings.

'There is something fundamentally wrong with the system,' says Colm O'Carolan, who has been seeking appropriate education and therapy for his 14-year-old autistic son Lewis for two years. 'You have clerical officers making decisions on issues which they have no comprehension of. Yet these are decisions which are affecting people's lives.'

As if taking care of a child with autism isn't energy-sapping enough, finding the stamina to battle for what your children are entitled to can push parents over the edge, says Mikala Gourney. 'It's very depressing. You're up all night writing letters, you're looking for therapies. We don't live. We just exist. The health board seem indifferent to us. They don't seem to care. But what about our children's rights to be allowed to reach their full potential?'

The Health Service Executive yesterday declined to comment on the status of services for children with autism in the State. The Government, however, has made much of the last Budget, which promised to spend a record amount on services for people with special needs. The gap between what parents want for their children and what the State is providing is reflected in the number of court cases being brought against the State. The Department of Education has confirmed it is facing 110 High Court cases in which parents claim their children's inability to access appropriate education or therapies is an infringement of their rights. It has settled almost 130 cases since 1996.

Against this backdrop, support groups are taking an increasingly sceptical look at the Government's Disability Bill which, they say, plans to either refuse rights or sharply limit the grounds upon which rights of any kind would be meaningful. Tellingly, they say, it would block off the courts as a right of access for some categories of people whose needs have been assessed, but not met, by health authorities.

The Government, however, insists that the new legislation represents a major step forward for people with disabilities, introducing rights to needs assessments and putting in place complaints and appeals procedures for people who feel they are not receiving adequate services.

The O'Haras' case, meanwhile, has become a lightning-rod issue for the disability community, capturing all the fear and frustration of a section of the population which feels increasingly ignored and isolated by the State.

'My husband said to me last week on his way out to work to have a bag packed, to make a quick getaway in case they came knocking at the door,' says Mikala Gourney. 'That's what it's like. I keep getting flashbacks to what happened on the Friday night. On and off I'm okay, but then I sit down and cry. I can't shut off the pictures of what happened.

'I went over to the house last Sunday and it was like a morgue. It's one of the most traumatic things that can happen to a parent: to have your children taken from you when you've done everything you possibly can to help and protect them. You don't need to be found guilty of anything. That's the most frightening thing of all.'

MONDAY, 14 MARCH 2005

US Happier without Gandhi with a Guinness

Mark Steyn

For the first time in a decade the official observances will not be disfigured by the presence at the White House of Gerry Adams.

When President Bush declared his 'war on terror' after September 11th, most of us assumed it was a euphemism. As the eminent British historian Corelli Barnett endeavoured to explain 'It is misleading to talk of a "war on terrorism". You cannot in logic wage war against a phenomenon, only against a specific enemy.' But it seems the president begs to differ. His predecessor was a great performer, and as such he was happy to go along with the performances of others – in this instance, the charade that Gerry Adams had somehow transformed himself into a man of peace, a Gandhi with a Guinness. Alas, the current occupant of the Oval Office is not a performer and thus has less of an appetite for play-acting, particularly when it's as unconvincing as Sinn Féin's: Mr Bush is who he is, he's a what-you-see-is-what-you-get kinda guy. And when he sees Adams, he gets him – which is more than can be said for the British and Irish governments.

So instead of one more chorus of *The Wearing of the Green* it's the wearing out of the welcome for

Sinn Féin at the White House. In their place, President Bush will welcome the fiancée and five sisters of Robert McCartney to Washington. As is now well known, Mr McCartney was beaten with iron sewer rods, slit open from neck to navel, and none of 70 witnesses to his killers saw a thing.

Depravity-wise, what exactly is the difference between Robert McCartney's murder and the lynching and torching of the four US contractors in Fallujah? None – except that the organisation responsible for the former has enjoyed 10 years of White House photo-ops plus the enthusiastic support of the London and Dublin political establishments. For the last 3 1/2 years one of the most persistent streams of correspondence I've had is from British readers sneering: 'Oh-ho. So America's now waging a war on "terror", is she? Well, where were the bloody Yanks the last 30 years? Passing round the collection box for IRA donations in the bars of Boston and New York, that's where.' They have a point. Blowing up grannies and schoolkids at bus stops and shopping centres is always wrong, and the misty shamrock-hued sentimentalisation of it in this particular manifestation speaks poorly for America, the principal source for decades of IRA funding. On the other hand, it was London and Dublin, not Washington, that decided they were going to accommodate the IRA, Her Majesty's government going so far as to make Martin McGuinness the minister of a crown he doesn't deign to recognise.

By contrast, America's role was mostly confined to some platitudinous glad-handing by Bill Clinton – lots of maudlin speeches about how 'I truly believe that two sides riven by bitterness and mistrust can learn to coexist on a small island. Look at me and Hillary on our post-Monica vacation on Martha's Vineyard.' (I quote from memory.) It wasn't the bloody Yanks who thought Mr McGuinness had such unique talents to bring to the job of 'education minister' – though he and his pals have certainly done a grand job educating the citizenry in west Belfast: keep your head down, mind your own business, don't step out of line, nobody saw nuttin'. My British readers' anger is misdirected: it's their own government that's spent 10 years cynically indulging IRA thuggery as nothing more than a little 'internal housekeeping'. It's George W. Bush who's decided enough is enough.

Recognising they had a problem on their hands, the IRA made their now famous offer to Mr McCartney's loved ones. You're right, they said, it was all a mistake, but don't worry, we're really sorry about it – and, just to show how sorry we are, we'll murder his murderers for you. As an afterthought, they acknowledged that, as a lot of folks were upset by the brutality of the McCartney whack-job, this time they'd eschew the sewer rods, abdomen-slitting, etc, and just do it nice and clean with a bullet straight to the head. Very decent of them.

There's a lesson there in the reformability of terrorists. The IRA's first instinct is to kill. If you complain about the killing, they offer to kill the killers. If you complain about the manner of the killing, they offer to kill more tastefully – 'compassionate terrorism', as it were. But it's like Monty Python's spam sketch: there's no menu item that doesn't involve killing. You can get it in any colour as long as it's blood-red.

Even without the IRA's ties to Colombia's Farc and the PLO, American political reality requires Gerry Adams to be persona non grata. Even if one accepts the view that Northern nationalists are an artificially created minority trapped in a gerrymandered state, so what? The same could be said of Iraqi Kurds, whose gerrymandered border dates from the same year and the same source – London, 1922.

The point is the Bush administration is admirably clear-sighted about the world's tinpot thugs. They concluded, rightly, that Yasser Arafat was a waste of time: the Nobel Peace Prize winner did more for peace in the Middle East by dying than he'd done in the previous 40 years. And right now the Sinn Féin/IRA leadership is looking a lot

Paula McCartney, sister of Robert McCartney, the Belfast man murdered by IRA members, shakes hands with President Bush in the White House on St Patrick's Day. Also pictured are, from left, Mr McCartney's fiancée Bridgeen Hagans, other sister Catherine, and Taoiseach Bertie Ahern. Photograph: Eric Draper/AP/White House.

like the PLO's – men who use the lavish patronage of European political leaders as a useful cover for lining their own pockets and eliminating their enemies.

The only difference is that in this case the European leaders concerned – in London and Dublin – are not monkeying with the lives of faraway people of whom they know little, but with their own countries. And, given that Sinn Féin's conversion to a shadow kleptocracy that's a cross between Hizbullah and the Russian Mafia poses a far greater long-term threat to the fundamental identity of the Irish Republic than of the United Kingdom, Dublin's behaviour has been even more foolish. With hindsight, the 1990s were the apogee of terrorist mainstreaming, with Yasser and Gerry given greater access to the White House than your average prime minister of a friendly middle-rank power. And in return for what? The people of Northern Ireland, quite reasonably enough, enjoy being able to go to the pub without having it blown up mid-pint. But peace is more than merely the absence of bombs. And in the past decade, under cover of the 'peace process', Sinn Féin has, as Kevin Myers puts it, utterly transformed Ireland's political map – to a degree they could never have accomplished with mere bombs. Some peace process. It is not Bush's job to be tougher on Sinn Féin than Blair or Ahern. But at least in years to come, if they're asking 'Who lost Ireland?' we'll know who not to blame.

Veronica Walsh from Kentstown, near Navan, Co. Meath, at Fairyhouse races. Photograph: Bryan O'Brien.

WEDNESDAY, 16 MARCH 2005

The Madness of the King George III Turf Bucket

Orna Mulcahy, Property Editor

It's old, it's mahogany and it's brass bound but it's a bucket nonetheless. Still, it's now among the world's most expensive buckets, having sold for €145,000 at auction yesterday in the James Adam Salerooms in Dublin. Two well-known Dublin property developers fought it out by phone to buy the large Georgian peat bucket, for which Adam's had expected to fetch no more than €20,000.

'Even at that price we had a lot of viewers saying "that's a very expensive bucket"', said Adam's director James O'Halloran. 'There were four other bidders in the room and others who didn't get a look in.' According to Mr O'Halloran the bucket, which dates from the time of George III, is special because of its size and its general quality. 'It's very large – you could fit a family in there – it's beautiful timber and it's in lovely condition which makes it rare. Rarity will always draw people out, but we certainly didn't expect it to break the €100,000 mark.'

A particularly Irish item of furniture, peat buckets were used to haul fuel from room to room and were designed to sit by the fireplace, sometimes with their counter part, the plate bucket, which was made to take plates to the diningroom and keep them warm by the fire. A slot opening in the side allowed the plates to be taken in and out with ease. Because they were practical, hard-working items, original peat and plate buckets in good condition are hard to find and imitations abound.

Far larger than the traditional bucket, this one stands 66 cm high and has a scallop shell on the

That bucket ... all €145,000 of it. Photograph: James Adams & Sons.

front, a typical motif in Irish Georgian furniture, though not often found adorning buckets. The size and the decoration suggest that it was made for one of Ireland's grand houses. However, its provenance is not completely clear.

'We don't have a lot of information about it, except that it was in Dublin up to 20 years ago, and then went to the UK where it was owned by a dealer,' said Mr O'Halloran. Now it's back and on its way to a good home. The buyer, like the underbidder, has a large residence in Dublin 4.

THURSDAY, 24 MARCH 2005

These Men Scare your Children

Arminta Wallace

Ghoulies, ghosties and long-leggety beasties? Forget it. Today's kids are more likely to be reading about shape-shifters, shadows and streetwise vampires. Horror is the new Harry Potter. The green slime department is becoming a permanent fixture of many bookshops as publishers scramble for a slice of an increasingly lucrative market; and with the age range targeted by horror fiction writers now stretching from six to adulthood and beyond, monsters are moving into areas where no monsters have gone before. 'Reader Beware! You're in for a Scare!' is the tag-line on the cover of the Goosebumps series. Scoff if you like. The Goosebumps books clocked up average sales of half a million per volume internationally – which, when you think about it, is a pretty scary number of real live children.

The problem for parents is two-fold. Bring your children to the bookshop – or even the local library – and you'll find it difficult to avoid this type of literature. On the other hand, with electronic wizardry grabbing more and more of your children's time and energy, you may be happy if they read anything at all. Even Darren Shan?

'Yep,' says Darren O'Shaughnessy, long-time resident of Limerick and creator of a top-selling 12-volume vampire saga. 'Occasionally I get a critic saying "Oh well, it's good that boys are reading – even if it's only Darren Shan". But as people who are actually out there trying to get kids to read will tell you, kids are very demanding. If a kid doesn't like a book he'll put it down right away.' A regular visitor to schools and libraries all over the world – he's huge in Japan – O'Shaughnessy was bitten early by the vampire bug, and says he spent his teenage years up to his neck in 'vampire movies, fantasy and adventure books. By my early 20s I'd got a bit bored with vampire books, because so many of them just repeated the same old Dracula story. I mean, Dracula was a brilliant book, but it's been done over and over and over. So I wanted to do something a bit different. But I still loved the idea of vampires.' Why would any sane person love the idea of vampires? He laughs. 'Vampires are cool. There's no other way to put it. The fact they drink blood, that they come out at night; they're

Ciara Callanan-Ryan (left) from the Ryan Dancing School in Tipperary, Sara O'Brien from the Cowhey-Ryan Dance School in Cork, Nakita Cassidy from the Costello Dance School in Galway and Ciara Moran from the Sylvan Kelly Dance School in Ballina, Co. Mayo, warming up for the World Irish Dancing Championships in Ennis, Co. Clare. Photograph: Marie McCallan/Press 22.

more believable than a lot of other monsters, you know? Zombies and so on?'

Drogheda-born Oisín McGann, author of *The Gods And Their Machines* and *The Harvest Tide Project*, also cites childhood reading as a major influence on his adult writing career. 'The writers who made me want to write were the likes of Roald Dahl, and Tolkien, and C.S. Lewis – so I suppose when the imprint has been made, that's the one that's going to stick with you.'

Parent, beware? 'I've never seen any formal proof that if children read anything at all, they'll inevitably progress to reading something "better",' says Robert Dunbar, a regular reviewer of children's books for *The Irish Times*. 'On the other hand, I suspect there's a large body of people who read Point Horror and then go on to Stephen King, or whoever – and good luck to them. Adults who read literary fiction are very much in the minority of readers, in any case.' Even within the category of 'horror' fiction, says Dunbar, there are books which have some literary merit and books which have none at all. On the whole, it's pretty easy to figure out which is which. Books which rely too obviously on formula, contain racist or sexist overtones, or are produced by a nameless corporation – as opposed to a real author – are ones to avoid, he suggests, while he would place Francine Pascal's Fearless series, whose heroine is a cross between Scully from *The X Files* and Buffy, among those which cleverly subvert the expectations of the genre.

Ask someone who disapproves of horror books what they expect them to consist of, and they'll most probably say 'gore and guts'. Ask a child and they'll say something like 'the guy pulls his face off and all the maggots fall out'. The authors, however, tell a different story. 'It sounds strange, given that I'm writing about vampires and circus freaks and so on,' says Darren O'Shaughnessy, 'but I think the books are moral books. They're about making the right decisions, trying to do good things, being loyal to your friends. I'm not interested in just grossing readers out.'

The crucial component of 'horror' fiction, it turns out, is that old chestnut – a rattling good yarn. Nobody knows how to spin one better than Anthony Horowitz, author of the BAFTA-winning TV series *Foyle's War* and the million-selling *Alex Rider* series of spy novels for children. Having written two volumes of scary stories, Horowitz is about to take a major plunge into horror with a five-part sequence called *Raven's Gate*. 'I don't think that gore and violence are necessarily important parts of horror – indeed, horror is more effective if you keep the blood count fairly low,' he says. 'I don't enjoy extreme violence. What I'm much more interested in is poking at the imagination; looking into the dark corners of the mind. There is a limit to how much I want to scare children. On the other hand, with this new series I want to push that limit as far as it will go.' This from the man who once wrote a story called Bath Night: 'one mother told me that after she read it, her daughter refused ever to have a bath again.'

Blood, then, isn't necessarily bad. In fact, the high-camp style of gothic horror is often more hilarious than horrible. 'I find that black comedy aspect of it quite appealing, I must say,' says Robert Dunbar. 'I suppose any book that has a lot of corpses and death and decay gets to the point where it's sending itself up.' Some of the titles – *Graveyard School* by Tom B Stone, or *Spine-Tinglers*

Darren Shan. Photograph: Brenda Fitzsimons.

Deirdre Ryan competing in the high jump at the European Indoor Athletic Championships in Madrid. Photograph: Stu Foster/Getty Images.

by MT Coffin – are, ahem, a dead giveaway. 'I would find it hard to believe,' says Dunbar, 'given the sophistication of today's children, that they're reading books like Goosebumps for much more than a laugh. Tomato ketchup on the corpse, sort of thing.'

At the older end of the market, matters undoubtedly get more serious. Death is a recurring theme in many books for teenagers, as is the situation where a child is isolated, with adults either physically inaccessible or unable to see that there's a problem. This is usually – though not always – turned around when the child solves the problem, thereby taking control of the story.

In a similar way, the presence of monsters or supernatural beings allows horror fiction to play with such themes as fear of the unknown while using the safety net of metaphor. After all, vampires are not something we expect to meet at the supermarket. (Although, now that supermarkets stay open all night ...)

There's nothing particularly new about any of this. One horrible plotline runs as follows. A pair of evil shoes condemn their youthful owner to a life of perpetual motion. She is promptly condemned to death for dancing on the Sabbath – only to be spared by a 'kindly' executioner who cuts her feet off instead. As the reference to the Sabbath might suggest, that plotline has been around for quite a while. In fact, Hans Christian Andersen's sinister story, Red Shoes, was first published in 1835.

One thing is for certain: children's horror fiction isn't going to vanish in a puff of smoke any time soon. Oisín McGann has already written two books for the eight-plus age group, *The Evil*

Damien Duff jumps in celebration towards his manager, José Mourinho (left), after scoring Chelsea's third goal in their Champion's League second leg knockout match against Barcelona at Stamford Bridge in London. Photograph: Dylan Martinez/Reuters.

Hair-Do and *The Poison Factory*; his sequel to *The Harvest Tide Project*, *The Fragile Stone*, is scheduled for publication in the autumn.

Darren O'Shaughnessy has embarked on a series about demons, of which the first volume, *Lord Loss*, will appear in June. As for Anthony Horowitz, he is unrepentant about the fact that his new series pits five blameless children in a battle against evil. 'The idea is that evil and black magic and witches and devils and monsters exist in the real world. That orcs, or whatever, walk the streets at night, just out of your sight. The truth is, we like being scared. There's no greater pleasure than to gather close around the fire in the dark and tell scary stories. And better to be scared by devils and demons than … well, today – for example – they're talking about America bombing Iran. Now that's much scarier than anything I can come up with.'

SATURDAY, 26 MARCH 2005

How Pupil-Power brings McDowell to Book

Paul Cullen

Olukunle Elukanlo got lucky. Hundreds had gone before him, people without a name, or people with a name but no friends, all of them deported back to Nigeria. Gone, forgotten, history, after their brief sojourns in Ireland.

However, Olukunle (Kunle) had a mobile phone and the confidence instilled in him by some years of Irish education. He had mates, too, back in Palmerstown, Dublin, where he had spent three years at the community school until he was deported last week. His friends mobilised effectively on his behalf, protesting spontaneously outside the Dáil on the day after he was deported. Fringe left and anti-racist groups rushed to help, as could be expected, and Opposition parties made political capital with the usual noises. So far, so predictable. In the past, small-scale campaigns had helped to stave off deportation for a few asylum-seekers but none had succeeded in having a deportee returned to the country. This didn't look any different.

Then something strange started to happen. The students kept banging away, showing a surprising level of media savvy. Parents and teachers turned out on their demonstrations. The public, more accustomed to youthful apathy towards politics, was intrigued. The Minister for Justice, Michael McDowell, who had signed the orders that led to the deportations of Kunle and 34 others, wasn't for turning. In last Tuesday's adjournment debate in the Dáil, however, he didn't seem to be on top of his game, prompting Opposition deputies to claim he hadn't read Kunle's file before deporting him. But it was Holy Week, a traditional time for religious reflection and national self-examination, and a quiet one for the media. The only Government TD in the Palmerstown area, John Curran, made sympathetic noises as constituents put him under increasing pressure. The Archbishop of Dublin, Dr Diarmuid Martin, made a rare but crucial intervention.

And so McDowell – of all people – buckled. Three days on, he effectively ate his adjournment speech, admitted he was wrong and agreed to let Kunle back on a six-month visa. Given the publicity and the phlegmatic nature of the asylum system, it's unlikely the 20-year-old will have to get on any more aircraft to Lagos for a very, very long time. So where does this leave McDowell's 'I stand by the asylum system' speech of Tuesday night, and his assertion that 'part and parcel of fairness and

Olukunle Elukanlo with friends at a 'welcome home' party in Lucan, Co. Dublin, after his return from Nigeria following justice minister Michael McDowell's revocation of his deportation order. Photograph: Fran Veale.

Ballymun's McDermott Tower comes crashing down after demolition experts set off explosives to remove the block, part of an urban regeneration scheme that will see the end of the unpopular north-Dublin flat complex. Photograph: Haydn West/PA.

effectiveness [in the system] is that deportations must take place'?

The Minister insisted his change of mind was a 'once-off' but as every pressure group knows, a politician's once-off decision is often followed by another once-off decision. Now the clamour is on to have others who were on last week's deportation flight returned – from whole families deported from Castleblayney to mothers split from their children in Athlone. Another deported Leaving Cert student has popped up and no doubt more will follow.

The nature of the cat-and-mouse game played over immigration is that any exemptions or concessions offered in any Western country are bound to stimulate their own demand. If McDowell were to let only left-handed, high-IQ 10-year-olds stay, he would suddenly find himself besieged by just that category of people, such is the desperation of people to make a better life in the West. But as the Minister told the Dáil before his volte face, it would be 'indefensible' not to deport good students while sending back the less academically gifted. 'The same applies to athletic prowess and participation in church activities. I cannot discriminate against those who are less gifted or on grounds of religious activity.'

So it isn't a beauty pageant, but the trouble for McDowell is that people don't think that way. They respond sympathetically to tales of good citizens, hard workers, cuddly children; they are indifferent to or ignorant of the fate of nameless, faceless, unintegrated 'statistics'.

Besides, he has now discriminated. As Peter O'Mahony of the Refugee Council points out: 'It now seems that having a strong case is of little value in itself unless the applicant has been lucky enough

Fireworks over the Liffey celebrating St Patrick's Festival 2005. Photograph: Matt Kavanagh.

to get the backing of a politician with influence to lobby for leave to remain.'

The asylum wars pit two directly conflicting protagonists against one another. On the one hand, the securocrats of the Department of Justice point to the need to control our borders, and to protect the 'integrity' of the asylum process by deporting failed applicants. They tend to talk in the abstract, and their heads spin with numbers, graphs, regulations and the minutiae of international conventions.

In the opposing corner, members of the anti-deportation lobby personalise their appeals; they talk of gifted young non-nationals, students torn from their books, and mothers sundered from their children. They relay the stories given by asylum-seekers as fact, even when these accounts have failed to convince those processing the applications. In a small voice, they say they accept the need for deportations, but they always plead against the particular deportation in question.

Most of us veer from one view to the other. We want to be humane, hospitable, generous, and we respond sympathetically when presented with individual cases. We are not completely comfortable with our new-found wealth and we are still conscious of our own history of emigration.

Yet we also respond positively to claims that the asylum process is being abused. We are fearful of the rapid changes which are happening in our country, of which the arrival of thousands of Nigerians, Romanians and other asylum-seekers is only one facet. We want less immigration, but are unwilling to do the low-paid work that immigrants do. We also want fewer asylum-seekers, but squirm when presented with the brutal facts of deportation.

Anyone who disputes these latter views has forgotten the thumping majority by which voters approved the restriction of citizenship rights for the Irish-born children of non-nationals last year. They are also ignoring the anti-immigrant chatter on radio phone-in shows, where the so-called silent majority can vent its spleen without fear of identification by the liberal left.

McDowell is painted as the bad guy in the asylum debate, but his policies are little different from those of his predecessor, John O'Donoghue. The processing of asylum applications and appeals is a far more streamlined and efficient operation than it was a few years ago; it has its critics, but many observers accept the overall fairness of the process. For those whose applications are rejected, there is still the possibility of being granted humanitarian leave to remain. It is here that McDowell has taken a tough line; last year, only 75 failed asylum-seekers were successful at this stage; eight times as many were deported.

It is this failure by the Minister to use the flexibility available to him that led law professor William Binchy to call for 'an infusion of humanity' into McDowell's thinking. Ultimately, too, it led to the political blunder of sending a student back to Nigeria, just three months before his Leaving Cert.

TUESDAY, 29 MARCH 2005

In Search of Truth for Kirsty

Tony Clayton Lea

More than four years on, nobody has been held accountable for the death of Kirsty MacColl. Her family and friends hope to change that.

She was, by no great stretch of the imagination from critic or fan, coming into her prime. Born in 1959, the daughter of 1950s folk legend Ewan MacColl and teacher/choreographer Jean Newlove, singer and songwriter Kirsty MacColl had been put through the usual blender process in terms of the record industry, but by the release in 2000 of *Tropical Brainstorm*, MacColl was back on track. Widely recognised as the best album of her career, it matched wit with insight, sex with love, spite with understanding, disappointment with resolution.

She had experienced up to this point a frustrating recording career – lots of critical acclaim but few commercial highs. To this day, it's arguable that most people know Kirsty MacColl best for three songs she didn't write: cover versions of The Kinks' *Days* and Billy Bragg's *New England*, and her part (a pivotal one) in The Pogues' *Fairy Tale of New York*. 'She never followed a hit with another hit,' says former husband, producer Steve Lillywhite. 'She had quite a few hit records, but had the same amount of flops – that next record after the hit never did it for her. And in the early days she never went out and toured, which meant that she was always back at square one.'

A period before the 'early days' included a tour of Irish ballrooms, organised by her then manager Frank Murray (who would subsequently go on to manage, as much as anyone could, The Pogues). The experience of playing to handfuls of people in vast auditoria around Ireland – in particular at the Parnell Ballroom – put MacColl off touring for years. By the early 1980s, she was a memory on the live circuit; her songwriting talents, however, provided chart-hit material to the likes of Tracey Ullman (the superlative teen angst love song, *They Don't Know*), while her voice graced many recording sessions overseen by her boyfriend and then husband Lillywhite.

When sons Jamie and Louis came along, her recording career was put on hold. 'We had children very quickly,' says Lillywhite, 'and that seemed like a good enough reason to not think of touring. But after we'd recorded *Fairy Tale of New York*, The Pogues went on tour to Germany and asked her to come out to Berlin, just for the Berlin show, and then she could go home. So she went out, did the gig, and I'll always remember her phoning me up after the gig and – with all The Pogues behind her – asking me if I minded if she did the whole tour. I didn't see her for another 10 days, and that was the beginning of her coming back. It was a win-win situation for her, because when she came on stage everyone knew that *Fairy Tale of New York* was going to be next, but she wasn't the centre of attention.'

For reasons no one would have wanted, MacColl has been the centre of attention for the past four years for something other than her music. Following the release of *Tropical Brainstorm*, the success of which prompted renewed media attention and even tour dates (including one in Dublin's HQ, now Spirit), she decided to bring her sons to the island of Cozumel. Also with her on the trip was her partner, musician James Knight (MacColl and Lillywhite had divorced in 1995).

Known as Mexico's crown jewel, Cozumel is located 12 miles off the Yucatan peninsula and boasts the second-largest coral reef chain in the world. It was here on December 18th, 2000, while scuba-diving with her sons and their divemaster in the restricted area of Chankanaab Reef, about 300m offshore, that MacColl was killed by a powerboat owned by Guillermo Gonzalez Nova, chairman of the holding company Controladora Comercial Mexicana, which is the second-largest retail operator in Mexico after the WalMart chain. More than four years later, no one has been made accountable to the satisfaction of MacColl's family and friends.

From her home in Ealing, London, Kirsty's mother Jean tells *The Irish Times* of the progress of the campaign known as Justice for Kirsty (JFK). In her early 80s, Jean's tireless and tenacious demeanour has driven the campaign from the start. Support from friends and musicians Bono and Billy Bragg and actor Tracey Ullman – along with thousands of fans – has helped maintain the thrust.

'Support for the campaign is going terrifically well. As regards our activities, in relation to prosecution, it's also going very well now. Initially, we started with no help at all – nothing from the Mexican authorities or the Foreign Office or the British government. But that's all changed. We've spoken to the head of the diplomatic corps, Sir Michael Jay, and we have the support of the Foreign Office. We have even gone to the attorney general in Mexico. I believe that Mexico's President Fox is aware of what we're doing.' Jean states that if the present campaign drive doesn't work, she's going to the International Court of Human Rights, and 'from there we can bring a case against the state of Mexico'.

But, as Jean says, JFK needs all the help it can get. 'The fans have been writing to their MPs, and we want more people to do that to publicise the campaign. Publicity helps the funding, which comes from the fans. A woman in Lincolnshire ran a coffee and croissant morning, which raised £300.People ask me what they can do – well, they can look at the website, and they can send for leaflets, which have the bare bones of the case, and a postcard already addressed to President Fox. He has probably received about 10,000 already, but the more the better.'

Political pressure is maintained from media exposure, says Jean. Some weeks ago, the documentary *Who Killed Kirsty MacColl?* was broadcast on BBC terrestrial television (following its première on BBC4). Yesterday, *From Croydon to Cuba*, a three-CD anthology of Kirsty's music, was released. Every little bit of exposure will help, says Jean, to cut through the bureaucratic red tape which she says she and other JFK personnel have encountered in the past four years.

While the CD set will raise MacColl's profile higher in certain political circles than it has been since her death, it might also arouse interest in her back catalogue, which remains (despite its relatively poor commercial placing) one of the strongest of any UK female songwriter of the past 20 years. Not

Kirsty MacColl. Photograph: Charles Dickens/EMI.

for her the witterings of the pop brigade; rather, in no uncertain terms, she made highly intelligent, often autobiographical correlations between male and female interaction; the pull and push of life in all its contradiction and dysfunction.

'She would always say that the songs were about everything,' recalls Lillywhite. 'Maybe there was a bit of me in there, maybe her whole life. She was certainly happier than a lot of her songs made her out to be, although after we were divorced I think she started analysing what she did more. She once said that a lot of the songs might actually be about me, but I'm not sure if that was true. How would I rate her as songwriter? Oh, I think she's up there with Shane MacGowan and Elvis Costello. She was a poet. Bono's a great songwriter, as such, but a lot of what Kirsty would write would be more poetic.'

She was a frighteningly honest songwriter, too, says her former husband. 'She could nail what she wanted to say in one sentence. She could be the most vitriolic, put-down person you could ever meet. If she wanted to say something that cut you to the bone – both in her songs and as a person – then she could. The term "fiery redhead" was probably invented for Kirsty.'

Lillywhite's involvement in the JFK campaign is mainly one of support. 'Any campaign like that can only be driven by someone who has lost a child, because the love you feel for your children is quite frightening. To Jean, Kirsty is her little girl. That's how we feel, no matter how grown up our children are.'

Says Jean, 'In a way she spoke for all of us and she was not afraid to say how things were – she didn't cover anything up. That's one of the things that people liked about her. She was very open, very frank, honest, and she could quickly see through anything that was false.'

The music on *From Croydon to Cuba* proves this with its songs of shrewd insight, feminine instinct, determination for fair play, and a few swear words. No matter how frustrating things could be, says Jean, she never gave up trying to see the good in people and in certain situations. 'I'm in my 80s, and I'm not giving up either. You do these things for your children. We just battle on.'

MONDAY, 4 APRIL 2005

An Eerie Calm Fell as Death Announced

Paddy Agnew, in the Vatican

Sixty thousand people stood so quietly in St Peter's Square that from 100 yards away one could clearly hear the water gently flowing in the square's two handsome fountains. Just minutes earlier, a huge wave of applause rippled across the square as the voice of Archbishop Leonardo Sandri relayed the news of the death of John Paul II to the crowd: 'Pope John Paul II has returned home to the Father.' It was 10 p.m. on Saturday night. About half an hour before, the Pope had died.

Archbishop Sandri's announcement came as a brusque interruption to a prayer vigil that had started more than an hour earlier as pilgrims and tourists alike had gathered to pray for the Pope. After the round of applause, an eerie calm descended on the square, a quasi-silence that lasted seven or eight minutes. Some people got down on their knees to pray, some wept openly, but the vast majority of those gathered in St Peter's simply stood quietly, as if trying to assimilate the rite of passage, the historical and unique moment of the death of John Paul II.

Even those TV reporters doing their 'live' reports from the square were practically whispering into their microphones, relating the news in serious and grave tones.

Even though the Catholic Church is a 'universal' church and even though a few Polish flags fluttered amongst the crowd, the gathering had a peculiarly Roman feel to it. As the news of the Pope's death spread, the already-crowded square became even more filled up as Romans, complete with babies, dogs, bicycles and *fidzanzati* (courting couples) streamed in. In these parts, they have seen emperors, empires and Popes come and go for much of the last 2,000 years. Il popolo too has its rituals to respect. So it was last Saturday night as the popolo once more got out on the street to pay tribute to a Pope called 'un uomo buono' (a good man) on posters throughout the city yesterday.

About an hour after the Pope died, the Campana Sant Andrea, the huge bell high up on the right-hand side of the facade of the Basilica of St Peter's, tolled long and loud. The bell tolled for 84-year-old Karol Wojtyla, the 264th pontiff to sit on the seat of Peter and the second-longest serving Pope in church history after Pius X1 (1846–1878). Even as the bell tolled, the lights in all the rooms of the pontifical apartment were turned off as some of the Pope's closest collaborators re-enacted age-old rites following the death of a Pope.

The Pope had died at 9.37 on Saturday evening. About an hour and a half before his death, Mass for Divine Mercy Sunday had been said in his bedroom, presided over by his long-serving private secretary, Archbishop Stanislaw Dziwisz. During the Mass, both the Viaticum and the Sacrament of the Anointing of the Sick, once colloquially known as the last rites, had again been administered to the Pope. Throughout Saturday a steady stream of senior Curia figures had visited the papal apartment to bid farewell to the Pope, kneeling briefly by his deathbed to pray for him. Vatican medical bulletins reported that the Pope had begun to drift in and out of consciousness throughout Saturday while the official Vatican death certificate records that he died of 'septic shock' (sepsis or blood infection) and 'heart collapse'.

Present with the Pope at the time of his death were his extended Polish clerical 'family' comprising his two personal secretaries, Archbishop Dziwisz and Monsignor Mieczyslaw Mokrzycki, as well as Cardinal Marian Jaworski, Archbishop Stanislaw Rylko, Father Tadeusz Styczen, Sister Tobiana Sobodka and three Sacred Heart of Jesus nuns. Also present, of course, was the Pope's personal physician, Dr Renato Buzzonetti. It was the latter who, having verified that the Pope was dead, then passed a candle in front of his face. According to this ancient rite, if the candle's flame does not flicker, then the Pope is dead. At that point, a linen veil was placed over the Pope's face.

Shortly after the death, the Pope's closest collaborators, including the cardinal secretary of state, Angelo Sodano, Cardinal Joseph Ratzinger, Archbishop Sandri, the camerlengo (chamberlain) Cardinal Eduardo Martinez Somalo, and the vice-camerlengo Archbishop Paolo Sardi then arrived in the apartment. In accordance with tradition, it was the camerlengo, Cardinal Somalo, who formally announced in the papal apartment, 'Vere, Papa mortuus est' (Truly, the Pope is dead). He did this after first removing the linen veil and then calling out the Pope's baptismal name (Karol) three times.

The camerlengo then used a small silver hammer bearing the papal coat of arms to destroy the papal ring, the pescatorio, or 'Fisherman's ring', thus re-enacting a custom that goes back to the Middle Ages. Once, the camerlengo would also have used that same hammer to strike the Pope three times on the forehead as another way of verifying death, but that custom has been dropped.

Back out in the square, the initial calm had been interrupted by Cardinal Sodano who formally began an hour-long prayer service that included the recital of prayers for 'eternal rest', the Lord's Prayer, Hail Marys and readings from scripture including Psalm 130. At the end of the service, Archbishop Sardi told people: 'The prayers are over. Now go back to your homes or, if you like, stay here in silence.'

Pall bearers, escorted by Swiss Guards, carry the body of Pope John Paul II through St Peter's Square in the Vatican past grief-stricken mourners. Photograph: Dylan Martinez/Reuters.

WEDNESDAY, 6 APRIL 2005

'How Can you Not Attend the Funeral of one's Father?'

Daniel McLaughlin, in Warsaw

The lucky ones gripped their tickets a little more tightly and hurried past the growing scrum. Dozens of restless bodies obscured the international ticket

Pilgrims who have arrived at Termini railway station in Rome struggle to board buses bound for the Vatican. Photograph: Yves Herman.

office at Warsaw's main train station and scores of impatient eyes strafed the dim cubicle for signs of life.

The website of Polish state railways had collapsed within minutes of announcing plans to provide special trains to Rome for Pope John Paul's funeral, and the result was this: a mass of impatient Poles clutching precious zlotys in their pockets, demanding the chance to exchange them for an even more precious passage to the Eternal City. Across Warsaw and Poland, a deeply Catholic country of 40 million people, mourners looked for ways to get to the Italian capital to bid farewell to their national hero and purveyors of all conceivable means of transport looked for ways to oblige.

In the bowels of the Warsaw station, dozens of people quietly gathered on platform four, apparently a little embarrassed at not being part of the ensuing throng upstairs. They shuffled along the platform with their bags, some travelling light, others lugging bulging supplies of solid Polish food and drink, eyeing the notice board all the while, willing it to clatter round and declare their train ready to depart.

At a little after 9.30 p.m., it finally dissolved into a sea of swimming letters that gradually coalesced into the desired form. The train called Chopin – the composer who is now perhaps Poland's second-favourite son – would leave at 21.37 for Vienna. 'Thank God, we are on our way,' muttered one elderly traveller to her companions, who helped her onto the train and waved her off with the entreaty: 'Pray for us!' She was on the first leg of a journey that millions of her countrymen were desperate to make and which a few dozen were now starting on the night-train to the Austrian capital, a city that for centuries has been one of Europe's great crossroads.

'From Vienna we are not sure what to do,' admitted Tomas Sokolowski, who was travelling with his wife, Elzbeta, 'but we wanted to get moving south no matter what, so we just decided to go.' The couple were lucky, they said, because as retired teachers they had a little money put aside and could leave home quickly after packing up their two small bags. 'Who knows how many people will make it to Rome, have the chance to actually see our Pope or be there at his funeral?' added Tomas. 'We had to go early to give ourselves a chance.' Despite not having accommodation booked in Rome or a detailed plan of how to get there, the 62-year-olds showed little apprehension of the journey ahead. 'Millions of pilgrims are on their way to the same place,' said Elzbeta. 'We will all look after each other.'

As the high rises and smokestacks of Warsaw suburbs passed by in the gloom, yesterday's travellers on Chopin, the daily overnight train to Vienna, could not predict what lay ahead but knew they were leaving travel chaos behind. In the central station from which they had just departed, news agencies reported that many would-be pilgrims had bedded down on the floor to be sure of getting tickets on one of only six special trains that were announced to run between Polish cities and Rome. National airline LOT said it had sold every seat to Rome until Friday and was laying on 'our biggest Boeings' and an extra flight to the city yesterday.

'And how can you not attend the funeral of one's father?' one pensioner, Malgorzata Jurowska (65), was quoted as saying in LOT's Warsaw ticket office. 'I am giving my savings for a holy thing,' she said, after paying for the flight to Rome.

For thousands of others, the prospect of a 30-hour journey by road, spending two nights on a bus, paying at least €150 for a ticket and staying as much as 200 miles outside Rome appeared to be no obstacle. 'I was a small boy when he was elected the Pope,' wrote Piotr in an advert posted on Poland's Onet.pl website to find a seat in a private car to Rome. 'He paid us so many visits and now it's time for me to go on a trip and say goodbye to him.'

City officials in the Pope's home town of Wadowice in southern Poland have chartered four buses to take some 200 locals to Italy. Many will be given free lodging in private homes in Carpineto Romano, a town near Rome that is a sister city to Wadowice, though potential pilgrims from the nearby city of Krakow were still waiting for a response to their travel requests.

'We already have 400 pilgrims who want to fly,' said Mariola Peknicka from the Krakow diocese, where Karol Wojtyla was archbishop from 1964 until he became Pope in 1978. 'We have to wait to see how many charter flights we can get. With every minute there are more and more people coming and asking how we can help them to get to Rome.'

On board the Warsaw-Vienna express, as it wound down through the Czech Republic towards Austria, some slept while others talked of what their pilgrimage would bring and why they were so intent on making it. 'This is expensive for us, but Friday will be a national occasion for Poland, there in the Vatican,' said Ana, a student from the southern industrial city of Katowice. 'It is only right to be there; it is the last chance to see our Pope,' added her companion, Dorota. 'We will try and take a bus or train from Vienna to Italy. I've heard there is another overnight train straight to Rome.'

In Marek's compartment, Polish sausage and two empty bottles of the popular Zywiec beer were clustered on the little folding table. In the corridor outside, wreathed in smoke from the first cigarette of the day, he watched dawn cast a pink glow over the steel and glass skyscrapers that marked our approach to Vienna. 'He was the only man like that,' the 28-year old engineer said of John Paul, 'and there is just one chance to say goodbye to him. I hope to make it, but if I didn't even try, I would always be sorry.'

FRIDAY, 8 APRIL 2005

Young Differ on Faith but Unite in Affection for 'Papa'

Eyewitness in Rome: Kathy Sheridan

A sign – in English – to 'Keep off the Lawn' stands in the middle of the Piazza Risorgimento. But for a nice, sheltered spot of soft greenery less than a kilometre north of St Peter's Square, it was never going to happen.

Cheek by jowl with the sign, 19-year-old Tom is sound asleep on a floor sheet, his Polish flag draped over his face. A few yards away, 22-year-old Jaime is running the Spanish flag up a pole before attaching it to a handy piazza sapling beside his tent. A little Polish group is having a picnic on the grass, breaking out the tinned fish rations. Beside them, three skinny boys are stretched out, their T-shirts pulled up to their chins, the better to roast their pale torsos in the hot Roman sun.

Nearby, a young entrepreneur is doing a nice trade in 'Goodbye Papa' T-shirts. Another is flogging last Sunday's newspapers announcing the death of the Pope. Further on, a morose-looking individual is selling the usual religious kitsch of Papal busts, paperweights, and rosary beads in little boxes adorned with the papal image. For the young followers of 'Giovanni Paolo', as they call him, this is about as good as it gets, short of setting up camp in St Peter's Square itself.

Showing a commendable grasp of reality, the city authorities chucked away the rule book and made the best of it. A mobile hospital has been set up yards away, the usual coterie of civil defence volunteers are virtually begging all-comers to take the free bottled water, and big screens and speakers are in place, relaying images, prayers and music from the basilica.

Apart from yesterday's Polish invasion, with its throat-catching displays of regret, emotion and proud flag-waving, the outstanding image of this week has been the hordes of young people in their teens and early 20s pouring into Rome. To call them 'young people' is to imply a homogeneity that simply is not there.

While the American satellite TV station CNN devoted much of their schedule one morning this week to a young British rock duo, Raindown, singing *Crucifying You* (recipient of senior church approval, by all accounts), down in St Peter's Square young, exuberant Italians danced and wiggled and belted out the songs they learned when Giovanni Paolo invited them to Vatican World Youth Day in Rome in 2000.

Five years on, it seems that the sense of loss at his passing is melding with nostalgia for that amazing time when two million of them travelled from all over Italy and experienced what was – for their age – the nearest thing to a parentally approved 10-day rock concert. These were the youthful followers with their football chant of 'Giovanni Paolo' who were dubbed the 'Papa boys' by the media here.

Ask them what they mean when they say they 'love' him – which they say repeatedly – and they talk about him as a 'man of peace', 'someone who brought all the people together', but above all about 'that happy time' back in 2000. 'What I am doing now,' says bright-eyed, 21-year-old Nicoletta, 'is thinking about the jubilee when we were all so young and we made a celebration for the Pope. We have come here today to say "thanks for all you did".'

Many, when pressed on Catholic teaching and the Pope's orthodoxy on sexual matters for example, simply shrug and admit that not only are they not regular Mass-goers, but they don't think about any of it very much at all. 'I can pray at home better than in church,' says Rita. 'You can be just as near to God there.' Nicoletta nods happily: 'Many are not here as much for the Pope as for the man. To us, he seemed like the loveliest father in the world. Even atheists have come here for that reason.'

Four young clean-cut Americans, also in their early 20s, present a very different take on their religion. Assertive and certain of their righteousness, they loved him for his conviction, reflected in their own. 'We love him because he never compromised the faith,' says Natalie. 'He had the truth and he called the youth to be the future of that truth. He never tried to change the faith to get the youth to come to him – he made the true faith appealing to the youth.'

All four – who attended the 'very orthodox' Christendom College in Virginia – are assiduous Mass-goers. Jeremiah, a construction worker, attends daily. 'That's how I was raised by my parents.' 'My Mom also,' adds Natalie. 'She was Jewish and became a convert because of this Pope.' They all voted for George Bush in the last election, 'mostly because of his pro-life stance'. Three of the four are of Irish descent.

Talk to young Polish people, by contrast, and their sense of loss and regret is like that for a father. Wrapped in the Polish flag and often wearing Solidarity scarves – a movement dating to before they were born – they admit that their adoration of John Paul has an element of political as well as religious fervour. Again and again, they talk about a man who never forgot his people, who crushed the oppressors and continued to mind them like a father.

'When we could not speak "God" out loud, because of the government, he did it for us,' says a thoughtful 23-year-old Beata. 'And I think we must accept that whoever is the head of the church cannot be seen to change the teachings. But of course, we in Poland also find the issues of sexual behaviour very difficult to deal with. The difference I think is that my country is still quite conservative compared to yours so not many people are questioning this ... that is, for now.'

Meanwhile, back in the Piazza Risorgimento, the mood is calm. Not a Smirnoff Ice in sight or bottles of anything apart from water. Not for the first time, it is notable that tens of thousands of young Europeans can mix easily without resorting to alcohol. It's also notable that young Irish and English people are conspicuous by their relative absence from this week's phenomenal events.

SATURDAY, 9 APRIL 2005

Pageantry that was Poignant as well as Powerful

Eyewitness in Rome: Paddy Agnew

In Rome, when the wind blows through St Peter's Square, there are those who say that it is the Holy Spirit at work. If that is the case, then He did a good job yesterday as the blustery, grey April day provided a fittingly solemn backdrop to the funeral service for John Paul II, a service that was both stunning in its choreography and moving in its content.

This was a Vatican ceremony that was much more than a display of institutionalised Petrine primacy. Behind the pageantry of a ceremony sung in Gregorian chant and spoken in Latin, there was the palpable sense that the princes of the church, the political shakers and makers, and the 300,000 pilgrims gathered in the Vatican, had all come together to mourn the loss of a dear friend.

For the 200 or so world leaders gathered to the right of the altar, it may well have been edifying to find themselves back about 800 years in a service that owed nothing to the post-Vatican Council II vernacular but more to Byzantine and medieval rites. Edifying, too, to find so many friends and foes clustered together into the same small space. One unnamed member of a delegation from an Islamic country said: 'He [John Paul II] is still at work amongst us. Look at the atmosphere of dialogue and listening around us here today.'

The service began in truly dramatic fashion. As the *Requiem aeternam*, sung by the Sistine Chapel choir, sounded across the square, and as the

Pilgrims throng St Peter's Square in the Vatican for the funeral Mass of Pope John Paul II. Photograph: Dylan Martinez/Reuters.

Sant'Andrea bell tolled, more than 165 cardinals filed on to the steps after emerging from the red-curtained main doorway to the basilica.

Following the cardinals was the cypress-wood coffin of John Paul II, carried by 12 Vatican sediari and escorted by two Swiss Guards. Its emergence was greeted by sustained applause as the pallbearers carried it slowly round to the front of the altar. Throughout the service the coffin lay on a carpet in front of the altar, with a book of the Gospels on top. The wind blew first the pages, then finally shut the book. Behind the steps of the basilica, a tapestry portraying the resurrection of Christ hung from the closed curtains at the door.

Cardinal Joseph Ratzinger, deacon of the College of Cardinals and Prefect of the Congregation of the Doctrine of the Faith, presided, and his solemn opening words, In Nomine Patri, et Filii, et Spiritus Sancti, set the tone for the next three hours. Throughout his homily, spoken in Italian, he had to stop several times as applause swelled from the square, usually prompted by the mention of the name John Paul. He spoke of the sense of 'sadness, yet at the same time of joyful hope' with which 'we bury his remains in the earth'.

He also spoke of a Holy Father who was 'a priest to the last'. He concluded: 'None of us can ever forget how in that last Easter Sunday of his life, the Holy Father, marked by suffering, came once more to the window of the Apostolic Palace and one last time gave his blessing Urbi et Orbi. We can be sure that our beloved Pope is standing today at the window of the Father's house, that he sees us and blesses us.'

Following Vatican tradition, the Swiss Guards dipped their halberds, got down on one knee and saluted with the left hand during the Eucharist. As 320 priests from the parishes of Rome went out among the crowd to offer communion, they were confronted with banners saying 'Santo Subito' (Make Him a Saint, Now).

Two of the most poignant moments came after the Eucharist when the Litany of the Saints boomed across St Peter's Square as the cardinals paid their last respects. Minutes later the patriarchs of the oriental churches recited their Greek prayers for the dead, in solemn but ancient tones: 'For you, oh Christ, oh God, are the resurrection, the way and the repose for your servant John Paul, Pope of Rome who has gone to sleep.'

The service climaxed with the pallbearers carrying the body back up the steps of the basilica, accompanied by the Magnificat; the lugubrious tolling of the Sant'Andrea bell; and by a crescendo of applause. At the threshold of St Peter's, the pallbearers turned to face the crowd, holding the coffin aloft for one last salute.

The ceremony then passed out of the public eye and down through the 'door of death' on the left-hand side of the main altar, down to the crypt where John Paul II now lies buried alongside John XXIII and two pious women, Queen Christiana of Sweden and Queen Carlotta of Cyprus.

Cardinal Joseph Ratzinger (centre) at the coffin of Pope John Paul II. Photograph: Franco Origlia/Getty Images.

SATURDAY, 9 APRIL 2005

Day of Tears and Pride as Poles turn Rome into their City

Eyewitness in Rome: Daniel McLaughlin

A Roman woman, apparently managing to sleep late on this extraordinary Friday morning, opened her shutters and called down to an acquaintance on Via Ottaviano. In response, thousands of Poles glared up at her and hissed, as politely as they could, 'Sssshhhh!' The funeral of Pope John Paul II was about to begin, and in St Peter's Square, as in this nearby street, the red and white of his homeland dominated the day.

Between a blue sky and the heads of more than a million tired Polish pilgrims – who spent precious money and dozens of hours getting here in buses, cars and trains – banners streamed in the breeze and told of a nation's devotion to its favourite son. Many flags carried the names of towns and villages from across Poland, including Bialystok close to Belarus and Rzeszow near Ukraine, held aloft by pilgrims who revered the pontiff both as the leader of their church and as the strongest keeper of the flame of Polish identity through the darkest days of communist rule and martial law.

He was, several Poles remarked, the embodiment of the Polish spirit's victory over communism,

Polish pilgrims arriving in St Peter's Square for the funeral of Pope John Paul II. Photograph: David Sleator.

and the nation's re-emergence as a strong, free and still intensely Catholic European nation. That, they said, was why celebration triumphed over sadness yesterday.

'It took 20 hours to get here and the Austrians tried to turn us back at the border,' said Pawel Jasynski (25), a medical student from the town of Sedziszow, who arrived with 18 friends of all ages in three cars and a bus. 'They thought we were coming here to look for work, and said not to go to Rome because the roads were closed. So we went to another border post and drove through.'

Krzystof Cyzio (30), the organiser of the trip and bus-driver, had called his brother back from Belgium to make a journey that he started planning after the Pope's death last Saturday night. 'We stood 12 hours in a queue to see his body,' said Krzystof. 'He was the best man in Poland and in the world, and we had to say goodbye. It is important for us.' The grief of last weekend was now replaced by gratitude, Pawel added. 'We are so proud that he is Polish and we have to wish him well on this last trip. Lots of special people have come here to do the same thing,' he said, referring to the unprecedented gathering of national leaders and dignitaries on St Peter's Square.

The Sedziszow pilgrims, who included several elderly men and women, had slept in their vehicles at the Stadio Olimpico, where thousands of Polish cars were parked after the long journey south to a city besieged by more than four million mourners. For Krzystof, a highlight of the trip was a chance meeting at the Coliseum with Viktor Yushchenko, Ukraine's new president. He congratulated him on an election hailed in Poland as a victory over malign Russian influence. That win was also a triumph for Poland's president, Alexander Kwasniewski, who helped broker a final political deal, but he did not win applause from his massed countrymen when his face flashed across the big screen erected on Via Ottaviano.

That privilege was reserved for Lech Walesa, who was Poland's first post-communist president after leading the Solidarity union, a movement John Paul supported in its fight for democracy throughout the 1980s. Walesa, whose political star fell quickly in the 1990s, was among the dignitaries at the funeral, and his former Solidarity comrades were in the crowd a few miles away.

'We have so much sorrow,' said a former Polish deputy from Solidarity, Ewa Tomaszewska, who was among the mourners. 'For Poles, and for Solidarity, it's hard. He is no longer behind us to help and defend us as he did during the siege'. She was referring to the siege the communist authorities imposed in a 1981 attempt to break the trade union, which has lost much political influence in recent years. 'At the same time, he is not suffering any more,' she said. 'He has left us an enormous legacy, hundreds of thousands of pages of encyclicals, books and homilies. We must study them now, reflect on them to know how to live in the years to come.'

Holding red-and-white Solidarity flags aloft on Via Ottaviano, two stalwart members of the union said they had come with two busloads of comrades on a 35-hour trip from Warsaw. 'John Paul II was our greatest supporter,' said Grzegorz Orlowski (51), 'a great ally in social defence'. His friend, Jan Karwowski (55), added: 'We are sad but, also, he was such a great man, and here we are now together, one people, unified. There is a feeling of brotherhood here today.'

Daybreak found many Poles huddled under blankets after a night in the open, but they rose as one to greet the coffin of the former archbishop of Krakow, Karol Wojtyla, for a final farewell. Watching the funeral procession on the huge screens, they seemed stunned with pride at the sight of so many of their countrymen in St Peter's Square, and many cried at the display of national devotion.

While the Italians applauded the progress of the Pope's coffin towards the altar, most Poles fell silent, clasping their hands before them, reverential and contemplative. They turned down the Polish stations on their portable radios, and such was the hush over the packed street that their flags could be heard fluttering in the chilly breeze.

Later in the day, when the Pope's coffin was already in the Vatican crypt, that breeze would bring cold rain to a city that had seen only sunshine over the past days.

Three hours on, some cried and hugged friends and family as they bade farewell to John Paul. Many had hoped he would come home for ever in death, and the pontiff's final testament showed that he had considered burial in Poland.

Several Polish mourners said the scale and formality of yesterday's ceremony made them feel oddly distant from a man to whom they always felt so close. Others described a feeling of bewilderment, of being almost fearful of imagining their country adrift in the world without the guidance of Karol Wojtyla. Others acknowledged that an era was over – a time of struggle and ultimate victory with leaders such as Walesa and, above all, the Pope – but that the future had to be faced with the strength, determination and faith that John Paul showed to the end of his days.

'We Catholics know that he is before God and praying for us now,' said Waldek Matuszak (29), a computer engineer from the town of Kalisz. 'He is closer than ever to us now. He is our protector.' Waldek travelled for 30 hours to Rome on a bus with 58 other people, including five priests and his friend, Jarek Perskawiec (23), who said he hoped to have time to look around the Italian capital before heading home.

But as a million or more of his countrymen drifted back to their vehicles, or gathered to talk and sing in the rain that began falling on St Peter's Square, he knew he had been part of a unique pilgrimage, one his nation would never forget. 'We are united here, in solidarity and love,' Jarek said. 'Today, Rome is a Polish city.'

A warrior monk displays his Kung Fu skills at Songshan Mountain near the Shaolin Temple, build in AD 495. It has been earmarked by Unesco as a World Heritage Site. Photograph: Cancan Chu/Getty Images.

TUESDAY, 12 APRIL 2005

Farmers Riot over Chemical Plants' Emissions

Clifford Coonan, in Huaxi, Zhenjiang province

Thousands of Chinese farmers overturned buses, smashed cars and attacked policemen during a riot in a village in eastern China against chemical plants they say are destroying their crops. Villagers said 3,000 police officers descended on the village of Huaxi before dawn on Sunday. Armed with electric batons and tear gas, they had come to clear roadblocks the villagers had set up to stop deliveries to and from 13 chemical plants built where rice and vegetable farms once stood.

The scene yesterday was one of devastation and anarchy – 40 buses lay smashed in the grounds of a local school, while 14 cars were piled upside down in a side alley, some draped with police uniforms. There was debris everywhere and no sign of law and order.

The chemical plants produce fertiliser, dyes and pesticides and farmers say waste from the factories is poisoning the well water they drink and periodically causing stinging clouds of gas. The effluents are also allegedly causing stillborn babies and birth defects.

'I'm afraid my children won't live to reach my age. I want my land back, I want my food back and I want my water back,' said one 60-year-old

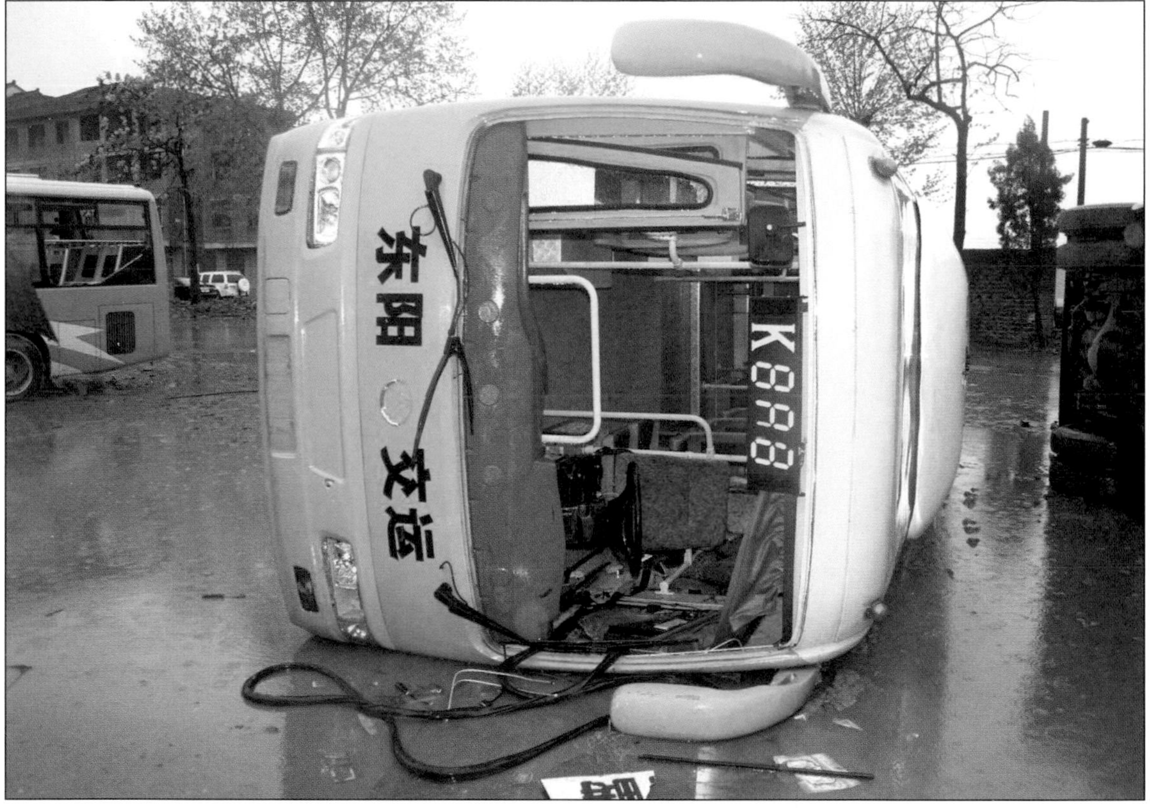

Bus overturned by rioters in Huaxi, Zhenjiang province, China. Photograph: Clifford Coonan.

woman with the surname Wang, which is carried by one-third of the village of 30,000. She was speaking at a makeshift shelter put up at the local old people's association, which displayed police riot shields, identity cards and helmets, as well as machetes and scissors which the locals said had been used against them. Elderly women were eager to tell their tale of the night they drove the police out of the village. The atmosphere was jubilant.

Soon after leaving the village, I was stopped by police on the highway on the way to the county town of Dongyang and detained by government officials for almost six hours. In a surreal experience I was shown wonderful hospitality and fed delicious food before my notes were confiscated and photographs deleted from my camera. I then signed a statement saying I had entered the village illegally and broken Chinese reporting laws. There were unconfirmed reports of two deaths during the riots. The local hospital could not confirm the reports and none of the villagers actually named a victim.

Recent riots in China have been sparked by reports of such incidents that have turned into demonstrations of public anger with local corruption or abuse of privilege.

Dongyang government spokesman Chen Qixian denied that anyone had died in the riot. He said 1,000 officials had taken part in the operation to remove the roadblocks. 'Of those 1,000, around 100 were police. The rest included officials from the Dongyang Women's Association. They were sent in because we did not want to be accused of manhandling elderly female protesters,' he said. The roadblocks were set up on March 24th and

The statue of Daniel O'Connell that dominates the southern end of O'Connell Street in Dublin gets a facelift from conservator Jason Ellis of Cregg Stone. Photograph: Matt Kavanagh.

had stopped production at the chemical plants, which have been operating since 2002.

Local hospitals treated 128 people, of whom 36 are still hospitalised. Of these, three were villagers and the rest police or cadres. Five of the injuries were serious, Mr Chen said. The factories have suspended operations for the time being because the workers are scared. Some of them are locals. Many come from Dongyang and go back every night in the shuttle bus. The factories also employ migrant workers.

In China, farmers do not own the land they till. Instead, they receive the land from the government on 30-year leases, which means when the government wants to change the use of the land, it does not need to ask individual farmers but can ask the village committee, which is what it did in Huaxi. Mr Chen insisted they had tried to contact as many farmers as possible to assuage their fears and that the purchase of the land had been approved by the majority of the village committee.

He promised that the government would take steps to ensure the plants followed regulations on pollution and said they would be shut down if they broke the rules. He also said the city would try and gather evidence to jail the 'handful of people' involved in causing the trouble.

Farmers have been given compensation for land lost, but for many this was not enough. 'It's not compensation we want, we don't want these plants beside us,' said one smallholder, Wang Weikang. 'I tried to grow cauliflower last year, but the plant didn't grow bigger than a walnut before it shrivelled and died. The groundwater is completely poisoned,' he said.

'When the village committee agreed to rent the land to the chemical companies, they didn't tell many of the villagers. A few years ago the county leaders told the villagers to go home, they guaranteed they would solve the problem and ensure the plants reach an adequate environmental standard. But it never happened.'

Accidents are a regular occurrence around the plants, villagers say. 'Last year a pipeline exploded around 500 metres away from a vegetable market. Everyone in the market had tears running down their faces, the chemicals in the air irritated their eyes so badly,' said another villager, also with the surname Wang.

Land-grabbing and rural land rights are major political issues in China and the Beijing government has made public commitments to bridge the gap between urban rich and rural poor. 'In the creek in the village, you get itchy feet when you cross it barefoot and the fish from the Huashui river doesn't taste good anymore,' said one old man.

He too was called Wang.

MONDAY, 18 APRIL 2005

So Now, What Can We Do for the GAA?

LockerRoom: Tom Humphries

So what happens now? Nothing probably. Do the GAA place somebody beside a phone and wait for people to call about the For Rent ad in the *Evening Herald*?

Remember to tell them that there's an upstairs

Prince Charles and his new wife, the Duchess of Cornwall, after their wedding at Windsor registry office in Berkshire, England, and subsequent service of prayer and dedication in nearby Windsor Chapel. Photograph: Getty Images.

and a downstairs, all completely remodernised. Mention that there's hot and cold running water and a nice place to eat. If they ask about the neighbours, say they are very old and we'd have to insist on no parties and no animals – and if they sound like they're from Roscommon, no party animals.

We'll look back on the Rule 42 debate in years to come as one of the more bizarre interludes in Irish life. In the end, the GAA had no choice, so badgered and bullied were they by a coalition of the sanctimonious and the incompetent.

Opening the place up is the right thing to do if only for the sake of peace, but in hindsight we will wonder how we managed to let Rule 42 obscure the realities of Irish life. Namely, that in just about every county in Ireland the GAA have managed to put in place better facilities and more facilities than the FAI, rugby and the Government together have managed to do. Croke Park is available for rent now. The last weapon which the GAA rule book offered for their critics to beat them with has been decommissioned. What will happen now? Will the perception of the GAA change so that we see that, clearly, it is worthwhile and necessary to pump public money into the heritage that is our national games?

We take it so entirely for granted that it is absurd. Are we moving into an era now wherein the GAA rule book has been straightened out and there are no more controversies to devour and we just ignore the most remarkable sporting organisation in the world, leaving it to fend for itself against the pervasive influence of huge professional sports?

A book popped out of an envelope on to the Sports Editor's desk last week. There is an old rule in newspaper offices concerning the reading of books. You may sit with your legs on the desk all day long reading newspapers, but be caught reading a few lines of a book and you are deemed to be taking the mickey. The Sports Editor panicked at the sight of the book. He quickly put down his cheroot and said, 'Here, take this', and urgently shoved the offending tome into the hands of your present correspondent who was at the time entreating the Sports Editor to sign for some expenses which would help pay for expensive cosmetic surgery because the movie star good looks on evidence at the top of this column are beginning to fade slightly.

The book is called *Engineering Archie – Archibald Leitch, Football Ground Designer.* It's written by Simon Inglis, who only produces books of great wonder anyway. I'd only previously associated Leitch with the wonderful, elegant and angled stands at Highbury and Aston Villa, and had no idea his influence practically determined the character of English football. In fact, the list of his triumphs is almost endless: Ibrox, Goodison, Roker Park, St James' Park, Twickenham, Molineux, Old Trafford, Ewood Park and on and on and on.

The book is a treasure trove of detail and anecdote and leaves you with a residue of sadness. The coarsening of football and the eventual post-Heysel, post-Hillsborough need to replace the old stadiums has produced a landscape dotted with cookie cutter stadiums which while pleasant and comfortable lack the detail and love and character of Leitch's works.

The filigreed wrought-iron trim in Craven Cottage, the boardroom at Ewood Park, the latticed middle tier in Goodison, the marble halls of Highbury, the weird old north stand at Stamford Bridge. Every work by Leitch had its own character and sympathy with the area it was built in, and the aerial shots of the grounds show football clubs living cheek by jowl with the factories in which their fans worked and the houses in which they lived. Beyond the triteness of cliché and jaded sentiment, you can see just through geography and architecture how English soccer was once a people's game.

What is sad is that we move on so quickly. What is impressive is the series to which Inglis's book belongs is called *Played in Britain* and is published by English Heritage as an attempt to celebrate and commemorate the role of sport within English heritage and culture and 'to ensure that

The way in to Croke Park? Photograph: Brian Lawless/Sportsfile.

rare and significant treasures are not lost or left unrecorded in the inevitable march of progress'. To that end, near the finish of the book we see a little housing estate in Middlesbrough which occupies where Ayresome Park once stood. There is a bronze football fixed into a grass verge where a penalty spot once was. Studmarks are set in concrete where the centre circle lay; the roads are named after terraces and stands. A scarf cast in bronze drapes over a wall and there is a bronze puddle at the very spot from which North Korea's Pak Do Ik scored the goal which knocked Italy out of the 1966 World Cup. Wonderful and imaginative.

In Ireland, the inevitable march of progress has brought big-time pro sports into the field built for and used by the amateurs of the GAA. The unique incompetence of certain governments and sporting bodies meant that in the end it was necessary for the GAA to make the big gesture, but it is incumbent upon all concerned to remember and respect the living culture that is the GAA.

It's no great triumph for anything that Keano and Drico may be playing in Croke Park before long. It's a failure, the mire of which we have been bailed out of by the GAA.

In the meantime, the living heritage of the games which the GAA nurtures and promotes needs some thought, lest we find ourselves at ceremonies to place bronze sliotars in the parts of housing estates where Ring would once have stood. Rule 42 is gone and the air is a little clearer, and hopefully those outside the GAA can begin to see the games as the wonderful, living artefacts of our culture which they are. From Bord Fáilte (do we really need more golf tourists?) to the Department of Education to the Department of Health to the arts and culture bodies, we should be looking at ways to give special protection to native games which have survived despite the absence of Murdoch millions or the 'international dimension' which we poor, cringing culturalists deem necessary to validate any activity we partake in.

The field which Frank Dineen bought for the GAA in a fit of optimism all those years ago and which Luke O'Toole chose to develop instead of spending money on a more formal monument to Archbishop Croke is open to all.

It's a big gesture without strings. Any big gestures of reciprocation out there?

SATURDAY, 23 APRIL 2005

No Doorstep Hosannas for Trimble

Deaglán de Bréadún, in Portadown

David Trimble is walking up the path to knock on a constituent's front door. This could be his last battle, and there is something oddly moving about the sight of the UUP leader making his solitary way towards an uncertain welcome.

The orthodox historical view is that Trimble led his community into the Promised Land of peace and reconciliation when he signed up to the Belfast Agreement. Never mind that he appeared full of doubts and hesitations himself at the time, he took the risk and signed on the dotted line. But there's no gratitude in politics and certainly not in Portadown. Far from being greeted with hosannas, Trimble is desperately fighting for his political life. He has tried to make the point that Northern Ireland is as stable and peaceful as any other place in Europe and that credit is due to himself and his party for this achievement.

Wasted words: nobody is listening. The anti-agreement forces are in militant mood; the pro-agreement people apathetic and uncertain. Always at his best under pressure, Trimble proved in the past he had at least nine political lives, but even well-wishers feel he may have used up his quota at last.

The UUP leader gets a mixed reception at the 'blue-rinse' Kernan area of Portadown. Reporters accompanying candidates on an election canvass frequently get the sense that the whole thing has been carefully stage-managed in advance, with joyous supporters rushing to embrace their hero, but Trimble would never stoop to such a stratagem and, as a no-nonsense Ulsterman, he wouldn't be very good at it anyway. His Democratic Unionist Party opponent, affable gospel-singing Orangeman David Simpson, has forecast that Upper Bann will be 'under new management' after the election. Trimble laughs: 'The DUP are good at talking. They are not much good at real politics.'

The unionist vote in Portadown is badly split, and this is reflected on the doorsteps. Asked if she would be voting for Trimble, a housewife responded: 'Oh yes, he's great!' But another woman barely opened the door to declare, with nervous politeness: 'I vote for another party.' There were no prizes for guessing which one. An ex-policeman didn't even come to the door: 'You sold us out!' But another man, drinking a cup of tea outside his house, told reporters his vote for Trimble was 'guaranteed'.

Trimble is at bay, and the DUP knows it. The mood in the Paisley camp is buoyant and bullish. To make a point, the DUP held its manifesto launch in Trimble's own constituency, at the remote but scenic location of the Edenmore Golf and Country Club, near the village of Magheralin. High good humour would be an understatement to describe the mood of 'the Doc' and his followers, many of them fairly recent defectors from the UUP.

It was a long way from the panicky desperation of Paisley and his followers when they arrived at Castle Buildings on that dramatic April night seven years ago, in a last-ditch effort to block the Belfast Agreement. Even their website is known as www.dup2win.com as the party has never shied away from triumphalism.

Negative speculation about Paisley's health simply does not stand up to the sight of the man, who has just turned 79 but looks as sprightly and robust as ever. Taking a turn on the canvass at Dollingstown with the party candidate, Paisley is greeted like a rock star. 'It's lovely to see you! Golly, this is a surprise, so it is,' says Margaret Hall, at a doorway in Gilpin Park.

Even the kerbstones around here are a loyal red-white-and-blue. But a well-dressed woman packing her kids into the family car on Regency Avenue tells Paisley she won't be voting DUP even though her mother-in-law once worked for the party leader. She said she was voting Green but didn't know the candidate's name. In fact, the Greens aren't running in Upper Bann.

The only thing that can save Trimble at this stage, according to the pundit class, is the moderate Catholic and Alliance Party vote. But the Alliance is running its own candidate this time; self-styled 'young gun' Alan Castle bounds from door to door with a zeal and enthusiasm that contrasts with the measured pace of his canvassing team.

On the nationalist side, Sinn Féin polled better than the SDLP in the last Westminster elections. At the Sinn Féin office in Lurgan, former chef John O'Dowd is cooking up an election plan with his team. Better known as chairman of the Garvaghy Road Residents' Coalition, Breandán Mac Cionnaith is now working as political adviser to Sinn Féin. He is deeply sceptical at the prospect of nationalists 'lending' their votes to Trimble. 'He didn't convince people he was 100 per cent pro-agreement.'

The Lurgan headquarters of the SDLP is, poignantly, across the street from the office of the murdered solicitor Rosemary Nelson whose death is the subject of a public inquiry which opened this

David Simpson of the Democratic Unionist Party campaigning against Ulster Unionist Party leader David Trimble in Portadown. Photograph: David Sleator.

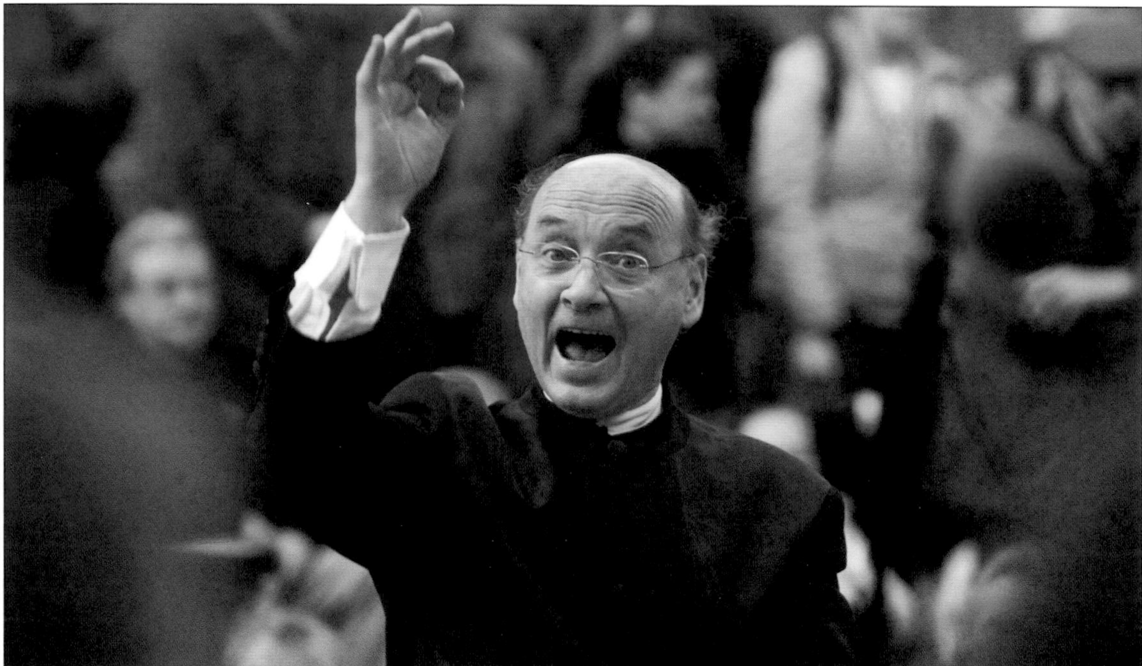

Proinnsias Ó Duinn conducting an outdoor performance by Our Lady's Choral Society of Handel's Messiah *in Fishamble Street, Dublin, where it was first performed in 1742. Photograph: Frank Miller.*

week. The vivacious SDLP standard-bearer is Dolores Kelly, former mayor of Craigavon and the only woman candidate. The Workers' Party is fielding one of its best-known faces, Tom French, on a platform of class unity: not a tune that tops the charts in the heartland of Orangeism.

Despite a lingering suspicion that 'Teflon Trimble' will, in the words of one observer, 'magic it again', the balance of probability is that the DUP will get its revenge on Trimble at last.

SATURDAY, 30 APRIL 2005

Blood, Sweat and Tears

TV Review: Hilary Fannin

Perhaps it's safe to laugh now, more than 800 years later, though with 'recent scientific evidence' suggesting that 'one in every 200 men alive today can trace their genetic lineage back to Genghis Khan', I'm not so sure.

Genghis Khan was a portrait of the Mongol warrior from his auspicious birth in 1162, when he entered the world clutching a blood-clot (like, hello!), to his death, by which time he and his meritocratic army controlled an area twice the size of the Roman Empire.

'I am the punishment of God,' Khan said to the Persians before annihilating a million of them, and on the evidence of this bloody biopic he wasn't joking. At times it was almost like watching a wildlife documentary: while Khan was still a child, his father was poisoned by an enemy chief, his family were deserted by their tribe, and Khan, proving his singular determination to survive, shot and killed his younger brother with an arrow for refusing to share the spoils of a hunt. In a nasty, short and brutish life, 'the greatest riches a man could have', according to Khan, were to 'conquer his enemy, steal his riches, ride his horses and enjoy his women' (one suspects his modern-day descendants might change the order).

Life on the Steppes was no garden party – inter-tribal warfare, rape, pillage, lousy weather and some deeply uncomfortable-looking headgear were the daily round. No surprise then that 50,000 Mongols chose to cross the Gobi Desert into northern China and beyond to Persia, Russia and eastern Europe. There were some deeply unpleasant vignettes en route, such as the siege of Beijing, where the determined Chinese pelted the invading hordes with huge clay pots full of chemicals, crude oil, molten metal and excrement. Not that they should have bothered; when Khan prevailed, he ordered total extermination, and a year later it was reported by foreign ambassadors that the streets were still slippery with human fat.

But the most tooth-watering moment was when the most successful military leader in history (if success can be measured by battlefields of corpses strewn like felled logs) was reunited with Jamuka, his former blood brother turned bitter rival. Jamuka, who had previously been boiling Khan's captured generals alive in a vat the size of Monaco, was delivered to Khan by a couple of treacherous guards.

'My noble lord,' Jamuka implored, refusing Khan's uncharacteristic offer of mercy. 'There can be only one leader just as there is only one sun. Give me a noble death, shed no blood.' They took him away and broke his back – that delicate snap, crackle and pop of the vertebrae still resonates. Well, Gordon Brown should be thanking his lucky cufflinks that he wasn't born in 12th-century Mongolia – or Bolton for that matter.

In *Peaches Geldof: Teenage Mind*, the physiology and psychology of adolescence were explored by the articulate daughter of Bob Geldof and the late

The former Taoiseach, Charles Haughey, with his wife, Maureen (left), after the funeral of his sister Bridie Dore in Donnycarney, Dublin. Photograph: Eric Luke.

Peaches Geldof.

Paula Yates. The well-heeled and confident 15-year-old visited various parts of Britain to find out whether teens were a rebellious and anarchic bunch of narcissists or victims of a fashion and music industry that's never been so competitive for their attention. Peaches slummed it in Bolton to investigate some 'yob culture', which involved a few hours in front of the mirror with a gang of girls and their juicy tubes, followed by a bag of chips and a night hanging out at a bus stop with about 40 lads with spotty necks and identical footwear.

Peaches asked some journalistic questions, such as 'Is this it?'

When the answer was 'yes', she scarpered to Wolverhampton and an alcohol-free youth club, where she interviewed a punk band called Nihilist, nice boys who used a lot of sugar to make their hair stand up and who thought Prince Philip was a bit of a legend. Peaches was obviously pining for London and the chattering classes who inhabit coffee shops with couches.

She and her girlfriends chatted about collective responsibility and whether if you weren't cool, you were a loser – to which Peaches answered a resounding yes.

She then went on to meet a bunch of adenoidal teenage environmentalists cleaning up a forest in Brighton, who couldn't care less about the undesirability of their undershot jaws or their M & S runners. 'I will never, no way ever, in my life, pick up litter,' said an indignant Peaches, her voice ringing with incredulity.

She discovered on her mission that human brains continue to develop until they are 25 years old, and that the planning and decision-making function is as underdeveloped in teenagers as that bloke at the back of the class with a crush. Having been freed thus from responsibility for losing and forgetting everything, Peaches was happy, although the Brighton environmentalists had rocked her cradle.

'I should start speaking to everyone!' she told the producer. When asked if she saw herself as an individual or part of a tribe, however, Peaches answered with candour: 'I might be the most stereotypical teenager of all.' I think not, but it was good to see a warm, confident teenage girl on the box. 'When I'm 30,' she confided, 'I'll probably be having a midlife crisis.' Actually, Peaches, I think you'll be leader of the Green Party.

Teenagers were proliferating this week. *Mono* returned with a gentle profile of the Levey family, in which former Irish jockey Micky Levey moved his wife, Tini, and their two sons, Seán and Declan, from the beautiful but ravaged Swaziland (where 40 per cent of the population of one million have

Aids) to Cashel in order that his sons could have the opportunity to work with trainer Aidan O'Brien at the Ballydoyle stables.

Micky Levey was an energetic and arresting raconteur, recalling how, when his sons began riding in Swaziland, they crawled around the course on their hands and knees, hopping over two-and-a-half-foot jumps themselves to show the astounded horses how to do it.

The programme, ostensibly focusing on 16-year-old Seán, who is about to become Ireland's first black jockey (he works in Ballydoyle stables seven days a week), became instead a moving tribute to his father, who had been diagnosed with terminal cancer. Filmed on his final journey to bid farewell to friends in Africa, Micky described (against the deceptively beautiful background of a luscious Swaziland) how he brought a dowry of 17 cows to secure Tini's hand in marriage – 'an absolute bargain', as he said. Things could be tough for women in this polygamous country and Tini had children by her previous marriage. Micky explained, however, that he preferred to have one wife and three extra kids. He went on to recall that when they decided to have a child of their own, he predicted that it would be a boy called Seán who would become a world-famous jockey.

Back in rainy Cashel, Tini was adjusting to a new society, with the support of her friends and neighbours. 'He left Swaziland for us to have a better future,' Seán said. Micky Levey 'was pulled in at seven furlongs'. He died just days after watching Seán's first race for O'Brien at the Curragh from his hospital bed.

Genghis Khan should have been employed to boil the pop-music section of the RTÉ archive in

One of three white rhinoceroses from South Africa settling into their new home at the African Plains area of Dublin Zoo. Photograph: Eric Luke.

elk oil before some bright spark decided it merited a series.

With the dullest crop of musical mementos available and an assembled punditry that looked a little dazed and confused (hang on, which RTÉ archive show is this?), the screamingly obvious solution would be one decent half-hour of Dickie Rock in a sequined catsuit or Joe Dolan with his lime-green-silk-shirted band. Instead we will be treated to hours of reruns with a self-conscious and not very funny commentary from the normally interesting Des Bishop: 'This song is called Pogue Ma Hone, Yankees, which I'm told means "we love America".' Stop it, Des, you're killing me.

In fact, there is no contest: faced with a marauding horde of Mongol nomads with weird fringes or more grisly reminiscences about comedian Jason Byrne's brother's hand-painted Iron Maiden jacket, I'll take my chances with the sartorially challenged barbarians.

TUESDAY, 3 MAY 2005

Early Dementia Presents Different Problems

Sylvia Thompson

It started with little things, like when Eileen couldn't remember her pin number on her banker's card and then when she went into the bank to retrieve her card after it had been swallowed by the cash machine, she couldn't remember her name. Then, later that same year, when she was on holidays with her son, she couldn't remember her middle name when asked by immigration officials at a Canadian airport.

Ruth O'Reilly (20) a second year college student and the eldest of three children of Eileen and Kevin O'Reilly speaks matter-of-factly about how in 2001, she, her Dad, her younger sister and brother began to notice things were just a bit off with Eileen who was then working as a fulltime solicitor in the civil service. 'She just wasn't able to keep up with her work so she went to her GP who is also a friend of the family and he picked up very quickly that it was something more than depression so she was sent for tests and in August, 2001, Alzheimer's disease was confirmed,' explains Ruth. 'It wasn't a huge shock to me. I was expecting it really because I had spent a lot of time with my mum and had noticed the changes.'

Following one year's sick leave, Eileen O'Reilly took voluntary retirement from her job. At 54, Eileen O'Reilly was young to be diagnosed with Alzheimer's disease yet, recent estimates suggest, there are over 3,500 people under 60 with early onset dementia in Ireland. The vast majority of these individuals have Alzheimer's disease. 'In the early days, Eileen was aware of having Alzheimer's and that must have been a horrendous realisation for her. She was very astute and followed the press details of the drug trials for Alzheimer's disease. We thought a solution would be found before the illness took hold,' says Kevin O'Reilly.

Although the symptoms of the disease are often similar to those diagnosed at a later stage, there are a different set of circumstances. For instance, those diagnosed at a younger age are usually still at work at the time of diagnosis. They may have young children and heavy financial commitments. They may also be physically fitter and have more challenging behaviour as a result. Some will also, like Eileen O'Reilly, be more aware of their disease in the early stages. 'The symptoms for early onset Alzheimer's disease are similar but there can be more pronounced language difficulties early on and more difficulty with learned motor movements such as dressing and undressing,' says Prof. Brian Lawlor, professor of old age psychiatry at St James's Hospital and Trinity College Dublin. 'There can also be a more rapid rate of progression of the disease. The care burden is greater because these people are at the peak of their productivity and the impact and distress of a diagnosis of dementia is higher,' he adds.

Eileen O'Reilly now spends her days in the family home in South Dublin. On Mondays, she goes out to lunch with two of her friends and an Alzheimer's Society home help comes to spend time with her on Monday and Wednesday mornings. She often spends Fridays in an Alzheimer Society daycare centre. Otherwise, she muddles through her days, grasping opportunities to spend time with other family members when they present themselves.

'She doesn't like being on her own and as things progress more and more, she is more distressed and agitated although she's still quite easygoing and we have a laugh,' says Ruth. 'She's happy to sit in my room when I'm doing my college work. But she gets upset when we leave the house and I've missed quite a bit of college and my Dad has missed some work days. But, it has brought us together as a family. We've had to pull together and my dad is great – he encourages us all to get on with our lives. We spend our time juggling schedules. You'd get frustrated and angry with her if you were there all the time.

'My sister and brother are brilliant cooks so they do a lot of the cooking, as does my Dad. It's funny really, my mum used to be a really healthy eater and conscious of what she ate – now she only wants to eat chocolate and yoghurt. I often take her with me to do the food shopping and, the other day, I found her in another aisle of the supermarket,

Ruth O'Reilly (left) and her mother, Eileen, at home in Dublin. Photograph: Bryan O'Brien.

eating a bar of chocolate. The only thing you can do is laugh. The playfulness is part of how we deal with it. Things have got more difficult in the last week or so and she has started to wander away from the house. She wouldn't be able to tell people her name or where she lived if they found her so we leave her contact details with her. Soon, we won't be able to leave her on her own anymore.'

The Alzheimer's Society has been very helpful, but there isn't a respite care facility for younger people with Alzheimer's disease, she points out. Families of those with early onset Alzheimer's disease also find it distressing to leave someone with early onset Alzheimer's disease in the company of elderly people, some of whom are in the advanced stages of the disease.

Anne Mescal, manager of training with the Alzheimer's Society of Ireland, confirms there are problems with lack of services for those diagnosed with early onset Alzheimer's disease and the younger age profile of these patients is the central issue. 'We do our best to strike a balance between not raising hopes of those looking for specific services for younger people with Alzheimer's disease (because we know that many of the services are geared towards older people who may already be attending community-care day centres) and encouraging people to look at what is available in their areas by making contact with public health nurses and other healthcare professionals.'

Prof. Brian Lawlor adds that there are no dedicated services for those with early onset Alzheimer's disease. 'Although the numbers of those with early onset dementia are not increasing, the population demographic is shifting and the number of people with dementia will double by 2050. Right now, we are not geared for that and there will be a lot of catch up needed in services,' he says.

In Britain, advocacy groups have stressed the importance of dedicated services for those with early onset dementia. Meanwhile, Ruth O'Reilly is determined to remain upbeat about her mother's condition. 'I was quite close to my mum and would meet her for lunch when I was at school. When I look at other friends' relationships with their mums now, it's kind of hard to accept. We realise that her health will deteriorate but if you thought too much about it, it would be too upsetting. You realise that you can't get too self-absorbed because you have to take someone else into consideration,' she adds.

SATURDAY, 7 MAY 2005

Far from a Plain Jane

Conor O'Clery

Astonishingly, Jane Fonda was alone when she went to Hanoi in 1972 to protest against Nixon's bombing of irrigation dykes. Already a Hollywood celebrity, she did not have an adviser or a press agent. On her last day she inadvisedly sat, laughing, on an anti-aircraft gun. Only afterwards did she realise how this would be used against her.

She was Henry Fonda's privileged daughter thumbing her nose at 'the country that gave me privilege'. Worse, she was the sex bomb of *Barbarella* who had embodied men's fantasies and was now the enemy. It was 'the largest lapse of judgement that I can ever imagine,' she writes. The confession is typical of this extraordinarily candid biography, tapped out on a computer by a woman who often found herself alone, making misjudgements along the way. Jane Fonda had several incarnations, as anti-war protester, Oscar-winning actor, mini-skirted bimbo, committed feminist and aerobics guru.

Born Lady Jayne Seymore Fonda in 1937, she says she was driven by a desire to please the men in her life, starting with her famous and cold-hearted father, Henry Fonda. Watching his callous treatment of her socialite mother, Frances Seymour, she concluded that it was better to 'side with the man if you want to be a survivor'. Her mother didn't survive: she slashed her throat while Henry had an affair with a 'tomato'. Jane was 12 and was told it had been a heart attack. She learned the truth from a magazine six months later.

Soon afterwards, her father married his 'tomato', Susan Blanchard (whom Jane came to love), but had to cut short his honeymoon when Jane's brother, Peter, shot himself (not fatally). The trauma helped bring on the bulimia from which Jane Fonda suffered for 20 years. The next man she tried to please was the hedonistic Roger Vadim, with whom she went to live in Paris. One night he brought home a red-haired call girl to share their bed. This was the Swinging Sixties. It never occurred to her to object, and she threw herself into the threesome 'with the skill and enthusiasm of the actress that I am'. Sometimes there were more than three, and sometimes Jane herself did the soliciting. Looking back, she feels she betrayed herself through a lack of self-worth.

The second act of her life began when she rejected the 'permissive, indolent' existence with Vadim and threw herself into the protests against the Vietnam War, motivated by desire 'to be a better person'. A GI draft-resister gave her an anti-war book, *The Village of Ben Suc* by Jonathan Schell, which fuelled her outrage. She was also profoundly influenced by the autobiography of Malcolm X, the drug dealer turned black militant turned Muslim, which convinced her of the possibility of profound human transformation. As an activist, Jane Fonda became strident and humourless.

Looking at taped interviews now, she wants to shout: 'Will someone please tell her to shut up!' But again there was no-one to tell her what to do. She concedes now that there was some truth to what was said about her, that she was a puppet, and needed a man to come along and pull her strings. The new man who supplanted Vadim was Tom Hayden, an anti-war campaigner whose 'Irish juiciness' brought 'welcomed moisture to what I felt was my arid Protestant nature'. They named their son Troy O'Donovan Garity, the O'Donovan bit after the Irish hero O'Donovan Rossa and Garity from Hayden's mother.

Jane Fonda. Photograph: Frederick Brown/Getty Images.

Throughout all this she pursued her movie career, winning an Oscar for a call girl in *Klute* and, with incredible timing, starring in *The China Syndrome* about a nuclear mishap just days before Three Mile Island happened. But she and Hayden drifted apart – long absences on film locations didn't help – and on her 51st birthday he told her he was in love with someone else. Through all this, Fonda struggled for the affection of her father and tried to find it, to no avail, in *On Golden Pond* in which she and Katherine Hepburn played alongside the 80-year-old Henry Fonda. Hepburn found him 'cold, cold, cold'. To which Jane added simply: 'Yup'.

Ted Turner came into Jane's life with a booming phone call out of the blue and they got married on her 54th birthday. They moved to Atlanta where Turner's CNN was located. A month later she caught him having a 'nooner' with another woman in a hotel room. She hit him with the car phone, thinking at the time what a good movie scene it would make. He apologised for his 'tic' and they stayed together seven years before breaking up. She turned to religion to replace the void she felt. Once again a book, *In a Different Voice* by feminist psychologist Carol Gilligan, had a profound influence, with its reflections on the damage done to women who fear abandonment by a man if they speak up.

Her divorce from Ted Turner was not the end of another phase but the emergence of her complete feminist self, she concluded. She stayed in Atlanta to continue working on a foundation she heads that promotes equality for women as the basis of strong relationships. She has not acted since 1990, apart from her role in a new movie, *Monster-in-Law*, which she took to make money for her foundation. After a life of emotional betrayals, activism and Oscars, Jane Fonda is still defined by Vietnam. She makes no apology for opposing the war. But to many vets she will always be 'Hanoi Jane'. One spat in her face at a book signing. 'If I was used, I allowed it to happen,' Fonda writes. 'It was my mistake, and I have paid and continue to pay a heavy price for it.'

FRIDAY, 13 MAY 2005

Child's Play will Sort Out Airport Fiasco

Ground Floor: Sheila O'Flanagan

The question I'm most commonly asked when it comes to my current career is: 'Where do you get your ideas from?' It's probably the hardest question to answer because, the truth is, I'm not sure where they come from. Sometimes a plot arrives in my head, fully formed. Other times, a niggling interest in a subject might get me thinking about how it might pan out in fiction. When I think too hard about it, I come up with no ideas at all, while sometimes, ideas compete with each other in my head and I wrestle with which might end up working better on paper.

Making decisions about what plot to go with is an intuitive thing, but decision-making in business is usually different. Intuition plays a part, but there's an army of consultants out there to tell you the best way to evaluate the problem and to come to the right conclusion. They all start with a very basic instruction, which is to identify the issue to be addressed or the purpose of your decision. Then you should gather information about the problem to help you understand the nature of the decision you must make. You should then look at the range of options available to you and evaluate those options based on their possible outcomes. Having done this, you should be able to decide on the best option. After making the decision, you evaluate it and try to learn from it. You should ask yourself whether or not you would make the same decision again and assess whether or not the decision you made resulted in the outcome you hoped for.

Alternatively, you could do like Takashi Hashiyama, president of the Maspro Denkoh Corporation, a Japanese electronics company. Hashiyama's decision-making process was my favourite story of last week and resulted in Christie's auction house winning the business to sell the company's art collection, which was valued in excess of $20 million (€15.6 million).

There's no information available on why Maspro Denkoh decided to offload its collection, although it might have been influenced by the fact that the one-year return on Maspro Denkoh is currently -5.256 per cent and the coffers need replenishing. The collection included paintings by Cézanne, Picasso and Van Gogh – you may

A section of the Seán O'Casey pedestrian swing bridge, linking the north and south quays near the IFSC, is lowered into place. Photograph: Dara Mac Dónaill.

remember that many Japanese companies invested in art during the 1980s and had something of a rollercoaster ride as a result. Hashiyama decided to get rid of the paintings, presumably using these criteria. His next decision was how to choose the auction house to sell them.

The choice was between Christie's and Sotheby's. Abandoning all of the means of decision that we expect from corporate leaders, Hashiyama elected to make the two companies compete against each other in a game of Rock Paper Scissors (RPS) – and the winner would get the contract. For those of you who think this is a game suited to the schoolyard, you should ask Lee Rammage for his views. Lee is the RPS world champion, a title he won at the World Championships in Toronto, Canada last year. Kanae Ishibashi, head of Christie's in Japan, didn't say whether she spoke to Lee about his strategies, but she did some research on the game before the competition started. There are many gambits in RPS – the crescendo (paper, scissors, rock), the avalanche (rock, rock, rock) and the fistful o'dollars (rock, paper, paper).

But Christie's strategy was to start with scissors which, according to the daughters of the international director, is a safe opening move. According to the 11-year-old twins, Flora and Alice, most novices anticipate their opponents going for rock, because it 'feels' strongest. Therefore, they'll choose paper which beats rock, which means you should choose scissors.

The girls were right. Sotheby's went for paper. Bang went the estimated $2.5 million in fees. Christie's made $142.9 million in their impressionist and modern art auction, $52 million more than the previous night's total at Sotheby's. It's hard to know whether or not Sotheby's would have achieved more than the $11.7 million realised for

Mark St John Ellis (left), curator of the Ashford Gallery, and Sam Stephenson, manager, with Death by Numbers, *a sculpture by Tom Fitzgerald, while they were setting up the 175th Annual Royal Hibernian Academy exhibition. Photograph: Brenda Fitzsimons.*

Cézanne's *Les Grands Arbes au Jas de Bouffan*, which had been estimated to reach between $12 and $16 million, but it was still a good result for Christie's. Hashiyama has his money and hopefully the girls were rewarded for their strategy.

Which all leads me to think that perhaps this is the way out of the Dublin airport debacle. This ridiculous state of affairs has turned into a battle of ideologies, in which the consumer is losing out. Reminiscent of the old adage that you wait all day for a bus and then three come together, the latest proposal is for a third terminal at the airport to assuage the desire for the PDs to have competition.

But the flip side of this is the issue of union power and the Taoiseach's unwillingness to crack the whip in north Dublin. The provision of basic, decent facilities is not one that should have become a political football, and the inability of the Government to make a rational and, above all, consumer-led decision on the running of any terminal is appalling.

Private enterprise may not always get the job done, and employers in the private sector may not always make the right decisions, but at least they make them quickly. The idea that this has been rattling round for years with nothing being done is ludicrous. Which is why Bertie, Mary and the unions should agree that the quickest, simplest way to agree on how many terminals are built and who runs them should be by playing RPS.

The rules and code of conduct are available on the RPS website, www.worldrps.com and the whole thing could be supervised by independent observers. We might not get the best decision, but at least we'd get one!

SATURDAY, 14 MAY 2005

One False Step on the Red Carpet . . .

Cannes Diary: Michael Dwyer

Around six o'clock every evening during the Cannes Film Festival, the upmarket Riviera town comes to a standstill. With 30,000 visitors doubling the population for the festival, Cannes suffers from M50-style gridlock throughout the event. Then the pedestrians hit the streets in early evening, swarming the Festival Palais that looms over the seafront.

Long established as the world's biggest, most important film festival, Cannes lays on the pomp and ceremony twice a night, when the officially invited movies have their gala screenings inside the Palais, and the bigger the movie, the bigger the crowds of locals and tourists gathered outside. Tomorrow's main movie is very big indeed, the world premiere of *Star Wars Episode III: Revenge of the Sith*, and thousands will throng the Palais area to catch a glimpse of director George Lucas and his cast – Hayden Christensen, Natalie Portman and Samuel L. Jackson – going up the red-carpeted steps.

The organisers have the procedure down to a fine art. A passage is cleared for the gleaming limos discharging their chicly attired passengers at the entrance. Tenue de soirée (evening dress) is

Actress Scarlett Johansson at Cannes. Photograph: MJ Kim/Getty Images.

mandatory at every one of the Palais gala screenings, and patrolled by fashion police. It is not at all uncommon for guests deemed to be wearing the wrong shoes, for example, to be sent back down the steps like a humiliated *Big Brother* evictee.

Gendarmes form a guard of honour on both sides of the steps as the slow procession of the red carpet begins – and the event turns into the Cannes Frock Festival before slews of photographers, who also have to be in evening dress. This is regarded as such an important photo opportunity that it's irresistible to people cashing in on the huge international media presence at the festival (around 5,000 this year) – even if they haven't got a film in the official selection. In 1993, at the gala for Mike Leigh's low-budget *Naked*, Arnold Schwarzenegger, in Cannes to plug some action movie, stole the thunder of Leigh and his cast by grinning and waving his way up the steps – and promptly slipping out a rear entrance as soon as he entered the Palais.

A celebratory party follows each gala screening. Some are relatively modest. When *The General* was screened in 1998, winning John Boorman the best director prize, the party was relatively modest and held in the only Oirish bar in Cannes. Other parties can cost more than many of the movies in the festival. The 1993 screening of *Raining Stones* – Ken Loach's socially concerned picture of a working-class man struggling to pay for his

Barrister Gerry Danaher (front row, second from left) amuses his fellow National Library of Ireland board members at their first meeting with (front row from left) Breda Kelly, board member; Danaher, chairman of the board; Arts Minister John O'Donoghue; Aongus Ó hAonghusa, Director of the National Library; and Susan McGrath, board member. Back row (from left) Niall McMonagle, Jim O'Shea, Brendan O'Donoghue, Noreen Whelan, Bob Collins (all board members); Margaret Toomey, Executive Officer National Library; Phil Furlong, Secretary General Department of Arts; Máire Mac Conghail and Patrick Clyne, both board members. Photograph: Bryan O'Brien.

daughter's First Communion dress – was followed by an extravagant bash at a villa up in the hills, where the champagne flowed and the tables groaned under gourmet fare.

And that pales in comparison with the excesses of the Hollywood studios at the festival. For decades, Cannes has walked a tightrope between art and commerce. People have to wear evening dress to watch low-budget movies about racism, torture, ethnic cleansing and social deprivation. High art is the aspiration of the festival competition, but if a megastar is available to walk the red carpet, a prestigious out-of-competition slot becomes available – as when Madonna generated a media frenzy with the documentary *In Bed With Madonna*, or when *Far and Away* closed the festival and Tom Cruise and Nicole Kidman did carpet duty.

It works both ways. Even the formerly publicity-shy Woody Allen is now a regular on the festival circuit. He was back in Cannes on Thursday for the world premiere of his new movie, *Match Point,* joined on the carpet by its handsome Irish actor Jonathan Rhys Meyers and his equally eye-catching US co-star, Scarlett Johansson, and securing front-page coverage around the world. Away from the red carpet, Paris Hilton – the hotel heiress famous for being famous and a sexually explicit video posted on the Internet – is doing a beach photo call today to plug her new movie, *Pledge This!* – 'the most hilarious, outrageous and sexy comedy', according to its hyperbolic publicity material.

The Cannes beach has been de rigueur for photo shoots since a breast-baring British starlet got up close and personal with Robert Mitchum for the cameras back in 1954 – even though the beach has been topless for decades. For variety this week, Kiera Chaplin, granddaughter of Charlie, was lined up to wear 'not a great deal' and ride a horse along the Croisette to hype up *Lady Godiva: Back in the Saddle*, which has yet to start shooting.

This year, and not for the first time, a movie showing outside the official selection at Cannes is the link to the hottest ticket of the festival. Stephen Chow's exuberant martial arts movie, *King Fu Hustle*, a huge hit in Asia, will be followed by a lavish party tonight, hosted by Sony and MTV at Le Palais Oriental. The invitation advises that it runs from 10 p.m. to 6 a.m. At festival time, Cannes never sleeps.

TUESDAY, 17 MAY 2005

An Irishman's Diary

Kevin Myers

The key, the essence, the kernel of attending an immensely dignified memorial service is to pack in a good solid breakfast beforehand. It settles the stomach and calms the mind and assures the constitution that though the person you are commemorating has already made the Great Journey, you are not ready to join him, not yet, at least. Otherwise, you can pay a terrible price.

The commemorated person concerned was Bala Bredin, the last surviving senior officer of the 38th (Irish) Brigade which had fought with such extraordinary valour in the Italian campaign of 1944-45. He is usually described as 'Irish', though necessarily, in a somewhat attenuated form. His Irishness was of the old imperial species, in which Irish ancestry and an undying loyalty to Irish regiments in the British army could outweigh his birth in India and an almost complete ignorance of the country whose identity he so enthusiastically embraced. His Ireland was largely a creation of his imagination, populated by sturdy, cheerful, brave and humorous soldiers: had he ever been to a cattle mart in Limerick on a wet day in November, he might have had different opinions.

No matter. It is sufficient that he called himself Irish, and the Irishmen who followed him into action were content with his definition. Part of his understanding of Irishness was in the raw valour which he showed repeatedly, both before, during and after the second World War. When incapacitated by wounds at the battle of Monte Cassino, he had himself tied to the bonnet of his jeep, from which he led his men forward into action. And indeed, it was as much to commemorate those men who perished on the stony wastes of the Appenines in the long arduous advance up Italy's spine, or who have silently faded away in their civilian beds, that I attended the memorial service for Bala Bredin in St Anne's cathedral in Belfast.

The eulogy was by Sir Roger Wheeler, the old general's godson, and himself a retired general and former commander of the Royal Irish Rangers. He is one of those ex-soldiers who never loses his military bearing: his eye is keen and penetrating, his back ramrod straight in a lean, athletic frame. He strode to the podium, cast his eagle eye around the congregation, and opened his mouth to speak.

And in that momentary silence, someone rolled a bowling ball down a corrugated iron roof. Or at least that was what it sounded like. It was in fact my stomach. I had not breakfasted before heading north, and had then wallowed in a handsome lunch, with wine: and my alimentary canal was registering the only protest available to it. You could have heard the duodenal din in Ardoyne. Sir Roger is cut from game cloth. He ignored the heckling belly, and proceeded onto Bala's Irish ancestry, with roots in Sligo, and I think, Roscommon. I can be forgiven for any uncertainty because just as Sir Roger paused again, somewhere nor' nor' east of my oesophagus, a geyser cleared its throat and then uttered a long low gurgle of satisfaction, which echoed through the cathedral with the resonance of a shepherd calling his sheep in the Tyrol.

There is only one thing one can do in the circumstances, and that is to stare around in innocent bafflement, like a cardinal who has just broken wind at the very moment of the pope's coronation. Very possibly I got away with it, for my stomach then went quiet. Sir Roger paused – somewhere I think between Monte Cassino and the Po valley – for a long and dramatic silence, or rather as it should have been. But instead, from somewhere mid-abdomen, erupted a perfect facsimile of bath-time at a boarding school with Victorian plumbing, as plugs are pulled out of a dozen baths simultaneously. Numerous down-pipes vie for possession of the main waste-pipe, with thwarted bathwater gurgling, sluicing and chuckling its way backwards and forwards. Finally the surging water hits an airlock, and hiccups violently, before bubbling its way back into the baths, yodelling as it goes.

Well, if you thought that one man could not impersonate the sonar turmoil of an entire plumbing system, built circa 1865, going into crisis, then in all modesty, I am here to tell you that it can be done. Indeed, it has been done, and I am the fine fellow that did it.

As the rumble of hydraulics going into thrombosis slowly abated, Sir Roger composed himself, drew breath and opened his mouth. At which point, my jejunum opened the valve to the ileum due south of it, and noisily propelled my lunch into a sloshing pool of digestive juices. It sounded like a cauldron of porridge coming to the boil. Against this uproar, Sir Roger nonetheless fought gallantly on, taking Bala up the Italian peninsula. Then, some three days short of VE-Day, and perhaps in anticipation of it, a sort of Hallelujah Chorus erupted in the vicinity of my umbilicus, complete with sackbuts, viols, cornets and other early instruments. To my ear, one of the boy sopranos was a little off-key, but there we are, no-one's perfect.

And so the memorial service proceeded, next, very possibly, to the sound of *The Water Music*, but without any assistance from the choir of St Anne's. I have no way of knowing, for my poor tormented mind has mercifully removed all memory of the rest of the proceedings from my brain. However, if you have need of a ventriloquist with a virtually limitless – though utterly uncontrollable – repertoire, you now know where to go.

Pupils from St Michael's Loreto school hold hands at the funeral of Claire McCluskey, one of five schoolgirls killed when their bus overturned on the road between Kentstown and Navan in Co. Meath. Photograph: Eric Luke.

TUESDAY, 24 MAY 2005

'They were Really Nice, Always Cheerful, Full of life'

Carl O'Brien, in Drogheda

The girl, still dressed in her school uniform, raised a limp hand from her hospital trolley and gestured towards her mother. 'It's OK, Mam,' she said. 'I'll be fine.' The mother, whose daughter's face was framed by a neck-brace, managed a painful smile.

It was a scene repeated dozens of times in the A&E unit of Our Lady of Lourdes Hospital yesterday evening as trolleys containing schoolchildren were rushed through the hospital's narrow corridors. Parents and school friends gathered in shocked silence, waiting for news of the condition of their loved ones. Some hugged each other when they heard an update of a child's condition, while others stood silently, still waiting for news. The father of a girl with serious head injuries said shattered glass had caused widespread damage to many of the children. 'Many kids were injured as shattered glass flew into their faces,' the father said. 'One young girl's face was riveted with glass such was the impact of the crash.'

The tragedy of yesterday's accident has been underscored by the fact that most of the 50 students on the bus were from the same parishes of Beauparc and Yellow Furze. Two school friends who would normally have been on the Navan bus, Shane Finegan (18) and Graham Crosby (17), were still coming to terms with the scale of yesterday's tragedy. 'I knew two of the girls from Loreto who were killed,' said Shane. 'They were really nice, always cheerful, always full of life.' He added: 'This is going to be devastating for the area, especially with all the funerals in the days ahead.'

Fr Richard Goode, a parish priest attached to the hospital, busily attended to many of the relatives who were still numbed by yesterday's events. He said everyone was praying that the remainder of the casualties would survive. In the midst of the chaos of the crash, Niall O'Connor, a spokesman for the hospital, said staff had responded 'magnificently' and added that six students were still in a serious condition last night and would be closely monitored over the coming hours.

WEDNESDAY, 25 MAY 2005

Tributes of Friends Paint a Picture of Five Sparkling Young Women

Carl O'Brien, in Navan

The group of schoolgirls, their faces drained with grief, sobbed quietly as they clutched each other for support. Like many other students they had gathered at the entrance to the Loreto Convent school in Navan, where four of the five dead schoolgirls were from, to leave a floral tribute to their friends. 'It's devastating that such an overwhelmingly good and honest girl had to leave the world through no fault of her own,' said one note. Another in neat biro read: 'You were the best prefect ever. Every day you had a smile on your face. Miss you loads.'

Yesterday, as the overwhelming shock at the scale of the tragedy began to subside, the moving, personal details of the five schoolgirls' hopes and aspirations began to emerge. They painted a picture of sparkling young women whose lives

Claire McCluskey

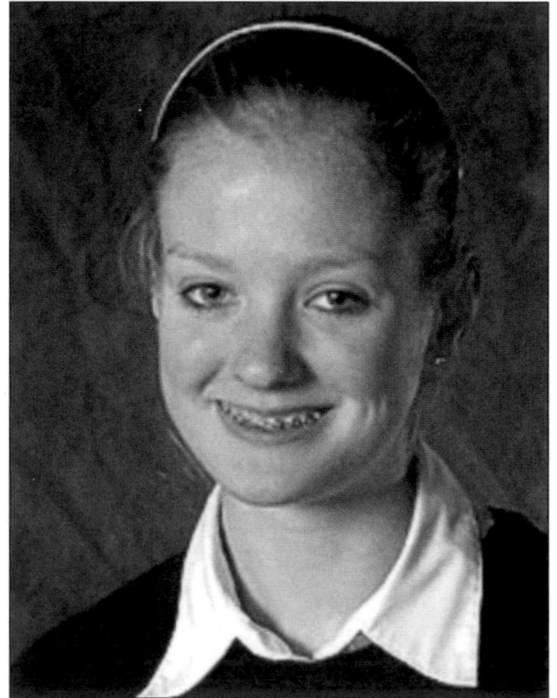

Lisa Callan

Sinéad Ledwidge

Aimee McCabe

stretched out ahead of them, full of possibility and opportunity. There was Claire McCluskey (18), a bright and bubbly prefect who always had time for younger students, and Deirdre Scanlon (17), who was quieter, more studious and a straight-A student. She loved singing and was a member of a local folk group. Lisa Callan (15), with her striking blond hair, played bass guitar and was intent on becoming an architect. There was Aimee McCabe (15), the leader of her class, the person everyone went to first when they had a problem. And Sinéad Ledwidge (15), another vivacious girl with a talent for playing the accordion, spent many of her weekends at music fleadhs.

As the community prepares itself for five funerals, those within are helping each other to grieve. Elizabeth Sheridan, a mother whose teenage son and daughter survived the crash, said: 'Even at the hospital last night it was like a community gathering, everyone knew everyone else … All of this is still very, very shocking.'

Deirdre Scanlon

TUESDAY, 24 MAY 2005

Tolerance of Racism Exposed

Fintan O'Toole

In 1992, the ludicrous English TV presenter and politician Robert Kilroy-Silk wrote a column in the *Daily Express* in which he referred to Ray MacSharry as a 'redundant second-rate politician from a country peopled by peasants, priests and pixies'. We did our collective nut. On the State's behalf, Ireland's then ambassador to Britain, Joseph Small, condemned the 'gratuitously offensive and indeed racist remarks'.

In 1994, Michael Woods, then minister for social welfare, told the Dáil on behalf of the government that he deplored the 'offensive remarks' of *Daily Mail* columnist Paul Johnson to the effect that: 'The Irish exploit Britain's welfare state as a kind of patriotic duty.' In 2003, Neville Sanders, the Tory leader of Peterborough council, was barred from holding political office because he had replied rudely to a letter from Carrickfergus council and had told the *Belfast Telegraph* that 'The f***ing Irish should learn to live in peace and bloody well get on with it.'

In the same year, the London Irish Centre called for a boycott of all the businesses owned by the English retailer Philip Green because he had complained about *The Guardian*'s financial editor Paul Murphy with the words 'He can't read English. Mind you, he's a f***ing Irishman.' Twice in 2001, the then minister for foreign affairs, Brian Cowen, told the Dáil that the government endorsed a report that condemned anti-Irish prejudice in Britain and that: 'Discrimination and disadvantage are as repugnant to the British government as they are to us. We remind them of the importance of sensitivity by public authorities towards the distinctive social and cultural characteristics of the Irish people with whom they have dealings. The embassy in London takes up with the British authorities specific instances of alleged anti-Irish racism or discrimination.'

Last week, a Minister in the department that instructs the Irish embassy in London to do these worthy things made an entirely gratuitous remark belittling Turkish people as 'kebabs'. The remark was not, as subsequently claimed, made 'in the heat of the moment'. It had no conceivable connection to the subject under discussion at the time – Aer Lingus. It was cool and deliberate and intended, in the context, to imply that the welfare of Turkish workers in Ireland was a piddling subject fit for the likes of Joe Higgins, who should therefore leave the big boys to debate important issues. And what was the reaction? Nothing. Conor Lenihan's boss, Dermot Ahern, told us within hours that the whole story was at an end.

And Conor Lenihan did not apologise for the offence he had caused. According to the official Dáil record, what he said was: 'I regret the remarks made and I apologise sincerely if any offence was taken from the remarks.' Note the if. But even this is, rather disturbingly, a cleaned-up version of what he actually said. In reality, he couldn't even manage to articulate his weasel words with any clarity. What he in fact said was: 'I regret the remarks made and apologise sincerely if any cause or offence was taken from the remarks made.' This may be a Freudian slip which reveals the underlying truth. The sentence is meaningless because the apology means nothing.

Imagine for a moment that a junior minister in Tony Blair's government had interrupted a debate on British aviation last week to tell an MP with ties to the Irish community in London that he should 'stick with the spud-gobblers'. The minister in question would have been gone before lunchtime. And if he wasn't, Irish outrage would have been revved up to a thunderous crescendo. Conor Lenihan's own department would, through the embassy in London, have been out with all guns blazing to remind the Brits of 'the importance of sensitivity by public authorities towards the distinctive social and cultural characteristics of the Irish people'.

Let's get this straight. Neville Sanders is officially unfit to be a member of a minor local council in England because he made some stupidly curmudgeonly remarks about the Irish peace process. Conor Lenihan is fit to be in charge of the major part of Irish relations with the developing world even though he chose to use our national parliament to belittle the people of one of those countries. This is not just a display of the grossest hypocrisy. It is also an indication of abject self-contempt.

It means that higher standards apply to the members of Peterborough council than to ministers in our sovereign government. This makes us, by the way, more tolerant of racism than the Republican Party in the US or the Tories in Britain. Trent Lott, the former party's leader in the Senate, had to resign because he said some nice things about a segregationist politician.

Iain Duncan Smith sacked a member of his shadow cabinet, Ann Winterton, for joking that Pakistanis were 'ten a penny'. He did so, he said, to show that the Tories were 'a decent party'. We, on the other hand, are apparently not too bothered about offensive jibes – so long as they're not directed at the Irish. And that's a real slur on Ireland.

A US soldier holds a child fatally wounded in a suicide car bomb attack in Mosul, northern Iraq. Photograph: Michael Yon/Associated Press.

FRIDAY, 27 MAY 2005

Amazing, but Let's Not be Fooled

Mark Lawrenson

There I was, sitting in the stadium in Istanbul at half-time, and thinking what those thousands of Liverpool supporters around me were probably thinking … let's get out of here as quick as we can. I'd imagine that's how the team felt too. The second half was just going to be about damage limitation. Restoring some pride. Trying to avoid humiliation. Then leg it to the airport and get home.

What followed? Well, the best, the most astonishing comeback I have ever, ever seen. Staggering. From getting it so spectacularly wrong Rafael Benitez managed to get it spectacularly right. I would give anything to know what he said to them at half-time – talk about inspirational. And what makes it even more amazing is you could not describe this Liverpool team as a great team, by any stretch of the imagination. In fact, if you made those players available today to other clubs around Europe there really wouldn't be too many takers.

So, if you had said to me a few months ago that Liverpool would have a night like that, would win the European Cup for the fifth time, I would have laughed. Out loud. I didn't expect them to go far in the competition, certainly not to get past Juventus, and positively not to win it. In the middle of it all I couldn't help but think of Michael Owen. At half-time he must have said: 'What a good decision I made leaving Liverpool.' By the end of it I'm sure it was: 'Crikey – how did that happen?' Which is kind of how I felt too.

How did that happen? When we won it 20 odd years ago – is it really that long? – we had a very, very good team. I can't say we were expected to win it, but everyone knew we had a chance. We had the players, we had the experience, we had the pedigree, I suppose. But I don't think even the most blind of Liverpool supporters could have felt that way about this team. Even now, regardless of what happened on Wednesday night, they know they don't have a very, very good team. How many of those players would you have in your first XI? Exactly, not many. We're talking about the Champions League and we're talking about a team that was beaten 14 times – 14 times! – in their own league this season. It's unheard of.

They beat Juventus, they beat Chelsea and they beat Milan along the way, so it was hardly an easy route. But, as fantastically well as they've done, they played those three teams at the right time, the right time for Liverpool and the wrong time, for various reasons, for the others. But when you win a cup competition that inevitably is what happens.

I'm really, really pleased for Benitez. I think everyone's delighted for him, not least because he seems to be a thoroughly nice man. In fairness to him, he never once moaned, unlike his predecessor, about his bad luck during the season, about being without Djibril Cisse, Xabi Alonso and others. He just got on with it. And he's earned respect for that. And at least he had it in him to change everything at half-time after making a massive boo boo – and he does do that quite often in games, he will change it tactically; he's not rigid, not afraid to concede he got it wrong. Picking Harry Kewell. Well, maybe Benitez just had too long to think about it. I don't know if he was trying to be too cute, maybe he saw it as his masterplan, one Milan wouldn't be able to cope with, but the opposite happened: Milan destroyed Liverpool in the first half.

By half-time he really had no option but to go for it. That was the key to the comeback, playing just three at the back and getting numbers in midfield. And everything changed spectacularly. Djimi Traore in the first half wouldn't have got a game as sub for The Dog and Duck, would he? But in fairness to him, he made two or three brilliant tackles in the second half and cleared one off the line – we were looking at a different person. And Stevie Gerrard was transformed. In the first half he was anonymous, but that was because the system Benitez chose meant Gerrard was too busy putting out fires. And Vladimir Smicer? The player with, arguably, the biggest yellow streak down his back you've ever seen, comes on and scores an outstanding goal. An absolutely extraordinary turn-around.

So will this signal a Liverpool revival, get them back to where they were in the 1970s and 1980s? Not with this team it won't. Ecstatic and all as Liverpool supporters are I don't think there's any danger of them kidding themselves over this, that somehow they now have a team capable of challenging Chelsea, Arsenal and Manchester United – because they don't. They know what they have and what they haven't got; this won't kid them.

With the players they've got at the moment I still wouldn't tip them to finish above Chelsea, Arsenal or United next season: I think those three teams are much better. Fourteen defeats in the Premiership? Really they need five, six new players, it's that drastic. And that's assuming that they'll keep Gerrard and that Alonso and Cisse are fit. If they can get rid of him, Kewell will go somewhere, although at £65,000-plus a week and with three years left on his contract you're looking at a bill of £10 million if you want to get rid of him. That's another problem Benitez has inherited, something else he has to deal with. Milan Baros could go, Jerzy Dudek too. They need a proper left back instead of Traore, God bless him. There'll be lots and lots of changes, finances permitting, of course.

And winning the Champions League obviously improves things financially (and I'm convinced UEFA will find a place for Liverpool in next season's competition: they'll have to find a way). I would imagine it will make it easier to attract good players, and I think it will probably persuade Gerrard to stay. It's very difficult for him to leave now. He must surely feel there is something to build on. When there was initially talk of him leaving it was about him going somewhere where he could win the Champions League – well he's done it with Liverpool. The next objective is to be

Liverpool captain Steven Gerrard celebrates after being awarded a penalty during his club's Champions League thrilling final victory over AC Milan in Istanbul. Photograph: Eddie Keogh/Reuters.

Rosemary McDonald from Tarbert in Co. Kerry with her award-winning Bantam hen at the Kingdom County Show at the Ballybeggan Race Course in Tralee. Photograph: Domnick Walsh/Eye Focus.

part of a team that can challenge in the Premiership.

It will be interesting to see in a year's time how many of this team are still involved at Liverpool. There'll be a lot of departures, but that speaks volumes for Benitez. He's won it with a couple of outstanding players, some good players and some average players. In that sense what he has achieved rivals much of what went before him at Liverpool, when several of his predecessors assembled genuinely great teams that went on to have fantastic success. Rafa Benitez has won the Champions League with a team that finished 37 points behind this season's Premiership champions, Chelsea. That is amazing. But not half as amazing as the second half in Istanbul on Wednesday night.

SATURDAY, 4 JUNE 2005

An Unbroken Chain of Indifference

Fintan O'Toole

To get a sense of how bad the situation revealed by the Morris report is, you have to think, not about the bad cops but about the good cops. In trying to mollify public concern about the shocking story that Justice Frederick Morris has to tell, the Garda and political authorities have relied on the evident truth that most people in Ireland still feel our police force has a solid core of decent, committed public servants. Yet one of the things that emerges from the report is how hard it is to be a good cop when those around you are feckless, incompetent or corrupt.

Consider the case of Supt John Fitzgerald, one of the senior officers criticised in the report. He was the district officer for Letterkenny when the cattle-dealer Richard (Richie) Barron was found dead on the roadway outside Raphoe, Co. Donegal, in the early hours of Monday 14 October, 1996. From then until early February 1997, he was in overall charge of the bizarre investigation into a death that resulted from a hit-and-run accident but that led to two local men, Frank McBrearty jr and his cousin Mark McConnell, being framed for a murder that never happened. Supt Fitzgerald, the report finds, shared with three other senior officers the overall responsibility for an investigation that was 'prejudiced, tendentious and utterly negligent in the highest degree'.

To anyone reading a quick summary of the report, it seems obvious therefore that John Fitzgerald was one of the rotten apples. In fact – and this is what makes the whole story so serious – he was one of the good guys. Justice Morris notes that he 'left the Garda force after a fine career with a high reputation' and that 'Time and again, I have heard evidence of the high regard in which those who worked with him, and served under him, held Supt Fitzgerald. I have no doubt that he was an able, experienced officer. I am also satisfied that his work practices were based upon an ethic of trust. He assumed that his fellow officers and those that served under him would behave in a proper and trustworthy manner.' He failed in his duty to the Barron family, to the McBreartys and to the general public, not because he was an amoral cynic, but because he was too decent. That's how bad things are: the very quality that the public most values in its police – decency – is, in the distorted world mapped out by the report, a vice.

Or consider the case of another good cop, Det. Sgt Sylvie Henry, a member of the team investigating Richie Barron's supposed murder. He seems to have been the one senior member of the team who refused to jump to the conclusion that the extended McBrearty family were the guilty parties. He tried to act like a policeman investigating a crime rather than a member of a lynch party. He interviewed a petty criminal called Paul Gallagher, whom he suspected of involvement in Richie Barron's death, and Gallagher fed him a line about hiding a billhook which was supposedly used in the murder. Although he reckoned that Gallagher's story was nonsense, he did his job and found the billhook in question. Garda Tina Fowler, who worked in the incident room for the Barron case, told the tribunal about the general attitude of the other gardaí to Henry's attempts to do his job properly: 'He became almost the subject of ridicule in relation to the investigation. He was nicknamed "Captain Hook" after the discovery of the billhook, and his pursuance of that aspect was almost a source of derision during the investigation. At a conference, if something came up in relation to Paul Gallagher, there'd almost be a sigh or a, not quite a laugh, almost a snigger, in relation to it.' The decent but naïvely trusting superintendent became a fool. The diligent detective became a joke.

In the Morris report, the word 'extraordinary' appears 18 times, 'astonishing' 13 times, 'bizarre' 10, 'unbelievable' seven times, 'absurd' three times and 'incredible' twice. And while all of this language is undoubtedly justified by the events the judge has to describe, it may, in a broader sense, be somewhat misleading. It suggests that Co. Donegal was a through-the-looking-glass world, a parallel universe where the normal rules of behaviour did not apply. Yet the disturbing reality is that Co. Donegal was not a law unto itself. It was an extreme expression of a set of problems that are now fundamental to the nature of policing, and indeed of governance, in Ireland. That is precisely why it took so long for the truth to be acknowledged by the leadership of the force and by the Government.

No to Asbos (anti-social behaviour orders) protesters skateboarding outside the Central Bank on Dame Street in Dublin. Photograph: Dara Mac Dónaill.

The story at the heart of the report is not about one or two exceptionally bad cops. It is a tale in which those who did their job with basic professionalism were the exceptions. From the mundane gardaí who were first contacted about Richie Barron's death, to the senior officers in Co. Donegal, to the higher echelons in Garda headquarters and on to the civil servants and politicians in the Department of Justice, there is an unbroken chain of arrogance and indifference.

It begins almost at the moment at which the Garda Síochána was told there was a body on the road outside Raphoe. Garda Pádraig Mulligan, who was supposed to be on duty in Raphoe at the time of Richie Barron's death, could not be found and did not answer his call from the Garda Central Communications centre in Letterkenny. He was drinking in a pub in Lifford with his off-duty colleague Garda John O'Dowd at the time. When the Communications Centre then called Lifford station, the crew of the Lifford Garda car deliberately delayed answering the call until after their meal break. When they eventually went to Raphoe they did nothing to preserve the scene or to initiate local inquiries. When they went to Letterkenny general hospital, where Richie Barron's body had been taken, they again did nothing. It was left to a hospital porter to preserve Barron's clothing.

When the investigation into Richie Barron's death did begin, it was blinded almost from the start by sheer prejudice against the McBrearty family. In Judge Morris's memorable phrase, it was governed by 'the ability of hatred to transform myth into facts'. A postmortem, had one been held, would have shown beyond doubt that there was no murder. Instead, the case would have been one of dangerous driving causing death. No forensic pathologist was called to examine the body. The Garda Technical Bureau was not asked to become involved. There were, according to the tribunal, four possible suspects for the driver of the car which had hit Richie Barron. The case against none of them was seriously examined by the Garda.

What happened instead was a rumour. At the traditional wake held for Richie Barron, people began to speculate that he had been murdered. One of those at the wake was Willie Doherty, a minor criminal and a garda informer who was also, in the eyes of Judge Morris, 'a deeply mischievous individual who would be prepared to lie in order to turn any situation to his advantage'. Although he had no real information to give, he was being used by Garda John O'Dowd as a source for fabulous claims about IRA activity which were passed on to Garda headquarters to gain kudos for the Donegal gardaí. At the wake, Frank McBrearty snr went in and out of the room where Richie Barron's body was laid out in an open coffin. He seemed genuinely upset. Instead of being taken for what it was – a mark of human decency – however, this display of emotion was taken as evidence of a guilty conscience. Willie Doherty told his handler John O'Dowd that rumours were flying at the wake that the McBreartys had a hand in Richie Barron's death.

In a professional police force, this was the kind of vague lead that ought to be investigated. Instead, it was treated by the senior gardaí in Letterkenny, not as a potentially interesting question, but as a final answer. Within an hour, the senior officers had 'translated rumour into fact'. Chief Supt Denis Fitzpatrick told Supt Fitzgerald: 'Mark my words, it is a murder and Mark McConnell and Frank McBrearty jnr did it.' The astonishing speed with

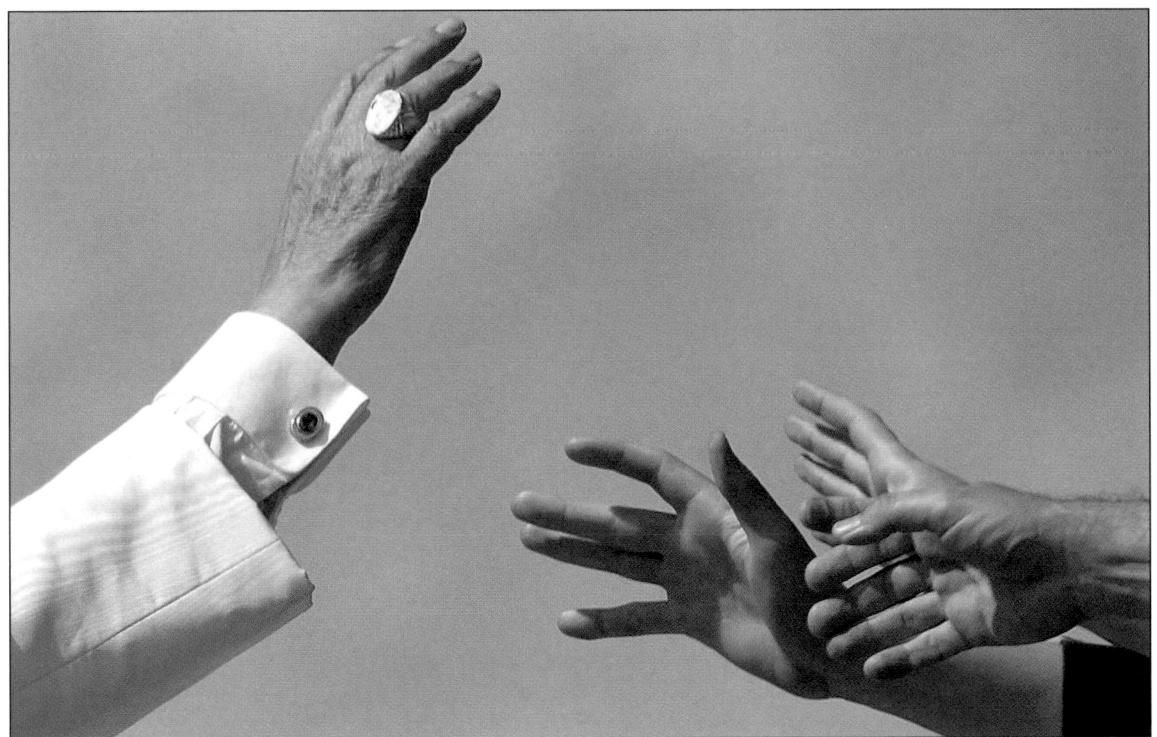

Pope Benedict and the faithful exchange waves in St Peter's Square in Rome. Photograph: Max Rossi/Reuters.

which this conclusion was reached can be explained only in one way: Willie Doherty was telling the Gardaí what they wanted to hear. They didn't like the McBreartys and from that moment, with what the report calls 'hysterical determination', they set about framing two of them for a murder that had never happened.

On the night of 29 November, Robert Noel McBride, whom his own counsel described at the tribunal as 'a gormless auld divil', was arrested on suspicion of stealing an aerial from the technical school in Raphoe. In the course of the questioning, he made a statement that he had seen Frank McBrearty and Mark McConnell on the night of Richie Barron's death near the scene of his alleged murder. In fact, McBride was not in Raphoe that night. The tribunal concludes, 'Whatever Robert Noel McBride was saying that night, it was doctored by the Gardaí so that it told the story that the other witnesses were not prepared to tell.' McBride made a number of subsequent statements implicating the McBreartys in the 'murder', but retracted them all in September 1997.

Using McBride's concocted statement as an excuse, members of the extended McBrearty family, including Frank jnr and Mark McConnell, were arrested and questioned. Frank jnr allegedly made a statement admitting to the 'murder'. The tribunal has yet to examine the circumstances surrounding this alleged confession. It notes, however, that two gardaí on the inquiry team have 'alleged that Det. Insp. John McGinley was seen practising, by way of some sort of a joke, as they rationalised it, the signature of Frank McBrearty jnr while he was in custody and purportedly made a voluntary statement'. Supt Fitzgerald was evidently so doubtful about the worth of this supposed statement that he took it with him in February 1997 when he left Co. Donegal.

The campaign to frame the McBreartys also had a public dimension. In March 1997, leaflets were circulated around Raphoe and the adjoining areas stating: 'The murdering McBreartys. See them live. Father and son at Frankie's nightclub on 8th March 1997 with Joe Dolan'. Slogans were painted on the road outside the McBrearty home: 'House for sale, owners moving to Mountjoy, contact Frank McBrearty.' There were also five phone calls made to an innocent couple, Michael and Charlotte Peoples, alleging that they had helped to cover up the McBreartys' involvement in the 'murder' and demanding money to protect them from prosecution. Four of these calls were made by the informant Willie Doherty and one was made from the home of Garda John O'Dowd. This, too, was 'part of the conspiracy to frame the suspects in this case, and particularly Michael Peoples'. It was these phone calls and the attempted extortion which ought to have blown the whole affair wide apart.

Michael and Charlotte Peoples made formal complaints to the Garda Síochána. But at this point an organised cover-up began. As the report notes, 'the reason why the Donegal Garda division did not properly investigate the extortion telephone calls to the home of Michael and Charlotte Peoples on the 9th of November was because senior officers, including Supt Kevin Lennon and Chief Supt Denis Fitzpatrick were determined to cover up the trail which led to Garda John O'Dowd. The reasons for this were to ensure that no light was shone on the unhealthy relationship between William Doherty and the Garda force in Donegal which had, among other things, contaminated the investigation into the death of the late Richard Barron.'

It is the cover-up, and the subsequent inaction of Garda headquarters and the Department of Justice, that makes the Co. Donegal scandal far more than an isolated and unfortunate episode. Garda headquarters should have known that something strange was going on in Co. Donegal. The bogus information supplied by Willie Doherty on alleged IRA activities was forwarded on a regular basis to the Crime & Security Branch at Garda Headquarters. Much of it was, as the tribunal puts it, 'dramatic', containing details of planned operations

Nan Pang and Shuang Jin, who are part of the catering staff at the National Gallery of Ireland, view the painting Le Chef de'L'Hotel Chatham 1921 *which is on loan from the Royal Academy of Arts in London, at a preview of the William Orpen retrospective* Politics, Sex and Death *at the Gallery. Photograph: Matt Kavanagh.*

and assassinations. If it was accurate, it demanded urgent action. Yet, 'none of the intended victims was ever notified. Nobody was ever arrested. Nothing was ever found.' Why did no one at the Crime & Security Branch, which was headed for a time by the current commissioner Noel Conroy, ask questions about this sensational information that was never acted upon? Or about the reason the flow of information stopped in July 1997 when the Co. Donegal gardaí realised that things were going awry and tried to distance themselves from Doherty?

According to the report, 'The witnesses from Crime & Security Branch maintained that it was not their job to act on the information received, nor could they act as they were an information-gathering and analysis unit'. Justice Morris concludes that the branch was 'negligent in failing to make the necessary inquiries'. He also notes 'the failure of the Department of Justice to impose order and discipline on the force'.

The department got its first inkling of what was going on in February 1997, when Senator Seán Moloney (the only local politician to take up the McBrearty case) wrote to the then minister Nora Owen about Frank McBrearty's complaints of garda harassment. (He was issued with 160 summonses on minor and trivial matters.) According to the current secretary of the department, Seán Aylward, this was 'processed as a piece of correspondence, among thousands of pieces of correspondence about the activity of the Gardaí and relatively junior people were forwarding it in a kind of post-box fashion to the Garda Commissioner's office to be looked at'.

After the McBreartys employed a private detective, Billy Flynn, and instituted civil proceedings, both the department and the office of the DPP received detailed complaints about the Barron investigation and the false confession. But even then, the department's attitude was that 'the civil claim was a distraction, an attempt by somebody who was under suspicion to throw dust in people's eyes'. There was, according to Aylward, a continuing 'assumption by the officials concerned that it was being handled appropriately by the Gardaí'. In July 1997, the then minister for justice John O'Donoghue was informed in a letter from a solicitor acting for the Peoples about the extortionate phone calls, including the crucial fact that one of them came from the home of a serving garda whose identity had also been made known to the chief superintendent in Donegal.

The response, however, perfectly expressed the deeper malaise. O'Donoghue asked the garda commissioner to look into the matter. He in turn passed the letter on to none other than the acting chief superintendent in Donegal, Kevin Lennon. In effect, an allegation that Kevin Lennon was covering up a crime by a garda was to be investigated by that garda's colleagues under the direction of Kevin Lennon. The attitude underlying this absurdity meant that the McBrearty and Barron families continued to be denied justice. By June 1998, the Department of Justice had a copy of the full McBrearty file, but the Gardaí were still contesting the allegations and, as Seán Aylward admitted, 'the department would have tended to take such a statement on trust'.

The internal Garda inquiry carried out by Asst Commissioner Kevin Carthy was thwarted by the ability of Co. Donegal gardaí to defy it with impunity. 'Gardaí', as the report puts it, 'looked to protect their own interests. The truth was to be buried. The public interest was of no concern.' Even when Carthy did identify some of the culprits, they were merely transferred with no stain on their reputations. The Garda Complaints Board failed to get to grips with any of the numerous complaints it received from the McBreartys. John O'Donoghue and the then attorney general Michael McDowell continued to resist all calls for a public inquiry.

The thread of injustice that began with a rumour whispered at a wake stretched all the way to the evasive mutterings of the highest authorities of the State.

SATURDAY, 4 JUNE 2005

The Great Unravelling

Denis Staunton

Over dinner in Berlin this evening, two haunted figures will pick over the wreckage of Europe's constitutional treaty, seeking desperately to salvage something that could keep the European integration project on track and possibly save their political careers. Gerhard Schröder and Jacques Chirac will find scant cause for cheer as they consider this week's resounding No votes in France and the Netherlands and the disarray the referendums have caused at the top of European politics. As the scale of the referendum defeats sank in among the European elites, it became clear that French and Dutch voters may have said No not only to the constitution but to the EU itself.

'We must acknowledge that many Europeans doubt that Europe is able to answer the urgent questions of the moment,' Schröder said after the Dutch vote on Wednesday. In fact, the referendums gave expression to a profound hostility many citizens feel towards the political elites at both national and European levels. Geert Wilders, a bouffant-coiffed, right-wing populist who featured prominently in the Dutch No campaign, summed up the message in his own crude way. 'The voters have stuck two fingers up to the elites in Brussels and the Hague,' he crowed as the results came in.

The referendum campaigns in France and the Netherlands focused on different issues and exposed different concerns about Europe's political direction. But the campaigns also had important similarities, such as the almost unanimous backing the constitution received from mainstream centrist politicians and the scrappy coalitions of the left and the far right that opposed it.

The debate was more intense in France, where more than 700,000 books about the constitution were sold and newspapers offered comprehensive daily analysis of the treaty's most important elements. Many No voters identified anxiety about the future of France's social model as their main reason for rejecting the constitution. They feared that the treaty tied the EU into liberal economic policies that could see well-paid jobs and comprehensive social protection threatened by cheaper labour from central and eastern Europe.

The Dutch debate was more low-key, not least because most government ministers refused to campaign in favour of the Yes vote they claimed was in the vital interest of the Netherlands. This was the first referendum in the country's history as a parliamentary democracy and many voters seized the opportunity to make their views clear on EU policies they had never been asked about before. The size of the Dutch per-capita net contribution to the EU budget, which is the biggest of any member state, and the perceived inflationary impact of the euro, became rallying points for No voters. Some used the referendum to express their anger at a system that obliged the Dutch government to make painful cuts to public services to comply with EU budget rules but allowed France

Ceallachan McDonald, aged 6, from Athy, keeps her eyes on a giant Atlas Moth from Asia in the tropical greenhouse of the butterfly farm at Straffan in Co. Kildare. Photograph: Bryan O'Brien.

and Germany to break the same rules year after year without sanction.

Beyond such specific issues, however, the campaigns in both countries revealed an enormous loss of faith in the EU's capacity to provide the prosperity that has been its hallmark for much of the past 50 years. In a climate of sluggish economic growth, persistent high unemployment and deteriorating public services, many continental Europeans fear that the pro-market solutions coming from Brussels could make their lives even more insecure. As the EU has expanded to 25 member states and taken on more responsibilities, its institutional workings have become more complex and more remote from citizens. The elites in Brussels and in the national capitals have become ever more defensive, eyeing with suspicion an ungrateful public that apparently fails to understand what is being achieved on its behalf.

Neither the French nor the Dutch outcomes took Brussels by surprise, but the high turnout and decisive margins against the constitution in both countries were unexpected. The EU President, Luxembourg's Jean-Claude Juncker, and Commission President José Manuel Barroso, insisted after both referendums that the process of ratifying the constitution must carry on regardless. Schröder, Chirac and Dutch prime minister Jan Peter Balkenende endorsed the call, claiming that it would be undemocratic to deprive the remaining member states of the chance to have their say on the treaty. Obliging other countries to put the constitution to a vote would also have the likely consequence of ensuring that France and the Netherlands would not be the only member states to say No.

For this reason, Britain has led calls for the ratification process to be abandoned rather than risk a series of demoralising defeats throughout Europe. Even before the French referendum, friends of Tony Blair were arguing that a French No would mean the end of the constitution and that there was no point in holding a British vote on it. Britain may have moved too soon to try to shut down the ratification process altogether and the consensus now emerging in Europe points to a postponement or suspension of ratification rather than a complete halt. This would mean that no further referendums or parliamentary votes on the constitution would take place while EU leaders engaged in a 'period of reflection'. The current deadline of November 2006, by which time all governments should have ratified the constitution, would be shelved. Such a decision, which would have to be agreed by all EU leaders at a summit on June 16th, would allow the Government to postpone Ireland's referendum indefinitely while the EU worked out how to address the concerns expressed by French and Dutch voters. Few observers in Brussels expect the constitution to be revived within the next two or three years and most believe that no progress will be possible until after Germany has a new – or re-elected – chancellor later this year and France has a new president in 2007.

In the meantime, Blair takes over the EU presidency next month, determined to launch a renewed campaign for economic reform in Europe. Barroso has made a drive for economic reform the central mission of his commission's five-year term, so far with no success whatsoever. Part of the problem is that most of the steps necessary remain the preserve of national governments and cannot be dictated from Brussels. EU-wide measures such as the proposed services directive, aimed at opening up the European market in services, are deeply unpopular.

The real malaise may have less to do with European institutions or policies than with the feeble democratic life of the EU, as Balkenende suggested after the Dutch vote. 'The idea of Europe has lived for the politicians, but not the Dutch people. That will have to change,' he said.

The Financial Times called yesterday for structured national debates on Europe in each member state, modelled on Ireland's National Forum on

Europe. Such a bottom-up approach may represent the best route towards giving the EU back to its citizens and building a stronger, more democratic union for the 21st century.

TUESDAY, 7 JUNE 2005

Night Couldn't Shield us from Death

Everest Diary: Grania Willis

Job done. Mission accomplished. In the early hours of Sunday morning I reached the highest point on earth – the summit of Mount Everest. But in doing so I had to dig into reserves of strength and courage that I had no idea I possessed.

Lowest moment of the longest day of my life came at 8,550 metres, at the top of the Third Step when I found the body of Slovenian climber Marco Linekah, part of the 7-Summits team. I knew he was there, but it was still a hideous shock to see him, frozen in the final agony of death as he tried to suck oxygen out of an atmosphere that simply wasn't enough to sustain life. His backpack sat about 10 yards downhill from where he lay, untouched by all the climbers that passed by his icy grave. Marco himself was on his back, arms stretched out above his head, his hands frozen in terrible claws as he tried desperately to cling on to life. It was the starkest possible reminder of the

Grania Willis's Everest Challenge: at base camp. Photograph: Grania Willis.

dangers of climbing Everest. Anyone taking on the challenge knows that there are risks, but seeing a body when you're already wondering if you're going to die yourself is spectacularly eerie.

My own summit push had started later than intended, but still before midnight, so the majority of the ascent was in the dark, with a light flutter of snow caught in the beam of my head torch. The darkness shielded us, not only from other bodies on the way, but also from the exposure – the mountaineering term for horrendous drops that would be unsurvivable in a fall. But even the darkness couldn't shield us from death. Himalayan Experience (Himex) leader Russell Brice rightly insists that all climbers maintain radio contact throughout summit day, but that meant we could hear every transmission throughout the night hours too.

At some stage – the hours passed by unnoticed – Scottish expedition leader Henry Todd contacted Brice from the south side to say he had turned his team around following the death of a 23-year-old Briton. A suspected heart attack had cut the young man down in his prime, exactly the same way my 19-year-old nephew Joe had died at college in England a month before my departure for Tibet at the end of March. It was a devastating blow to my family, so I dedicated my Everest attempt to Joe. It was an emotional moment when I set foot on the summit and Joe, the red-headed, blue-eyed youth, was there with me.

The moment was doubly emotional as I was with Paul Hockey, the one-armed Australian climber, who turned around just short of the summit 12 months ago. He was carrying his mother's ashes with him and, with only one hand, had to ask me to open the container before he could scatter its cargo to the winds. But things were about to get worse, as Hockey found the descent far more difficult than the ascent, even with the assistance of two sherpas. My sherpa Karsang and I got stuck behind Hockey on the traverse across the dihedral, the rocky outcrop just below the summit.

Hockey was seriously struggling, as the traverse meant that his left arm was away from the rock face and effectively useless. With serious exposure falling away beneath him, he was naturally keen to keep a hand on the rock, but had to twist his body through 90 degrees to do so. Towards the end of the traverse, he stopped and radioed Russell Brice. 'Russ, I'm in trouble,' he said, with death in his eyes. He had given up, just as so many people do on Everest and pay the ultimate price. It took all of Brice's skill to talk Hockey down, but he succeeded – with the help of four sherpas. And yesterday, after a very uncomfortable night at the 8,300m camp, Hockey was guided down by Nima Sherpa and Kiwi Dean Staples all the way to the 6,400m advanced base camp, having escaped death by a whisker.

But he had summited Everest and left his mother's ashes on the top of the world.

Others won't get the chance of a decent burial or cremation. Marco is one. And a member of the Indian Air Force team, who left only a crampon on the mountain for his colleagues to remember him, is another. But the body of the German who collapsed and died just above camp II after summiting was collected yesterday by four sherpas and will be flown home. It's an unusual mark of respect for those who die on Everest. Most are simply left frozen on to the mountain where they fell.

WEDNESDAY, 8 JUNE 2005

Syllabus Limited by Study of Words as Ideology

John Waters

'English', in the Leaving Cert sense, used to be about language and literature, about writing and comprehension, composition and criticism, a little bit about grammar and a wagged finger about spelling and syntax. It wasn't exactly a language subject, like French or Spanish, but

Grania Willis's Everest Challenge: going up the north face. Photograph: Grania Willis.

neither was it about everything the English language is about.

It was Yeats and Orwell; Maria Edgeworth and Dylan Thomas; Kavanagh, Kinsella and something about roast pig. It was hard to pin down, but you sort of knew what it was. You knew too that it wasn't really about language and literature – that there was an approved use of language in which sentences have subject, predicate and object and that there were skiploads of great books out there that never got mentioned.

But 'English' has changed. It's got bigger and broader, more varied and probably less predictable. But it still isn't what you might expect it to be. I did my Leaving Cert in 1973 and made another half-stab at the English course in 1980. It didn't change at all in between, nor for a long time afterwards. About four years ago though, they gave the course a complete overhaul, and the result is interesting for a lot of wrong reasons.

Looking at the 2005 curriculum, the most immediate aspect is what hasn't changed. *Wuthering Heights*, *Of Mice and Men* and *Silas Marner* are still there, on the required reading lists for both the higher and ordinary courses. Great novels, certainly, but are they that great? Less controversially, Shakespeare survives also. The list has been augmented with Hugh Leonard (*Home Before Night*), John McGahern (*Amongst Women*) Seán O'Casey (*Juno*) and, more mysteriously, David Malouf's *Fly Away Peter*. And it's all a bit like that: a light leavening of the eccentric and the obscure with the odd obvious choice. The higher level poets include stalwarts like Yeats, Kavanagh, Wordsworth and Eliot, but also Eavan Boland, Michael Longley and Seamus Heaney. The ordinary-level list extends to a few jazzier names, like Ciaran Carson and Roger McGough.

Most interesting is the list of prescribed 'texts' for comparative study, from which students must read any three apart from the one already selected from the required reading list. The most common characteristic of the comparative list, apart from inoffensiveness, is obscurity. It includes films like Baz Luhrmann's *Strictly Ballroom*, Kevin Costner's *Dances with Wolves* and John Huston's *The Dead*. There is a fairly eclectic mix of writers, from Sophocles to Maeve Binchy via Henrik Ibsen, Arthur Miller and Jung Chang. But many of the names, while worthy in their own way, would not suggest themselves as 'musts' for a grounding in world literature.

While there are some excellent writers on the list, many are far from obvious choices and most of the world's most celebrated writers are absent. It seems odd, at first sight for example, that someone appears to have gone to great lengths to overhaul

Grania Willis's Everest Challenge: on top of the world. Photograph: Grania Willis.

the English syllabus but never thought of making mandatory a Kafka, Tolstoy or Dostoyevsky. (There are no eastern European writers at all in 2005.) For a moment it occurs that perhaps the list includes only writers who wrote in English, but this is merely almost the case.

There are glaring omissions close to home: Joyce is acknowledged only by the inclusion of the Huston movie. Also missing are Beckett and Flann O'Brien, John B. Keane and Tom Murphy. Indeed, almost anyone you care to think of from any conventional understanding of the literary pantheon is likely to be missing: Rushdie, Rumi, Boll, O'Neill, De Lillo, Proust, Brecht, Mandelstam, Kundera, Freud, Greene, Williams, Sartre, Camus. Make your own list of 38 writers and I guarantee you won't get more than a dozen on the course, even including those I've already mentioned.

The extensive explanatory notes issued by the Department of Education are helpfully revealing not merely about the background reasoning but indeed about the, as it were, 'purpose' of 'English'. The syllabus, these notes aver, should 'provide opportunities for the development of the higher-order thinking skills for analysis, inference, synthesis and evaluation'. The point, we are told, is for students to become 'independent learners who can operate in the world beyond the school in a range of contexts'.

Our old friends grammar and syntax get a token mention and there is a nod towards the aesthetics of language, but mostly the talk is of 'texts' and 'genres', 'resources', 'language products' and 'learning outcomes'. A 'text' is anything from a memo to a movie to a political speech. All this is, on the face of things, unexceptionable. Detectable

Donna Rayner, Laura O'Reilly, Joy Stapleton, Karen Gleeson and Aoife Lynch from Dominican College, Griffith Avenue in Dublin, discuss the merits of the Leaving Certificate mathematics paper. Photograph: Matt Kavanagh.

also, however, is the shadow of an ideological view of both literature and language. 'Language,' the department's document elaborates, 'is not a neutral medium of expression and communication. It is embedded in history, culture, society and ultimately, personal subjectivity. In the contemporary world, the cultural reality of a person's own use of language needs to be highlighted. To achieve this end, a range of resources will be selected from different periods and cultures and students will be encouraged to approach them in a comparative manner.

'In encountering this diversity, students should develop an understanding of how the language a person uses shapes the way that person views the world.' All 'texts', we are assured, create their own view of reality by using a specific linguistic style within certain specific categories of language forms, which can be called 'genres'. Students are urged to approach 'texts' from a variety of critical viewpoints and to analyse and compare 'under such categories as gender, power and class'. If you didn't recognise this as straight out of the advanced feminist manual, the departmental notes provide a helpful dig in the rib-cage: 'Resources will be chosen to give the fullest recognition possible to the experience of both sexes.' The penny drops.

Of the 38 writers on the comparative list, 15 are women. Not a bad thing in itself, except that whatever way you look at it, the vast, vast majority of the great writers have been male. To attempt, therefore, to achieve even a relative balance of the sexes (roughly 60/40 here) is a recipe for mediocrity and, yes, subjectivity. Pat Barker, Muriel Spark and

Annie Proulx are fine writers, but hardly the most essential grounding for someone trying to get their head around the pantheon. Many of the male writers, accordingly, appear to have, where possible, been chosen both to harmonise with the relevant world view and to avoid shining over-much amidst the necessary relative obscurity of the female choices.

A dim memory returns of the doomed Exploring Masculinities project for transition-year boys: the same clunking hand, the same slithery agenda. This agenda, of course, extends beyond what is termed 'gender' (an interesting word for study in itself: having started life as a term for grammatical categories, it has become the ideological code for an insistence that the differences between men and women are essentially man-made).

Predictably – once you understand what's going on – there is a black African male writer (Chinua Achebe), a black female writer (Maya Angelou), a female Indian writer (Gita Mehta) and so forth, to most of which names the most immediate response of the average general reader is 'who?' Presently, one comprehends why there are no east Europeans: too European, male and white.

Barely below the surface of this syllabus is a sense of a neurotic ideological grievance, a message that certain categories of humans have been done down in, or by, literature and that this is the most important thing our young people need to learn. The purpose of literature in the Leaving Cert English syllabus appears to be the turning out of alert readers of 'texts' who will pounce on issues of alleged prejudice and discrimination rather than be inspired by the wealth of words in the canon of world literature. Its most striking aspect is not where it takes you but where it is 'coming from'.

While it purports to shine a light on the tendentiousness of culture, the English syllabus is itself deeply tendentious. What 'English' has become at its dead hand is the study of words as propaganda, with literature treated as though it were indeed no different from memos and speeches – a chronicling of experience and events rather than an imaginative exploration of human possibility.

SATURDAY, 11 JUNE 2005

Fighting to Make a Connection

Sean O'Driscoll, in New York

Russell Crowe lights up a cigarette and looks back at the 30 autograph hunters lined up behind his car. 'W★★kers,' he says. 'They're not the real fans, they're just in it for the money. They know exactly what they can get for each photo and poster. I used to be able to ask, "Who do you want the autograph for?" and if they didn't know a name, then I knew they were full of shit. But now they tell you that they want it signed for "John". Later they take out the alcohol rub and take "John" off the autograph and sell it. I wish they'd just leave me alone. It's ridiculous.'

For reasons I still don't fully understand, I am riding in the back of Russell Crowe's limo as he recalls his Limerick drinking tales and shares his love for the late Irish actor Richard Harris. I had asked for an interview and he had over-ruled his publicist and invited me into his dressing room at a Manhattan TV studio, where he stood half-naked as he discussed his Irish roots (Clare or Cork, he thinks). Afterwards, he invites me into the limo to hear an Irish track from his album, his first since he split with his band, Thirty Odd Foot of Grunts. As we veer down Broadway, he says he'd like to play a few other tracks from the album first. 'So whack on the album, mate. Stick on track one,' he tells the driver.

What's with the design on his jacket? (He is wearing a dark jacket with a bulldog and a shamrock design.) 'Oh, that's something I designed for the crew,' he says. The shamrock and bulldog are a tribute to James Braddock, the 1930s heavyweight champion he plays in *Cinderella Man*.

'Track one, from the beginning, really loud!' he says, puffing on a cigarette and blowing the smoke out the window. The first track is a tribute to the patience of his wife, Danielle Spencer, for enduring his moody personality. The lyrics are pretty timely, as he's arrested four days later for throwing a telephone at a hotel concierge while trying to call Danielle at their Australian home. 'I'm so hard to handle. My life is a suitcase that has never been closed. Don't know how you stand it. Don't know how you love me, God only knows,' he sings. He sticks his head out the window as he listens. His face is hidden behind a baseball cap and dark sunglasses but a woman in a taxi next to us screams in recognition and presses her face to the cab window. We turn a corner and he turns his head back into the car.

He'd like me to hear a track he wrote about Richard Harris and the Irish rugby team, which he hopes will become a terrace anthem for Irish rugby fans. 'Me and Richard were supposed to go to the test match at Lansdowne Road, Australia versus Ireland at the end of 2002, but he died about 10 or 14 days earlier. We kept talking as if he wasn't sick and we were going to go to the game and it would all be cool.' Harris's death devastated him, he says. After the funeral, he was supposed to return to Australia, but decided to stay in Ireland and go on a Harris pilgrimage. He travelled to Harris's native city, Limerick, to try out the Charlie St George's pub, which Harris had talked about many times while he and Crowe filmed *Gladiator* together. He was somewhat surprised by the decor.

'When Richard talked about it, it was always in such glowing and romantic terms. I was surprised to see that it was kind of a shop front. I was expecting some beautiful carved wood and traditional Irish pub built in the 1600s or something.' He had a

Russell Crowe. Photograph: Paul Hawthorne/Getty Images.

great time at the pub, he says, and travelled up through counties Clare and Galway for the Australia-Ireland game he was hoping to attend with Harris. Before the game, he asked then Irish captain Keith Wood if the team would wear black armbands in Harris's honour. 'He said that the Irish rugby union didn't do things like that. It was nice to talk to Keith. He's a legend.' He sat down to watch the game, expecting Ireland to be trounced. 'It wasn't expected to be much of a challenge for Australia. Maybe 20 minutes of rough and tumble up front but then they'd just amass points. So I'm standing there at Lansdowne Road and, at first, I'm feeling a little sad because Richard wasn't there but then the game got under way and Australia couldn't do anything right. George Gregan [the Australian captain] dropped the ball, I think, seven times at the base of the scrum.'

'The mist came down, everybody was singing *The Fields of Athenry* and the pressure just built and Australia lost. I couldn't help think from half-time onwards that Richard was on the field, that he was actually there.' Crowe throws his arms up, imitating an invisible Richard Harris catching the rugby ball in a line-out. 'I went to a pub after the game and wrote out lyrics on a beer coaster and put it in my pocket.' As the limo heads into Soho, he signals to the driver. 'Play that song, mate. Nice and loud. Track nine. Nice and loud.'

It is a surreal scene. We are barrelling down one of the world's trendiest neighbourhoods with the lyrics to his Richard Harris tribute blaring out the window, accompanied by equally loud bodhráns and bagpipes. People are starting to stare. He taps his finger to the lyrics: 'Mr Harris take the field and plays the 16th man. We'll sing of Athenry

Peter Murphy from Tallaght (left) steals a kiss from model Linda Evangelista who was signing autographs after appearing at Brown Thomas store in Dublin to help an Aids fundraising campaign. Photograph: Don Healy.

and you'll do all you can for the green, the glorious green. The emerald green of Ireland's pride.' A bicycle courier pulls up beside our car and turns to us, caught by the blaring music. 'We'll take the fight, we'll never yield, for Irish sons have Irish hearts and Mr Harris, Mr Harris take the field.' It's clear Crowe wants the song to be heard on the street, and when we stop at a traffic light the car gathers more attention from passers-by. I tell him I think Harris would have been very proud, both of the song and the attention it has brought.

'That's what I thought,' says Crowe. 'That's why I wrote it, as a galvanising thing for Irish rugby to reach for. Pretty much everything in your culture is steeped in the belief that there is more than you see. So here it is, here's the thing. If you call the rugby gods, maybe you can do it through Richard Harris. You can be assured that the rugby gods and Richard Harris are pretty closely connected.' He laughs loudly and takes another drag from his cigarette.

We pull up at the hotel and he gets out. (It's no secret now that it's the Mercer Hotel in lower Manhattan: its name was screamed all over the tabloids after his arrest on Monday.) One of his staff opens the hotel door. From the corner of my eye, I can see the man open and close the door repeatedly as Crowe stands on the sidewalk and talks and talks about rugby and Richard Harris. As a crowd gathers, he stumbles back on the pavement while imitating his trip to the Cliffs of Moher during his Harris tribute journey. He flounders around and comes back to me. 'I was leaning right into the wind, it was fantastic.' His eyes are wide and excited, like a young boy talking about a school tour.

I'm beginning to understand Russell Crowe. He likes uncomplicated situations and loves being a man's man. He loves rugby stories and clear-cut song lyrics. A concierge who can't connect him to Australia at 4 a.m. is being fussy and complicated and likely to suffer his telephone-flinging fury.

He suddenly changes the conversation and wants to talk about James Braddock. *Cinderella Man* is the first film this year to receive a solid nod for next year's Oscars. Crowe is proud of his work, but refuses to meet 60 journalists waiting at roundtable interviews the next day because of a tepid review he received from the *New York Times*. He has been inspired by the Braddock story since 1997, he says, and spent many years reading up on the subject. 'I didn't rely on family members for research,' he says. 'I just went through newspaper archives and things. He was an amateur boxer when he came to fight (heavyweight legend) Tommy Loughran, who gave him a bit of a boxing lesson so his stock went down and his confidence too.' Braddock's tumultuous fortune echoed that of the Depression-era US.

'The big thing for me is that the story stayed relevant because this change of fortune actually happened. Here was a boxer who was building a respectable wealth, he wasn't wasting his money, he was living very frugally, he had everything invested in stocks and everything he hadn't invested in stocks he put into a bank. So what happened to him in the stock market collapse was horrible and then there's this comeback. It took a long time for me to find people that would see it the way I saw it.'

He is delighted the Braddock family have already seen the film. Some 50 of them came to the studio and he was thrilled when they mistook footage from the film with real-life footage of James Braddock fighting. 'Braddock's heavyweight win was a gigantic *zeitgeist* moment. It was one of the few times when the complete working class fulfils what society needs from him at that moment and he was at 10-to-one odds at the most generous bookies,' he says. He has signed many photos for the Braddock family but is wondering how many more he will have to sign. 'James's son Ron said to me last night that he wanted another one and I was like: "God, how many do you need, mate?"'

Crowe's publicist is looking at her watch now; she looks like she is about to kill me but Crowe ignores her. 'Do you know what the greatest thing about Braddock was?' he says. 'That he re-achieved his normalcy. He didn't go around getting people to call him champion. He finished boxing, he joined the army for a bit, he ran a restaurant for a while, he had various businesses.' He discovered that Braddock was a bad businessman. 'He wasn't very good at restaurants in particular, because he couldn't charge people for food, given that he had come from the Depression.' He laughs quickly. He seems in very good form.

When he mentions Braddock 're-achieving normalcy' does he see a comparison with his own life, or is he still struggling with stardom? 'Well, I think to compare my struggle with Braddock's would be stretching it. Braddock's achievements were amazing and his legacy deserves its own attention and respect.' If there is a comparison, he says, it's only in the struggle to live a happy life. Crowe has his hand pressed to his face, trying to explain what he has learned from Braddock's life. 'You see, Braddock died desperately in love with his wife, having seen his children grow up and his grandchildren being born,' he says as he prepares to enter the foyer of the hotel.

'I just thought it was a really important American story,' he says. 'He didn't end up a drug addict or an alcoholic or a restaurant guy in Las Vegas, he just lived his life. It's kind of what I'm struggling to do myself.'

MONDAY, 13 JUNE 2005

McBride Ends Tyson Era

Keith Duggan, in Washington

It may not go down as one of the classic heavyweight fights but on an enthralling and elegiac night in the sweltering American capital, the Irish outsider Kevin McBride restored some romance and heart to the demoralised world of professional boxing. No matter what the generous and lionhearted giant from Clones goes on to achieve in the fight game, it is hard to imagine that any future experience in his sporting life will compare to the pathos and melodrama that unfolded on this steamy Saturday night in downtown Washington. With a show of courage and a boxing sensibility that few gave him credit for, McBride became an overnight sensation on what was the closing chapter to one of the most compelling and disturbing eras in modern sport. No matter what follows, Kevin McBride will always be remembered as the boxer who brought down the curtain on the fighting life of Mike Tyson.

The end came not with the cinematic haymaker from the blue which almost all experts believed McBride would have to concoct to have any hope against the menace of Tyson. But instead, the most explosively violent fighter of the modern sporting era just remained on his stool after six rounds after failing to make any impact on McBride's gigantic frame. 'Kevin fought a good fight,' Tyson would say later. 'I wanted to finish it out but my trainer Jeff Fenech was too sensitive to let me go back out there and get beat up on.'

Tyson's humble acceptance that his time has come and gone was all the more poignant given the presence of Muhammad Ali. The Greatest gazed on impassively as Tyson went through his last rites and the unheralded Irishman, derided and insulted on American television over the last few days, grew in stature and in confidence. By the sixth round, despite receiving a cut below his left eye from a head-butt by Tyson, McBride was raining uppercuts and thunderous hooks down upon the smaller man, who cowered and shielded himself in a way that would have been unimaginable in his prime. By then the majority of the 17,000 fans, the bejewelled and perfumed studs and honeys who shelled out up to $700 for what was supposed to be a night of celebration for Tyson, had begun to bay and jeer in disbelief.

Far up in the stands, the Irish Tricolours fluttered as the big Monaghan slugger began to take bold and confident steps around the ring, seeking out the man who was supposed to be the hunter. Late on in the sixth round, a lingering, heavy left hook, loose as the swing of a bear's paw, was enough to leave Tyson reeling and then falling against the ropes. For what seemed an eternity, he remained on the canvas and the night was poised on the terrible possibility that Tyson was on the verge of a breakdown there and then. But finally, he moved gingerly and with astonishing slowness back to his corner. He would not come out again. Seconds later, the referee took hold of McBride's massive fist and held it in triumph to a stadium trembling with emotional meltdown. As Paschal Collins and 83-year-old Goody Petronelli rushed on to the floor to greet the delighted Irishman, with half of Clones in train, the magnitude of what had occurred began to hit home.

'I came here to fight and to show everyone I am a warrior,' McBride said. 'Like, I'm not the fastest man in the world but I have a big, Irish heart. I just want to thank my mother and my father at this stage, Lord rest him.' It was fitting he mentioned his parents for even in his hour of glory, McBride's unassuming dignity and basic good manners did not desert him. Half way through his press conference, he received a whisper that the great Ali wanted to meet him and he jumped up from his chair like a child, begging forgiveness from his audience.

There followed a fairly remarkable few moments when the Champ drew the Irish man close to his ear and embraced him and traded a couple of mock punches while McBride shook his head in disbelief. Then he wrapped his huge hands, inherited from his father, around Ali's and told him he was the greatest. For the hard-boiled followers of American sport, it was a rare and unscripted departure from the usual choreographed scene. But

Kevin McBride celebrating his victory over Mike Tyson in Washington DC. Photograph: Susan Walsh.

then, the entire evening had a slightly surreal feel to it.

Although his skills have now unquestionably vanished, Tyson still possessed enough charisma to bring out the bloodlust in people from all walks of life. Seeing him destroy and ruin the gargantuan Ulsterman was to be the turn-on of Saturday night's entertainment, and the more gruesome and lurid the better. And as Tyson stalked the ring in his familiar black shorts, the gold teeth glimmering and those intelligent eyes shining black, the memory of all the men he reduced to desperate wrecks over the years came flooding back and it was impossible not to feel a shiver of apprehension.

But it was all a chimera. Sure, he feinted with flashes of the preternatural quickness that was his trademark and early on he punished McBride with those darting right hooks and thunderous body shots that used to be enough to fell all kinds of reputations. Not on this Saturday night, though, and not ever again. 'I just don't have the heart for it anymore,' Tyson would say later in a long and piercingly eloquent valedictory afterwards. 'Not so long ago, an old basketball player said to me in Phoenix, "I feel good, I look good but when I go out there I can't do it anymore." That's how it was for me. I wanted to win. But shit, I was dead. It was strange, I felt like I was 120-years-old out there.'

The fitting thing was that boxing, a sport which seems inclined to disgracing itself whenever possible, should have lucked upon a character as genuine and admirable as McBride to bid Tyson go gentle into the good night. 'Mike was probably one of the greatest ever but he has been on the road a long time,' said McBride. 'I happened to get him at the right time but it was a pleasure to be in the ring with him. And I don't know if it is the end of the road for Mike Tyson but it is just the beginning for me.'

No one would wish it otherwise. McBride may get the title shot he so covets soon after this night and no matter how long more he stays in the fight game, he will be talking about being the last man to step into a ring with Mike Tyson until he is an old man. Where Tyson himself will be by then, God only knows.

TUESDAY, 14 JUNE 2005

Sex, Lies and Videotapes, but Question was, Who Told the Lies?

Conor O'Clery, in Santa Maria, California

This was a trial that had the three ingredients of Steven Soderbergh's famous movie title: *Sex, Lies and Videotapes.* Lies were told about Michael Jackson's sexual behaviour with small boys and the jury had to decide who was telling the lies, with the help of no less than three controversial videotapes.

The first, the one that shocked the world and set in motion the pop star's prosecution, was the famous Martin Bashir tape. It came about when Michael Jackson was facing new charges of sexually molesting a minor. Jackson's friend Uri Geller persuaded him to allow the interviewer to spend some time in the singer's 3,000-acre Neverland ranch to make a documentary that would show that Jackson's love for children was – well nothing more than child-like. 'I didn't want to do a long drawn-out thing on TV like OJ and all that stupid stuff,' the star told Bashir. 'It wouldn't look right. I said "Look. Let's get this over with." I want to go on with my life. This is ridiculous. I've had enough.'

The resulting programme *Living With Michael Jackson* was shown on Granada Television in the UK on 3 February 2003 and later on ABC in the US. The documentary had the opposite effect to that intended by the performer. Viewers were shocked to hear Jackson admit that he loved to have young boys sleep in his bed. Jackson recommended others should do it as well. 'It's what the whole world should do,' he said. 'I see God in the face of children, and man, I just love being around them all the time.' He boasted about letting a 12-year-old boy with cancer sleep in his bedroom but denied anything improper had occurred, saying he himself slept on the floor.

It was the second video, shot some 22 weeks later, that proved the more damaging of the two. Prosecutor Tom Sneddon had watched the Bashir interview with more than passing interest. He had been looking for a chance to bring Jackson to court since 10 years before, when the parents of a 13-year-old California boy, Jordan Chandler, first accused Jackson of sexually abusing their son at Neverland, and then dropped their charge after an estimated $20 million settlement. He arranged for a taped interview with the boy in the county sexual abuse response cottage in Santa Barbara on 6 July, 2003. It showed the boy being assured by Sgt Steve Robel that he was in no danger but that in order to make a criminal case against Jackson he needed his co-operation.

The boy, in denim shorts and a blue shirt, described being molested. In contrast to his defence of the singer and his praise for helping him beat cancer in the Bashir interview, he said Jackson masturbated him five or so times, though he changed this during the interview to five times or less. He described what Jackson allegedly told him, including that boys need to masturbate or they would go crazy. 'He said that he wanted to show me how to masturbate,' the boy said. 'I said no. Then he said he could do it for me.' Jackson grabbed him, he said. 'He grabbed me,' he said, in 'my private area (for) a long time.' He said that Jackson 'put his hands in my pants. He started masturbating me. I told him I didn't want to do that and he kept on doing it. I told him no.'

The interrogator told the boy that he was proud of him, that Jackson was 'the bad person, not you. You and your mother and brother and sister are the good people.' The boy is now 15 and the testimony he gave in court at the start of the trial matched that on the second tape. He described two incidents of abuse, and his brother said he twice saw the boy being molested while asleep.

The prosecution asked to introduce the tape during its rebuttal case, which began after the defence rested earlier this week. Judge Rodney Melville allowed the prosecution to show the tape. It was the last thing the jury of eight women and four men saw when the prosecution wound up its case and before they began their deliberations on 3 June.

The charges levelled against Jackson eventually included molesting the boy in February or March 2003, plying him with alcohol and conspiring to hold his family captive so that they could rebut damaging aspects of the Bashir documentary. The prosecution was also allowed to bring in evidence

Singer Michael Jackson after a Santa Maria California jury cleared him of 10 charges of child molestation. Photograph: Haraz Ghanbari/AP.

of four other boys being molested which seemed to turn the case against Jackson. In the three months of the trial the jury saw other seemingly-incriminating evidence, including adult magazines found in Jackson's home with the boy's fingerprints. They also heard testimony from more than 130 witnesses including actor Macaulay Culkin, who said that as a boy he had slept in Jackson's bedroom and had never been molested. It became clear as the case progressed that the verdict would swing on whether or not the jury fully believed the accuser.

The defence tried to put the boy and his mother on trial, depicting her as a person who tried to con celebrities out of money and who had put her son up to giving false testimony. They called comedian Chris Tucker to testify that he once warned Jackson to be wary of the boy and his mother to whom he had given expensive gifts including a $39,000 flight to Miami, Florida. 'I said, "Michael, something ain't right",' he said, describing how the boy and his family came to the set of a film he was making and refused to leave. Other witnesses described her as a welfare cheat who used her son's cancer to get money from Hollywood stars. A welfare worker said the mother fraudulently failed to disclose when applying for welfare that she had received proceeds from a $152,000 (unrelated) legal settlement 10 days earlier.

Judge Melville refused to allow the defence to present testimony by CNN's Larry King that a lawyer who once represented the mother had told him she was 'wacko' and out for money. The defence did not call Jackson to the stand but among the 50 witnesses they summoned, some testified that the mother and her children had the freedom of Neverland and were taken on trips and shopping excursions while supposedly held captive, running up expenses totalling $7,000 in a week at a hotel. Defence attorney Thomas Mesereau said the boy was unusually 'cunning' for a 12-year-old.

While Jackson did not take the stand, he was allowed – to Sneddon's fury – to address the jury through a third video. It was a three-hour tour of Neverland. It showed a note written on a blackboard by one of Jackson's children, saying 'I love you daddy'. It showed children at play, amusement rides, animals, and a video library. There were happy ranch workers and numerous clocks, a point the defence made much of, as the boy's family said they were unable to find out what time it was when allegedly being held captive. The tape included scenes cut out of the Bashir documentary which showed the interviewer being more sympathetic to Jackson than in the final cut.

Mesereau made a point of declaring, 'Nowhere on the Bashir documentary does he say he slept with little boys', just that they slept in the room while Jackson used the floor. The singer protested in the video that his feelings for children were innocent and loving. 'I haven't been betrayed or deceived by children,' he said. 'Adults have let me down.'

THURSDAY, 16 JUNE 2005

Schiavo's Brain Badly Damaged – Coroner

Conor O'Clery, in New York

A Florida coroner yesterday reported that Terri Schiavo, the brain-damaged woman who died on 31 March amid national controversy after her feeding tube was removed, suffered from an irreversible brain-injury and would not have recovered as her parents and supporters insisted.

Dr Jon Thogmartin, medical examiner for Florida's Pinellas-Pasco County, also found that Ms Sciavo was blind and deaf, indicating that her apparent response to people in videos released by the family was without thought or consciousness. The coroner's report discounts rumours her husband Michael Schiavo brought about her persistent vegetative state through strangulation or drugs.

Mary Corduff (right), the wife of a Co. Mayo farmer, Willie Corduff, who was jailed for refusing to obey a court order. Mr Corduff was one of five fellow farmers protesting against plans by Shell to lay a pipeline beneath their land to take gas from the Corrib field off the Mayo coast. Photograph: Alan Betson.

'No evidence of strangulation was found and no evidence of trauma whatsoever,' the coroner told a press conference in Largo, Florida.

After examining 72 external and 116 internal photographs, he concluded that, at time of death, Ms Schiavo's brain was 'profoundly atrophied'. It weighed 615g (1.35lb), half the expected weight of a human brain. 'This damage was irreversible, and no amount of therapy or treatment would have regenerated the massive loss of neurons,' he said. The coroner was accompanied by Dr Stephen Nelson, who described Ms Schiavo's condition as 'very consistent with a persistent vegetative state'. This concurs with court conclusions over 13 years in favour of Mr Schiavo's requests to have her feeding tube removed to allow her die. The video of Ms Schiavo appearing to smile at a Mickey Mouse balloon and look up at visitors caused many of the parents' supporters to believe she could recover.

State senator Daniel Webster of Florida argued at the time, 'Here we have a woman who can smile, who can respond to her mom, who can follow a balloon around the room.' Her father, Bob Schindler, said in March: 'We have close to 15 doctors ... stating Terri is not in a persistent vegetative state. We have bona fide information from professional neurologists that Terri can recover. She can swallow.'

The coroner said she could not swallow and, if she was given food orally she would choke to death. The video, shown over and over on cable television, also prompted US Congress to rush through a law, signed by President Bush, requiring the Florida courts to review the case. Federal courts refused to intervene and Ms Schiavo (41) died nearly two weeks after her feeding tube was removed. The family tragedy became a very public and bitter feud that divided the country. Mr Schiavo was accused by some of the parents' more outspoken supporters, like anti-abortion campaigner Randall Terry, of 'murder' through starvation. Ms Schiavo died not from starvation but from 'marked dehydration', Mr Thogmartin said. The coroner could not, however, determine what caused her collapse 15 years previously.

The autopsy found no proof that she had an eating disorder like bulimia that could have caused a severe chemical imbalance and heart attack. The potassium level in Ms Schiavo's body was 2.0 where the normal is 3.5 to 5.0, said the coroner, but this could have been caused by treatment after her collapse. Terri's parents always maintained that she did not have an eating disorder and accused Mr Schiavo of abuse, which he vehemently denies. Mr Schiavo's attorney, George Felos, accused the Schindlers of continuing to engage in a 'smear campaign against Michael to deflect the real issues in the case, which were Terri's wishes and her medical condition'.

Mr Schiavo always maintained his wife never would have wanted to be kept alive in a persistent vegetative state with no hope of recovery. During the controversy, the Roman Catholic Church said the removal of the feeding tube violated fundamental religious tenets.

SATURDAY, 18 JUNE 2005

Ave Maria

Róisín Ingle

I have a cleaner. I know, I know. There are only two adults in the house. And no children. How much mess is it possible for two people to make? But it's not about the mess, exactly; it's more a problem with the distribution of labour. I don't do any labour, and as a result I suspected my boyfriend had been considering mutiny. I was under pressure to find a solution that didn't involve getting my hands dirty. A friend suggested throwing money at the problem. And now Maria comes to our house once a week.

Being a son of Iris, my bleach-obsessed mother-in-law-in-waiting, and John, my vacuuming-friendly father-in-law-in-waiting, it's no surprise that my boyfriend is more genetically disposed than I am to domestic duties. When I asked my mother to explain why I never developed natural housekeeping tendencies she said I was too busy making mud pies in the back garden to pay attention when she was giving lessons in ironing, folding and hanging clothes. The upshot is that the bulk – and by bulk I suppose I mean 100 per cent – of the labour in our house has always been done by my boyfriend. He didn't actually threaten to strike, but I could tell by the way he'd been clattering around the kitchen and wielding the vacuum cleaner aggressively that he'd had enough of this Cinderfella role.

The e-mail from my friend, who lives alone but has had someone cleaning his apartment for ages, was timely. His cleaner was looking for more clients; did we know anyone who would be interested? Did we what? A few days later I arranged to meet Maria on Talbot Street – which, incidentally, is one of my favourite shopping areas in Dublin. You can buy things there that you could never have imagined. That day, for example, I bought a Turby Towel, which you put on your head after you've washed your hair. It's a godsend for people who can never quite get their towels to stay on their heads after a shower. It was a bargain, too, at only €1.95. So after I'd bought something I didn't know I needed I met the cleaner I knew I needed but felt a bit embarrassed about. We chatted about our backgrounds for a while; then Maria, who is from Romania, asked whether I had children. It was the first hint that she was going to try to clean up more than one aspect of my life. 'Is terrible,' she said when she learned that I am childless. She looked me up and down with a look that clearly said: 'And you so old.'

Maria has limited English, so there were a few comfortable silences as we walked towards the bus stop. During one of them I thought it best to tell her that I wasn't sure I had all the equipment she might need to clean the house. She suggested we head for a supermarket. That's when Maria came into her own. I'd suggest that J Cloths might be good for, I don't know, dusting or something, and she'd tut-tut and swap them for what she insisted was a superior brand of cloth, which looked exactly the same to me. She'd also point knowingly at Cillit Bang while I'd wonder aloud if all those chemicals weren't a bit dangerous. Maria just looked at me pityingly and shoved it into the basket. I never knew cleaning required such a strange and multicoloured array of products. I'd spent our weekly karaoke budget already, and we hadn't even gone into the mop-and-bucket shop.

After buying a state-of-the-art mop and bucket we got the bus to my house. Maria tackled the kitchen and bathroom with gusto while I got on with some work. By the time my boyfriend came home she was still hard at it, and I could see he was feeling a little bit left out. Do you think she'll do everything?, he sighed, the yearning in his voice suggesting Maria might be charitable and leave him with a room to vacuum or some crumbs to wipe. But Maria is so thorough that it looks as if he is going to have to find other ways to amuse himself in his spare time. I've taken to leaving brochures for massage courses around the house. I can only hope.

I didn't enjoy watching Maria work, but part of me felt I might learn something. I certainly did. Cleaning a kitchen means wiping tiles and taking everything out of the fridge and the cupboards. Dust, contrary to what I have always believed, is the same as dirt and needs to be removed. From everything. Unfortunately, I could only watch for a little while, as we had a soiree to attend. Feeling pleased with myself in some new gear, I passed Maria in the hall. Not like that, she said, appalled; you are not going to a party like that. It took me 10 minutes to convince her that my dress was meant to be creased. She was still shaking her head in dismay when I waltzed out the door. I have a feeling she's going to be very good for me.

MONDAY, 27 JUNE 2005

Belief and Zeal are their Drugs of Choice

LockerRoom: Tom Humphries

People keep calling me up and asking me what I think of Michelle Smith de Bruin's showing in the recent Marian Finucane Show poll to find the woman who, in the opinion of many of the MF Show Listenership, is the Greatest Irish Woman Living or Dead, Clean or Unclean.

On the one hand, I am perfectly indifferent. Certainly Michelle (and Erik) have done much to promote cheating (aren't those matching his 'n' hers bans so cute) and those within the cheat community must be extraordinarily proud of them both. We can understand that, so if the listeners of the MF Show want to esteem and exalt a topline drug cheat above somebody like, well say, MF herself, who has made a huge contribution to Irish society, well than surely MF just deserves a better demographic.

On the other hand, I care deeply. I am outraged. I am frightened. Let me tell you about last weekend. It will explain all. I spent the weekend in Cork in the company of the Twenty-Four Greatest Living Irish Women, or the St Vincent's under-14 camogie team, as they are collectively known. We had the weekend of our lives. In fact, we had a holiday from life.

If you've never been to an All-Ireland Féile competition you should cleanse your palate of the faintly sour whiskey taste of congealed Smith

An owl flies above the crowd at the National Country Fair in Emo Court, Co. Laois. Photograph: James Flynn/APX.

de Bruin and hightail it to Limerick next weekend to refresh yourself at the football Féile. Restore your faith in sport. The trip comes with guarantees and recommendations. As part of my indentured slavery I have been forced to work at World Cups and Olympics and heavyweight title fights and golf thingies and at all manner of sporting shindigs. I've never enjoyed anything remotely as much as I have enjoyed being immersed in a Féile. I never will.

Anyway you'll be wanting the lowdown. What happened. And why. And how it all ties up. Well. The Twenty-Four Greatest Living Irish Women began the tournament in stately fashion. That is, slowly, and taking care to preserve their immense dignity. On Friday they drew a game with our generous hosts in lovely Inniscarra. It was a game which they might have won, but really should have lost. They withdrew to lick their wounds and to perform remarkable and scandalous syncopated samba routines in the Féile Parade through Cork that evening.

Saturday is a long, happy blur. A soft dream of a time. The most fun any group of people have ever had in a field in Ballincollig. You'd have to know the Twenty-Four Greatest Living Irish Women for as long as we, their noble mentors/caddies, have, to feel the curious mix of confidence and trepidation with which we travelled early in the morning. See, The Fab Twenty-Four can be both erratic and brilliant. They can die for each other or they can just be not in the mood for anything except the bartering of gossip with each other. They play and function as an aggregate of their two dozen separate personalities. They are beautiful and wild and basically nuts. Some days, they are just collectively hormonal and we are afraid to ask them to do anything in case they rage at us.

An example: On Friday, The Grand Chief Agitator (Howya, April), who had a wonderful weekend, incidentally, had sought to initiate a robust debate on team selection during the half-time team talk. This was like moaning about somebody's second-hand smoke as they drew their final puff when lined up against a wall to be shot. Nevertheless, we knew the Grand Chief Agitator would be most peeved about the curtailment of her highly valued right to free speech, even at such an inopportune moment. Discontent can spread quickly among the Fab 24. We had no certainty about how Saturday would unfold.

The Twenty-Four Greatest Living Irish Women set into a pattern early though. They'd take a lead on a team, then let them back into the game and then finish them off. Or else, they'd take a lead on a team, then let them back into the game and then battle like lunatics to prevent the others finishing them off. Whatever, it was a pattern of sorts. Against Ballincollig, we looked condemned to another draw when Gillian Smith (if MF Show listeners had to vote for a heroic Smith, well here was one) scored a goal with just about the last *poc* of the game. We hugged and danced and asked them what the hell they were thinking of, leaving it so late.

Not long afterwards came the final group game. Toomevara of Tipp. Fortunately, The Twenty-Four Greatest Living Irish Women are no great respecters of reputation and Toomevara of Tipp might as well have been Tooting of Timbuktu for all they knew. The game was one of those great epics which deserved a nationwide audience. The one and only Meltem Yazar thumbed her nose at the aristocracy with a hat-trick of goals, each one more wondrous than the previous one. Then a great big generous dollop of eight minutes of injury time got added, an allotment which the Fab 24 mistakenly took to be time added on especially for Toomevara's benefit. The 24 went into injury time three points ahead. They then conceded about 6,000 frees and watched about 17,000 balls whistle wide. They reached the final whistle two points ahead. And knackered.

There's always at least one moment in a Féile weekend that you'll remember forever. For me there were two. The first came maybe an hour and a half after the Toomevara win. The girls were getting ready for an All-Ireland semi-final. They were drained, emptied, shattered, wrecked. You name it. So the Mill Lodge Hotel became an army field camp. Twenty-four bodies lay around one end of the restaurant fast asleep in the middle of the afternoon. Legs getting massaged, wounds being tended too, words being whispered, the smell of liniments. The sight of them there, all huddled like a scattering of dropped commas, will stay with me forever.

As will an image from the end of the semi-final, a moment that has burned itself into a perfect picture in my head. The Twenty-Four Greatest Living Irish Women beat Glen Rovers. Beating the Glen meant getting into an All-Ireland final to the girls. To the rest of us, reared on the legend of how the hurlers of St Vincent's beat Glen Rovers in a famous challenge in December 1953, a game which half-filled Croke Park, it was something even more special. A gang of kids from Marino beating the Glen! I mean, jaysus, that was The Glen!

We were gathering up the sticks and the water bottles and the Fab 24 had paused 40 yards away to clap the Glen girls as they passed out the gate on the other side of the field. Our heroes stood in one long, spread-out line before the distant hill and as we paused our tidying all we could see were these kids whom we've known for half their lives, and beyond them their smiling, clapping parents and fans. There were Vincent's jerseys and flags everywhere. The sun was going down on a postcard day. There in the crowd, clapping, was Mark Wilson. Mark is our club president and was corner forward on that team that beat the Glen half a century ago. He was a great mentor to me as a kid. That little moment in Ballincollig brings tears to the eyes nearly a week on.

Sunday and an All-Ireland final. You have no idea. Those faces drawn and nervous sitting on the benches in the tiny dressingroom beneath Páirc Uí Chaoimh. Hearing the familiar names called out on the PA. Saying the familiar words to them. Sending them out with hope in the heart. Watching these heroes, one of them your daughter, out on the famous turf.

We were hammered by a brilliant side from Douglas. No complaints. Regrets maybe that we never got to show that we can play a bit, but hey, we shed our tears and we hugged each other and we moved on. Nobody said that they'd get drugs the next time and use them to cheat those wonderful Douglas kids. On our way out we passed Pauric McDonald and the amazing Kilmacud Crokes hurling side who were just about to win the Division One title. Their journey was as stunning as ours was emotional. And all those young, keen faces in Páirc Uí Chaoimh last Sunday and around Cork last weekend were the only fitting rebuke to a certain proportion of the morally challenged MF Show listenership.

So to The Twenty-Four Greatest Living Irish Women, to Ais, to Claire H, to Clairo, to Happy Gilmore, to Ciara O'L, to Niamh (Yo Foxy), to JoJo, to Jessie G, to April F, to Meltem Y, to Gillian S, to Shauna O and to Irene D, to Jenny R, to Leanna B, to Johanna C, to Fionnuala J, to Carol Mc, to Róisín D, to Eimear M, to Kate P, to Orla Mc, to Jodie C and to Molly in da house, love ye all, long may ye run and please don't ever become MF Show phone-in types, or Michelle S de B sports-cheat types.

You're better than that. A million times better. May you stay forever young.

FRIDAY, 1 JULY 2005

Master Strokes at Painting Village

Clifford Coonan, in Dafen, southern China

Dealers in the village of Dafen, home to 2,000 painters churning out remarkable copies of famous works of art, like to cut quickly to the chase when it comes to selling their wares. 'We can give you Tintoretto's View of Venice for 500 yuan,' says Xu Yi, a gallery owner, and occasional pointillist, in this painters' village, tucked away in the outskirts of the southern Chinese boomtown of Shenzhen. She asks where I'm from, then whips out a calculator to do the maths. 'Or we can do you a deal on a Matisse, just €15. Or a Van Gogh for €12. *The Sunflowers*. You like *The Sunflowers?* You can pay in Chinese money or euros. Renoir. Monet. What do you want?'

Behind her in the narrow gallery, carefully executed Gaugin rip-offs sit uneasily beside a startling 1970s prog-rock fantasy-album-cover style of blonde maidens kissing a green-skinned, winged nymph. Fin-de-siècle Toulouse-Lautrec knock-offs rub shoulders with alarming photo-realist Pamela Andersons in oils, all looked down upon by a stern-eyed portrait of an American bald-headed eagle.

The Dafen Painters' Village was originally an artists' colony set up by a Hong Kong businessman 15 years ago, who allowed local painters to live and work for nothing if they painted a sideline in good quality fakes. It's not a village in the traditional sense, more like Temple Bar in Dublin than a remote Chinese locality, but it is a locality given over totally to art, most of it reproduced. It's a business model that you see in many Asian countries, especially Vietnam. But like so many other things in China, it's the scale in the Dafen colony that takes your breath away – the thousands of artists working here are supplying at least 300 galleries. At the front you have the galleries, out the back the painters knock out the knock-offs.

'We have about 16 artists working for this shop. Different customers like different things. The Russians like Tintoretto. They also like this painting of the maidens kissing. We've sold 50 of these Tintorettos at least. We can do 100 copies for you if you want,' says Xu.

She's wearing a smart business suit – corporate clients are a big source of revenue. And the suits

Steve Fossett and co-pilot Mark Rebholz about to land near Clifden in Galway after retracing Alcock and Brown's historic first trans-Atlantic flight from St John's in Newfoundland. Photograph: Eric Luke.

come in droves from the rapidly expanding city of Shenzhen. Every office block you go to, the lobby has been decorated by Dafen's finest. Every plush villa you visit has at least some Dafen wares on the walls. Newly rich chief executives commission paintings in the style of their favourite artist – all perfectly legal, and all perfectly original. Others opt for a style, usually Impressionism, and have all the big names represented in their offices – Renoir, Manet, Monet, whatever you want. 'How about this?' Xu goes off to the back of the shop and re-emerges with the Mona Lisa herself, that discreet smile perfectly captured by an artist working on around €7 a day. The Norwegian national gallery recently had its copy of Edvard Munch's *The Scream* stolen. If they're stuck, they could do worse than ask Xu for a copy by their in-house painters. If they're interested, she has one ready to go.

The most popular work of art on offer, by a big margin, is Vincent Van Gogh's *Sunflowers*. There are thousands for sale in the shops of Dafen, which have been recently renovated and reorganised to deal with all the visitors. Walk through a door at the back of Xu Yi's shop and you come into a long corridor, lined with easels and painters busily working on the latest masterpieces. Neighbouring artist Lu Xingping is doing *The Flowers in the Vase*. By Van Gogh, of course.

'It takes about one-and-a-half days to do a Van Gogh like this one,' she says, dabbing blobs of oil paint onto the canvas, occasionally referring to a small catalogue copy of the original. 'I went to art school and I found it hard to make ends meet painting my own things. The most popular painting depends on market demands really. Sometimes one kind is popular, sometimes another kind is popular,' says Lu, who lives with her family in Dafen. She gestures to the painting with her brush. 'I don't know how many times I've painted this picture but I've been doing it for over 10 years. Probably hundreds of times.'

Something looks slightly wrong with the painting. It's a reasonably accurate representation, but something is askew, out of place. Are the colours different? 'Yes, some people want me to change the background – this painting had a white background originally. If people have a different colour scheme in their house, they might want a blue Van Gogh rather than a yellow one. It depends on the client. We'll do whatever they want.'

A green book of art history, *100 Great Paintings*, functions as a catalogue for the painters. The index at the back is a list of what you can buy. A Surrealist masterpiece seems like the most relevant choice in these circumstances. So, any chance of a nice René Magritte for above my sofa? No joy – not in the catalogue. A Dali, however, is do-able. 'Salvador Dali is very hard: lots of colours, and lots of detail. But we can do it. Just give us a bit of time.' She flicks through another catalogue until we come to *The Apotheosis of Homer* by Salvador Dali. Her eyes dart around the picture. She starts to nod. 'Give me a couple of weeks. I can do it.' Or perhaps her husband can do it more easily in the studio, she adds.

Walking the two streets across to her husband's studio, there are groups of people stretching large canvases and making big wooden frames. Dafen has plenty of room for both the sacred and the profane. In one shop is an enormous reproduction of Adolph von Menzel's wonderful *A Flute Concert of*

Xu Yi, a gallery owner in Dafen, southern China, with copies of Munch's The Scream *and da Vinci's* Mona Lisa. *Photograph: Clifford Coonan.*

Frederick the Great at Sanssouci. This is a wonderful piece, but not massively well known unless you had followed its progress from the Old National Gallery in Berlin to exhibition in London and back again. On the opposite wall stands a painting of the the Brazilian Holy Trinity of Ronaldo, Roberto Carlos and Rivaldo holding hands. Both works are painted with the same care and skill. You work out which is sacred, which profane.

Up five flights of stairs to the artist's garret and the smell of oils is strong. In the philosophy of Confucius, imitation is the sincerest form of flattery. Ling Junqi's studio is a truly Confucian place. There are racks of the inevitable *Sunflowers* on display, hanging out to dry, alongside a couple of other Van Goghs. Ling has been a painter for 12 years. 'When I graduated I was supposed to be an art teacher but the salary and the prospects weren't that good. So I left my home town and came to Shenzhen to try and find a better life,' he says.

In a country where everything can be counterfeited, Dafen is relatively harmless – fake paintings are less of a threat than fake car parts or medicines. And it's not exactly the fine art equivalent of the local pirate DVD shop. There are few enough works by living artists on show – the maxim that only paintings by dead artists sell was never truer than in Dafen. This is more about Renoir than Lucien Freud.

'I do my own work as well but I'm not as famous as the others so I can't sell them for a good price,' says Ling. 'I keep my painting as a hobby and I'm looking for an opportunity. I really want to be a professional artist but for the moment I'm doing copies. I don't really like doing commercial painting but it's the pressure of reality. I love art, I love Van Gogh, I love Monet.'

Ling is energetic and enthusiastic, though long hours of painting reproduction masterpieces is tiring him out, he says. But he'll stick with it: his wife and he have a child to support and, now, a gallery in the painters' village to fund. 'I remember the details of the paintings over the years,' he says.

The painters and gallery owners have a hard time making ends meet – 'rents have become expensive in the village since they modernised everything'. National pride is strong and Ling is keen to show it's not just the Old Masters of Europe. He pulls out a catalogue of work by one of China's top painters, Zao Wuji. 'I love him. I try to copy him too,' he says, grinning, and casting an appreciative eye over the canvas as he unscrolls a brilliant reproduction of one of Zao Wuji's better known pieces. 'Not as good as the real thing, maybe. But it's not bad, now, is it?'

FRIDAY, 1 JULY 2005

Youth in Vanguard of Forging Political Will

Carl O'Brien

They are young, naïve maybe, but more streetwise than previous generations of protesters. 'We know you can't change the world through donating money, but you can through changing awareness of issues,' says Edel McCabe (15), a fourth-year student, holding a Make Poverty History banner in Parnell Square, Dublin. 'It's gradual, it won't happen overnight. It's better to make people aware, to spread the message and put pressure on politicians.'

Twenty years ago Bob Geldof appealed to Live Aid watchers in siren tones that we needed more money. Today, the Make Poverty History campaign, and the broad base of campaigners it has attracted, recognise a solution is more complex. The campaign, which focuses on trade justice, debt cancellation and better aid, sees the G8 summit as a major opportunity to build the political momentum needed to secure progress on those issues.

Edel is one of thousands of young people who joined in yesterday's protest in what is one of the most unlikely of coalitions. There are missionaries, communists, anarchists, environmentalists, students,

Make Poverty History protesters marching from Parnell Square to Merrion Square. Photograph: David Sleator.

capitalists, feminists, all of whom have signed up to support one of the broadest campaigns in modern political history. Sr Máire Dillon (78), a Columban missionary on yesterday's march, is travelling to Edinburgh this weekend with her 13-year-old grandnephew. Having worked in Alongapo in the Philippines, nicknamed 'sin city' due to the widespread prostitution there, she says she became engaged in issues of global justice. 'I started to see the root cause of poverty and the structures that cause global injustice … to me, justice has a basic Christian dimension. We're called on to love each other, and that includes the poorest of the poor.'

Amid the heaps of white T-shirts, ID badges and posters at the campaign headquarters on Burgh Quay, Hans Zomer, of the development agency Dóchas, a long-time activist, says the campaign message is spreading. 'This is about awareness-raising, not fundraising. Tackling poverty isn't about donating a fiver, like with Live Aid. People are much more aware now that this is a political issue, and that what's required is political will. 'It's a structural issue. There are man-made choices which rich countries take that have an enormous impact on people across the world. The sense of global injustice is something young people feel particularly. They have an acute sense of what's fair. They're not as open to justifying it, or saying it'll always be like that.'

Make Poverty History has not been without its detractors. John O'Shea of Goal has angrily denounced aspects of the campaign, such as delivering more aid in the absence of dealing with corruption and military exports. In the wider Irish Make Poverty History campaign, an alliance of more than 40 NGOs, groups have had to bite their tongues on some issues in the interests of consensus building. Political parties may be banned officially from the campaign, but banners of parties such as Fine Gael, Labour, the Greens and the Socialist Party appeared among the thousands of marchers yesterday.

Standing at Parnell Square holding a red banner, Eugene McCartan (50), a member of the Communist Party, acknowledges there might be difference on ideological issues like trade. 'But we have things that we share in common, like a belief that economic structures are responsible. We can come together in solidarity with those people who are trying to bring about their own liberation,' says McCartan, whose two children, Almha (9) and Oisín, are carrying smaller banners. 'When you have belief and passion, you can look to the horizon and to hope.'

Nessa Ní Chasaide, one of the campaign co-ordinators involved in a range of NGOs over the last decade, agrees. 'In terms of ideology or whatever, our manifesto clearly states what we want to achieve. We may have different backgrounds, but there is a coherence and unity in our aims,' she said. 'We realise that progress on issues relating to poverty can be so slow, it can be difficult to see change. The Make Poverty History campaign is focusing on this problem, so we're coming together in a sense of global unity. We want to see concrete movement on aid, trade, and debt in 2005.'

Shelia White from Rathfarnham in Dublin celebrates with her FETAC certificates in Computer Literacy, Social History and Living in a Diverse Society, given to her the day before her 99th birthday. Photograph: David Sleator.

THURSDAY, 7 JULY 2005

Africa Needs More than Just Slogans

Paul Cullen

It's heady stuff, all this talk of making poverty history. World salvation, it seems, is only a few slogans away. Drop the debt! Double the aid! Tear down the trade barriers! In this way, we are told, a bright new future of affluence and equality for all is just around the corner – if only those elderly G8 men meeting on a Scottish golf course will play ball. But are campaigners selling just another miracle-fix for the new century? And are they guilty of oversimplification for propagating the notion that the poverty endured by half the planet can be eliminated by the wave of a few western leaders' wands?

The resort to simple statements is understandable, given the complexities of debt cancellation, aid conditionalities and tariff negotiations. Activists campaigned on these issues for years without success, until they translated their demands into easily understood slogans and enlisted the support of the rock glitterati.

Today they stand at a historic juncture, with the leaders of the rich countries finally poised to take action. In response to the effective campaigning of Bono et al on the poverty issue, the G8 leaders have come up with a debt relief package worth $40 billion. In September, many world leaders will tell a UN summit they plan to double their aid budgets (second time around for Bertie). Ongoing world trade negotiations are likely to lead shortly to a further dismantling of trade barriers.

It should be a moment of celebration, and yet the niggling questions won't go away. How effective is aid? Who benefits from the debt write-offs? Who will win from trade liberalisation? Haven't we been here before? Few of these questions have been addressed in the effort to build a broad coalition to put pressure on the G8 leaders. How many campaigners know, for instance, that academic studies are at best sceptical about the benefits of overseas aid? Or that aid programmes, Ireland's included, are not generally monitored and evaluated by independent referees not involved in the aid industry?

Over $500 billion of aid to sub-Saharan Africa over recent decades has not prevented the continent's slide into stagnation. Irish Government Ministers boast that we have the best aid programme in the world, because most of our assistance is 'real' aid that actually reaches the poor, but what does that say about other countries' aid efforts?

How many campaigners are aware that debt relief programmes have been ongoing for almost 40 years? Or that the easiest way for a state to get rid of its debt is simply to refuse to pay it? Argentina did this and hasn't noticeably suffered as a result. 'The truth is that much of Africa's debt has been fictional for a long time,' William Easterly, economics professor at New York University and a former World Bank official, points out. 'When the debtors had difficulty coming up with the repayments, creditors gave new loans, postponed the repayment of old loans, or forgave the old loans altogether.'

Further, how many campaigners calling for fair trade are aware that the EU already allows (or is about to) duty-free access to imports from the 50 least-developed countries? As Alan Matthews of TCD's economics department points out, the main tariff barriers affecting the poorest countries are increasingly not those imposed by rich states, but those which prevent them exporting to middle-income developing countries such as China and India, which happen also to have the fastest-growing economies.

The G8 decision to cancel the debts of 18 poor countries has been criticised as too little, too late. Éamonn Meehan of Trócaire observes that it won't wipe out all the debts in some countries; because of the exclusion of some debts, Ethiopia's indebtedness, for example, will drop by just 29 per cent.

But should Ethiopia be qualifying for this write-off? Or Uganda or Rwanda, two other countries included in the package? Ethiopia's government spent millions on a pointless civil war with Eritrea that killed 70,000 between 1998 and 2000. Last month, its soldiers killed dozens of unarmed protesters on the streets of Addis Ababa, a fate unlikely to befall their equivalents this week in Edinburgh. Uganda and Rwanda are among seven countries implicated in the civil war in Congo, which has led to millions of deaths.

Due up on the next list of qualifying countries are Sudan and Somalia, hardly paragons of tolerance and democracy. All of those countries spend multiples of what Ireland devotes to defence, notwithstanding their horrendous poverty. John O'Shea of Goal believes the debt relief package, while well-intentioned, is 'naïve and gullible'. 'Has it occurred to anyone that a country whose debt is relieved might go out and buy arms with the money?'

This is a key point; existing debt relief initiatives have helped some countries in small ways – by, for example, allowing more Tanzanian children attend primary school or by immunising more Mozambicans – but there are insufficient safeguards to prevent governments spending freed-up funds on arms or, indeed, borrowing more money for similar purposes.

Debt isn't necessarily such a bad thing – after all, no one in Ireland these days loses any sleep over our €38 billion national debt. There is a case for saying that the debt burden in some countries is so crippling that relief is necessary. However, this needs to be strictly monitored as well as being tied to the same standards of governance and good behaviour as we would demand closer to home. It isn't clear that such conditions are being attached.

It's the same story with aid. Meehan acknowledges that aid has 'a bad name in some quarters' because of the way projects were devised and the money disbursed. However, he places the blame for this on the fact that the programmes were built around 'pet projects' drawn up in headquarters offices in Europe and the US. The result was incoherence, and a large amount of politically-motivated aid, such as the support for Mobutu's dictatorship in the Congo during the Cold War.

The trouble is that the world is full of silver-tongued rulers who will argue persuasively that they are different from their predecessors and will put aid to good use. In the 1980s, Robert Mugabe was a highly regarded Jesuit-educated guerrilla leader who led Zimbabwe to independence. He was courted by Dr Tony O'Reilly and The Irish Times invited him to address a prestigious colloquium as recently as 1997. Today he's a corrupt and brutal dictator presiding over the destruction of his country.

It was the same story with Bokassa, Moi, Museveni and many others, all of whom had their admirers until the scales fell from their innocent eyes. O'Shea remarks: 'We're being taken for the biggest ride in history as we get caught up in the excitement of it all. Everyone loves to give out about the banks, but who's prepared to stand up to the tyrants?'

Co-ordination, too, remains a major problem with aid delivery. Dozens of donor states, hundreds and thousands of aid agencies, are often tripping over each other to deliver help in an emergency. Far more than aid or debt relief, trade has the potential to liberate Africa from poverty. Unfortunately, its share of world trade has been declining in recent decades.

Given the scale of the developing world's problems, doing nothing is not an option. The good news is that there are plenty of imaginative ideas out there. Economist Jeffrey Sachs has made practical proposals for tackling extreme poverty, by spending money on fighting HIV/Aids and malaria, and building infrastructure to encourage trade.

Security is the missing ingredient in the lives of many Africans, so a small arms treaty, the creation of a meaningful UN intervention force and the pursuit of tyrants should form part of any solution put forward by the G8.

Applying the principle of 'follow the money', western governments should also pursue their banks in order to retrieve the estimated $80 billion stolen by kleptocrats over recent decades. Western enterprises operating in Africa should be required to disclose the payments they make, so as to deter bribery, and a firm track should be kept of resources such as diamonds and oil, which are so often used to fund conflict.

Complex problems require complex solutions, much more than a rush to catchy phrases and celebrity endorsement.

FRIDAY, 8 JULY 2005

London Attack puts World on Alert

Frank Millar, in London

Major capitals around the world were on the highest state of security alert last night following yesterday's London bombings, which British prime minister Tony Blair says were clearly timed to coincide with the opening of the G8 summit at Gleneagles.

Over 50 people are believed to have died, with the toll expected to rise following four no-warning bomb attacks on London's transport network which left more than 700 injured, almost 100 of them described last night as serious. Doctors said many of those who survived the attacks would face multiple surgery.

British anti-terrorist police are working on the assumption that the atrocity was committed by an Islamic group, possibly linked to al-Qaeda. An unverifiable claim of responsibility was posted on an al-Qaeda linked website. 'Britain is now burning with fear, terror and panic,' a message claimed.

In fact, emergency services and ordinary people reacted with a mixture of professionalism and stoicism. The city's transport system was shut down immediately and a practised emergency action plan was implemented. As part of it, Metropolitan Police Commissioner Sir Ian Blair made mid-morning broadcasts urging people in London to remain where they were and others not to travel to the city.

Last night, all West End theatres were closed. There was evidence of the city's famed wartime spirit as the Salvation Army opened three of its churches where people could sleep if they could not get home. Hotels also provided stranded commuters with blankets and shower facilities throughout the day. The Thames clipper services ran a free service throughout the evening.

Mr Blair was forced to leave Gleneagles to chair a meeting of the cabinet's Cobra emergency co-ordinating committee in Downing Street. President Mary McAleese led Irish condemnation of the attacks. In a message to Queen Elizabeth, she expressed sympathy on behalf of the Irish people. Taoiseach Bertie Ahern deplored what he called 'wanton violence' against the innocent which would not influence how G8 did its business.

While not precisely simultaneous, the four attacks within the hour – three targeted at the

One of the defining images of the terrorist attacks on London was a series of camera-phone pictures taken by a passenger, Liza Pulman, as she and others were evacuated along tunnels beneath King's Cross Underground station.

One of the other defining images of the London bombings: a medical orderly helps a woman whose face is masked by an anti-burns cover as she is evacuated from Edgware Road Underground station. Photo: Gareth Cattermole/Getty.

Underground, one on a double-decker bus – evoked memories of the Madrid train bombings. Seven people died immediately in the first blast, on a train 100 yards from Liverpool Street station at 8.51 a.m. Five minutes later, 21 people died in the worst single bombing, which was on an underground train between Russell Square and King's Cross stations. At 9.17 a.m., seven people met their deaths in a blast on a train at Edgware Road Underground station and 30 minutes later, at least two people died instantly when a blast ripped the roof off a number 30 bus at Tavistock Place.

Before flying back to Scotland, however, Mr Blair vowed the perpetrators would not succeed in changing or dividing the British people. In a televised statement from Number 10 he said: 'It is through terrorism that the people that have committed these terrible acts express their values and it is right at this moment that we demonstrate ours. I think we all know what they are trying to do. They are trying to use the slaughter of innocent people to cow us, to frighten us out of doing the things that we want to do, trying to stop us from going about our business as we are entitled to do, and they should not and must not succeed.'

The London Underground network was not expected to re-open until this morning. Buses were running again last night in central London and rail services appeared to be operating from most mainline train stations. Heathrow Airport was operating normally although delays were inevitable as many passengers had difficulty reaching the airport. Eurostar's London to Paris rail service was running although passengers from the continent were being advised not to travel. Regular security checks were carried out on all buses, at bus stations and garages.

Questions about the absence of any intelligence alerting authorities to yesterday's attacks, the lowering of the official threat assessment and about the resourcing and efficiency of the security services, were effectively put on hold as opposition leaders Michael Howard and Charles Kennedy rallied behind Mr Blair's robust response to the bombers.

Queen Elizabeth led the British people in an open message expressing her sympathy to all those affected and the relatives of those killed and injured. Pope Benedict said the attacks were 'barbaric acts against humanity' in a message to the Archbishop of Westminster Cardinal Cormac Murphy-O'Connor. At Gleneagles, US president George Bush said there was 'an incredibly vivid contrast' between the work at the G8 to alleviate poverty and the 'evil' of those wanting to kill.

FRIDAY, 8 JULY 2005

'I Felt Blood and Knew it Wasn't all Over'

Lynne O'Donnell

In a city of more than a few survivors, Michael Hemmings yesterday described himself as one of the luckiest men alive. Standing outside the Royal London Hospital, his right eye swathed in a thick white bandage, the right side of his face and neck burned and lacerated, he described himself as 'an exceptionally lucky man'. Mr Hemmings was on the first London Underground train targeted in the co-ordinated terrorist attacks.

Having changed his normal weekday travel plans, he was sitting on a packed train taking him from Liverpool Street, among London's biggest and busiest stations, towards Aldgate, less than a kilometre away. At 8.51 a.m. as the first of four deadly explosions was detonated across an arc of London from east to west, Mr Hemmings saw a flash of yellow light and was showered with glass as the windows of his carriage imploded. Seven people were killed in that explosion.

'I wanted to get into the carriage where the explosion happened, but it was busy so I got into another carriage,' he said. 'The bomb must have been within 10 feet of me, but it was in the next carriage … I thought I wasn't going to get out of it. It was so dark. I touched my hand to my face and I felt the blood and I knew it wasn't all over [for me] yet.' In the darkness that followed the blast, there was silence, he said. 'Then the emergency lights came on and there was panic.' Many people around him began screaming, he said. Others attempted to calm them down while they waited for help.

After what witnesses said was a lapse of up to 25 minutes, help arrived and passengers were escorted along the tracks back to Liverpool Street or forward to Aldgate station. Ambulances and police cars swept in and out of both stations, which were rapidly cordoned off by police, throughout the day as the rescue effort continued.

Mr Hemmings was one of dozens of people ferried to the Royal London Hospital aboard a double-decker bus. The hospital treated around 200 people, including 10 seriously injured and six who were described as critical. Mr Hemmings said: 'Above ground there was general shock among the emergency services. I was angry at first at the type of people who had done this. I was shocked that emergency services didn't get there faster. I spoke to them about that, and they said there were concerns about another bomb.'

Across London, hospitals treated hundreds of people. Andy Trotter, of London Transport Police, said patients were treated for chest and blast injuries and broken bones. Some had limbs amputated. More than 300 were treated for minor injuries. The close proximity of medical professionals to the carnage helped save lives, said British Medical Association chairman Dr Peter Holden, who was among 14 doctors and a nurse who emerged from their blood-spattered building in Tavistock Place to use skills that haven't been needed since the height of the IRA's terrorist campaign.

'Many of these doctors had not used these skills for upwards of 20 years,' said Dr Holden. 'But it is amazing what the human body and mind can do when the skills are remembered.'

TUESDAY, 12 JULY 2005

Tolerating Corruption at Home

Fintan O'Toole

In all the debates about African poverty, there is now a broad understanding that change can't happen until the continent gets rid of its kleptocratic rulers. Using the polite euphemism for corruption, the Minister of State in charge of development issues, Conor Lenihan, told the Oireachtas Joint Committee on Foreign Affairs last month that we must 'treat the issue of good governance as an important development issue in its own right wherein we help, encourage and, where necessary, pressurise our partner governments'.

Two years ago this month, Bertie Ahern, launching the UN Development Programme's Human Development Report, told the world: 'If we are to retain public support for the level of overseas development assistance necessary to fight extreme poverty, the fight against corruption must be intensified.'

African kleptocrats: bad. Irish kleptocrats: wonderful.

That is the very word used by the same Bertie Ahern a fortnight ago on *The Last Word* programme on Today FM: 'I think that long after he's gone, people will say Charles Haughey was a wonderful person.'

And this was no rush of blood to the head. The Taoiseach is on a personal campaign to rehabilitate the reputation of his old mentor. He was on the *This Week* programme on RTÉ on Sunday, telling us that Haughey's government in the late 1980s is directly responsible for the State's current prosperity: 'The policies that were pursued in that 1987/89 government are why we are where we are today, and the person who helped to turn that around was Charlie Haughey.'

So while the Government is pressurising African governments to eliminate corruption, it is also suggesting that corruption doesn't really matter. Charles Haughey stole money from Fianna Fáil while Bertie Ahern was party treasurer. He stole taxpayers' money directly by using the Fianna Fáil leader's allowance, for whose bank account Bertie Ahern was a co-signatory, to pay for personal indulgences. He stole public money indirectly by functioning as the pinnacle of the Ansbacher Cayman tax evasion scheme for himself and his golden circle. And he is now being held up by the Taoiseach as a national saviour.

The notion that the Haughey-MacSharry government of 1987 to 1989 created the boom of the 1990s is mere propaganda, based on a classic logical fallacy: that because A happened after B, it happened as a result of B. The winter sun may rise after I have my porridge, but it would be rather odd to conclude that the consumption of porridge causes the sun to rise. The same is true of the sequence of events that preceded the Irish boom of the 1990s. That the economy began to grow rapidly after Haughey's government cut public spending and services is undoubtedly true. But if there is any relationship of cause and effect between these two events, it is at best a tenuous one.

In the first place, the fiscal crisis of the 1980s was partly caused by the corruption which Haughey embodied and protected. The Exchequer deficit came about partly from over-spending and partly from the failure to raise enough revenue because massive tax evasion by the well-to-do was tolerated. Ordinary workers paid penal tax rates to

Miss Piggy attempting to beat the world record for pig jumping from a five-metre platform at the Royal Darwin show in Australia after a month in training. Photograph: Peter Solness/Getty.

subsidise these rich scroungers, and this lunatic taxation of modest incomes devastated economic growth. The cosy relationship between a small golden circle of native business people and some key members of the political elite held back the economy.

Nothing stifles enterprise more than the knowledge that the system is crooked and that rivals with an inside track already have it sewn up. Nothing stifles innovation more effectively than the easy availability of nice little earners.

Haughey's sickening hypocrisy in pandering to reactionary Catholicism also had economic consequences. One of the eventual reasons for the Irish boom was the influx of women to the workforce. Haughey did his best to impede this critical social and economic development with his craven and stupid Family Planning Act, aimed at making access to contraception difficult and expensive.

When Haughey and MacSharry started to tackle the fiscal crisis in 1987, it was the path of least resistance, supported by the political opposition, the trade unions and the media. Crucially, Haughey made sure that the burden of adjustment fell exclusively on the poor and the vulnerable. He called a general election in 1989 because the Dáil had voted, against his wishes, to establish a £400,000 trust fund for people with haemophilia who had contracted HIV from blood products supplied by the State.

In the course of that election, Haughey, and his sidekicks Ray Burke and Pádraig Flynn, received substantial personal donations. Africa's most brazen rulers would surely have applauded the sheer effrontery.

WEDNESDAY, 20 JULY 2005

Touring Troubles on a Rainy Afternoon

From Malin to Mizen – stage 2, by Rosita Boland

Now, let's get this straight from the start. I'm Irish, and I know it rains in this country. I know it rains quite a lot, consistently, and that most years the term 'Irish summer' is an oxymoron. I'm used to it. Rain is entirely unremarkable, and to be expected. And naturally, I rarely carry an umbrella, because that's being defeatist.

I'm in Derry, on my leg of the Malin Head to Mizen Head run. And it's raining. Really raining. (This is the week before the heatwave.) And, as usual, I am umbrella-less. Bus is my mode of transport, although I won't be properly boarding a bus for some time yet. No, first there is The Picture to be got out of the way. Ninety-nine point nine per cent of the time as a journalist, you thankfully manage never to be the subject of The Picture, because you are rarely writing about yourself. Today, my luck is out. The lens is on me. And since the photograph has to indicate my location, it must include a recognisable Derry landmark, which of course means it must be outdoors.

So here we are, the very patient photographer Trevor McBride and me. I'm alternately grinning and grimacing like a prize eejit – with the Guildhall in the background. My aversion to cameras is so great that I've never owned one, and I find it almost impossible not to automatically scowl when a lens points in my direction. Plus it's raining. Did I mention that? Pouring. Bucketing. Lashing. There is no way it's going to stop for hours, so we have to do the picture now: Trevor is a busy bloke and has other jobs lined up. Passers-by are falling about with mirth at the sight of the pair of us streaming water like twin falls. Whatever about

En route... Photograph: Trevor McBride.

people and water, cameras and water definitely don't go together, so Trevor is even less happy than I am at the whole lark.

Finally, it's over. But I have to be honest. I'm soaked, it's still raining, and I feel a tad unenthusiastic about immediately exploring the highways and byways of the town Phil Coulter loves so well. I head for shelter and have black coffees instead. After this, my clothes have dried on me somewhat, and my temper has improved marginally.

While I've been staring out the window drinking far too much coffee, I have noticed that Derry has an open-top bus tour. It also leaves from the Guildhall, which is right beside me. As my mode of transport on this leg is bus, what better than a bus tour within the bus journey? Ergo, I get on the red City Sightseeing Derry bus when next it passes, and sit upstairs, under the roof at the front, since it is still raining.

I am the only person on the bus. Not just the only person sitting upstairs, but the only punter on the bus at all. Apart from the driver, and the knowledgable guide, Anna Connolly, who decides she might as well switch off the microphone and come to sit beside me instead of giving the usual running commentary.

She asks have I heard of the Troubles. I tell her I have. Once I open my mouth, she knows I'm Irish, and since I'm the only person on the bus, she also knows a potted history lesson isn't necessary on this tour. Past the Harbour Museum, up through the Bogside and the Free Derry gable wall. Anna tells me the political murals are very popular with tourists on the bus, but that if I get off to take pictures, can I be quick about it? I assure her I won't be taking pictures.

We pass gables painted with a portrait of a child killed in crossfire ('that one symbolises the death of innocence'), one of Bernadette Devlin and women bashing bin lids, and one of Bloody Sunday. 'In the 1970s and 1980s, it wouldn't have been possible to come into these areas on an open-topped bus. We'll be seeing unionist murals too, to balance it out.' And we do. We're deep in tough-looking suburbia, staring at more gable wall paintings, this time of UVF people, and statements saying such things as 'Here lies a soldier, killed by enemies of Ulster'. The place is coming down with Union Jacks and red, white and blue bunting. Both sets of murals are so aggressive they make my head ache. I don't find it interesting or enlightening: I just find it all incredibly depressing.

My final destination is Belturbet, which I plan on reaching some time the next day, so I head into the bus station to inquire about buses that will get me there. I'm trying to get there from Derry via whatever route I like, and I fancy an overnight in Armagh, a city I've only ever passed through.

'If you want to go to Armagh by bus, you have to go to Belfast first and then change,' the polite man behind the Ulster Bus counter says to me. I look at him. Is he joking? Belfast is a considerable distance east of Armagh. I would be going round the world twice to get to Armagh if I go there via Belfast. He's not joking. I stand at the counter and remember with blinding clarity why I finally learned to drive three years ago: I decided I was too old and cantankerous to hitch any more, and I had got fed up with Ireland's appalling public transport system that makes you do mad things like go to Armagh via Belfast from Derry.

So Enniskillen it is, and I get on board, still wet, and still cross as a weasel. At Strabane, however, I am cheered by a shop-front that declares itself to be The Holy Shop. This is a new one on me. Clothes shops, kitchen shops, bookshops, and now holy shops. Sion Mills is trim and tidy; a neat village with stone-cut buildings. So is Victoria Bridge. Past Newtownstewart, I see a sign by the roadside that makes me laugh out loud: Mountjoy B & B, which must qualify for a non-existent prize for the most unfortunately inappropriate name for paid holiday accommodation in Ireland. Soon after, I fall asleep and wake up when we get to Omagh, where I have to change buses.

Poor Omagh. People will only ever think of one thing now when they hear the name Omagh. At Ballinamallard, there is more loyalist bunting, and huge Union Jacks, as there are at several stops along the way. It's like die-hard smalltown America, where the flags are almost in your face at every turn. It's so simplistic – and crude – a statement that I feel myself getting depressed again.

At Enniskillen, where I didn't think I'd be that night, I go to the Tourist Information Office, and discover there is a choice of a one-star hotel or two two-star hotels. I ask the helpful woman in the Tourist Information office to recommend one of them. 'I couldn't possibly do that,' she tells me. 'Which one would you stay in if you were visiting Enniskillen?' I ask instead. But she says she can't tell me anything about any of them, that she's not allowed to, so I exit the Tourist Information Office and hoof it off to sound them out myself. It's still raining, by the way, in case you were wondering.

After checking in to the Ashberry, I beetle off to eat. At Scoff's, I look at the menu with astonishment and wonder if the restaurateur has a small zoo outside. Apart from the usual round-up of beef, chicken and fish, there is also on offer carpaccio of crocodile, chargrilled ostrich and seared kangaroo fillet. Not creatures I would have associated with Fermanagh. I opt for the less adventurous sea-bass.

Next morning, I'm all set for the 10.30 a.m. water bus tour of Lough Erne on the MV *Kestrel*, with a stop at Devenish Island. I wait at the jetty. There are seven others also waiting. But hey, someone comes off the boat, looks us up and down and says they need 12 for the trip, so they're not going. We can come back again at 2.30 p.m. and try again, we're told. Except I can't: I'll be on the bus to Belturbet. And guess what? Right on cue, it starts raining again.

It rains all the way to Belturbet, where I arrive just in time to find out that my onwards bus to Dublin has already left and I'll have to wait hours wandering round in the rain for the next one. Oh, the Irish summer. Nothing like it.

FRIDAY, 22 JULY 2005

An Irishman's Diary

Kevin Myers

The cathedral close in Salisbury is beautiful, and provides a perfect view of a Wiltshire heaven. The wisteria rambles in fragrant, muscular sinuousness over cottage and glebe-house, the hollyhock and lupins

Alan Stanford being made up for his role as Lady Bracknell in Oscar Wilde's The Importance of Being Earnest *by an all-male cast at Dublin's Abbey Theatre. Photograph: Matt Kavanagh.*

riot with an English decorousness alongside the cut-stone pathways, as the bells of the great spire chime their sonorous melodies on the quarter hour. Daily there is matins and evensong, the choirboys' voices drifting across the lawns of green linen.

This was where Sir Edward Heath lived alone over the last decades of his life. But in a way, solitude was his natural condition, for he was a man of few social skills, and none whatever when it came to women. Possibly he was just neutral, as some men are, with no serious interest in sex or marriage or abiding companionship. Or he could just have been a homosexual who repressed those natural instincts which would otherwise have enabled him to have been a happier man.

Instead, he became this other fellow, one who was driven by single-minded ambition, who became a singular organist, a brilliant yachtsman, a fine conductor and the man who steered the UK, and thus Ireland, into what was to become the EU. In doing so, he became one of the most important men in 20th-century Irish history, playing a vital part in the transformation of this country from an economic and cultural backwater into the dynamic, immigrant-inhaling country that it is today.

Yet he was a wretched prime minister, for he was utterly unable to assess how other people thought and felt; a Finnish pastor at carnival time in Rio. His insularity was compounded by his inability to confront. He was very much of that

Max from Circus Vegas, accompanied by his trainer Alexander Scholl, takes a shower using water from the lake at Kilruddery House near Bray in Co. Wicklow. Photograph: Joe St Leger.

wartime generation of British politicians who put unity of effort before clarity of thought. He was a political unitarian, and did not understand that even in a democracy, some issues – such as the trade union autocracy which was killing Britain – lay beyond all resolution by negotiation.

His initial stewardship of Northern Ireland was catastrophic, not least because he listened solely to the advice of soldiers and unionists. But the military were not the grammar-school officers of the people's army of his generation, but the professional military caste whose melancholy duty had been to supervise the imperial sun setting upon palm and pine. This was an often brutish, stupid business, and with brutish stupidity the British army set about the task of halting that imperial decline on almost its final frontier, the back-streets of Ardoyne and the drumlins of Armagh.

The tragedy that resulted was not of Heath's making alone. Armed with all that we know today, not one of us, from Gerry Adams to Ian Paisley, could travel back in time and give the wise counsel that would have halted the Troubles in their traps. Nonetheless, his own contribution to the Troubles was considerable, and allowing the Joint Security Committee of Unionist politicians, civil servants, RUC officers and a handful of senior soldiers to decide the policy of Her Britannic Majesty's Army, with virtually no input from Westminster, was a truly majestic one. The subsequent glories of the Falls Road curfew, internment, and Bloody Sunday were the result.

He was not so inflexible as not to learn, and learn he did: but he learnt little that was wise, and embraced much that was desperate. The power-sharing executive of 1974 was largely his confection. But with nationalist Ireland still refusing to support the very security forces that made the survival of the executive possible, as terrorists from all sides assailed the settlement the executive was in the long term doomed.

There was no long term. Heath's defeat in the general election in 1974 hastened the end of the Northern Ireland Executive, as unionist voters virtually extinguished executive-supporting politicians. His successor, Harold Wilson, managed to be simultaneously cowardly, inept, ill-informed, arrogant and foolish: and thus the cross-community power-sharing executive perished, as indeed did its successors, and as their successors are doomed to do also.

By this time the two countries were within the EU, which was to be Edward Heath's greatest triumph. But politically he was now fatally wounded, and he withdrew to the long grass where his political career faded and died in the sere Westminster Serengeti of failure. He was replaced by Margaret Thatcher who, aided by great good fortune and by her considerable tactical skills, took on the very enemies who had defeated him, and in turn defeated them.

So he retired to his yacht, his keyboard, his podium and his cathedral close in Salisbury. One by one these diversions faded, until only the close remained. Ted Heath spent his final decades in his delightful Avonside house, alone but for his two Special Branch officers. The three of them would spend much of the day in The Boot pub in nearby Berwick St James, each growing majestically in girth, jowl and chin, as Heath's face erupted with sunbursts of broken blood vessels and the grim brown stains of a surly, discontented liver.

Alas, infirmity did not weaken him nor hasten his end; he was condemned to live. So each dawn he woke in the close to yet another death-avoiding day: by noon, he was back in the pub, without conversation, friend or true companionship, silently, remorselessly drinking with his minders, bitterly contemplating the failure of the past three wasted decades. And so it continued, deathless year after bell-ringing, matins-singing, deathless year until, last weekend, mortality mercifully and finally intervened.

The cathedral close of Salisbury is beautiful, and provides a perfect view of a Wiltshire hell.

FRIDAY, 29 JULY 2005

A Long Time Coming

Editorial

It has been a long time coming and somewhat diminished for that. Yet, history could be in the making on the island of Ireland with the publication of the IRA statement ordering an end to its 'war' from 4 p.m. yesterday.

There have been many false dawns, most recently last December, when democratic Ireland was conned by the republican movement and demonstrated to have been so shortly thereafter, with the Northern Bank robbery, the money-laundering and the brutal killing of Robert McCartney. Only time will determine whether the IRA has gone into a new mode.

It will be a seminal day, nonetheless, if the republican movement does what it says it will do now. And there is reason to believe it may. The worldwide war on terror has changed the political climate for Sinn Féin and the IRA in ways that could not have been imagined a few years ago. Suicide bombing has devalued the so-called 'armed struggle' as a means of achieving political aims. And there is less willingness among the people of Ireland – nationalist and unionist – to tolerate ambiguity on paramilitarism, money-laundering and criminality any longer.

Former IRA prisoner Séanna Walsh who read, on behalf of the IRA's mythical spokesman P O'Neill, the organisation's statement saying its 'armed campaign' was over and calling on its members to 'dump arms'.

There is no doubt that yesterday's IRA statement is different to those issued before. For one thing, the republican movement is in total control of the commitments made. It is not dependent on any government or party to honour them. The republican movement is speaking to, and for, itself without any guaranteed parachute into the political process. And, to that end, the IRA leadership has ordered an end to the armed campaign and the dumping of all arms. It has instructed its members not to engage in 'any other activities whatsoever' – a phrase, one presumes, to cover criminality – and to operate from now on through exclusively peaceful means.

This seems to be the most positive and least ambiguous statement ever issued by the IRA's leadership. There is less republican theology. The language is more clear. The corollary is that the words can only have one meaning. The IRA seems to be committing the republican movement to an end to the IRA as an army and an end to its ancillary activities, like the murder of Mr McCartney, knee-cappings, robberies and thuggery.

Some will argue that the statement is unclear about the IRA's new mode. What is the IRA, which presumably still remains in existence, now? Yesterday's statement would suggest it is not about to disappear. Will recruitment come to an end? Is the IRA committed to the new dispensation in Northern Ireland whose status can only change if a majority so decides? Are the IRA and Sinn Féin signing up to the criminal justice system? What is Sinn Féin's commitment to policing? Many other questions can be raised.

But, for all that, a defining moment in Irish politics will be reached if yesterday's words are translated into actions. Then, and only then, can it be put validly to the Rev. Ian Paisley's Democratic Unionist Party that a new government should be formed in Northern Ireland.

Emma Garvey, aged nine months, from Knocklyon in Co. Dublin in playful mood with Shane Ryan of the Dublin GAA football team when the Leinster champions visited Our Lady's Hospital for Sick Children in Crumlin with the Delaney Cup. Photograph: Brenda Fitzsimons.

MONDAY, 1 AUGUST 2005

Winner of €115m Goes Away to Think About it All

Carl O'Brien, in Garryowen

Dolores McNamara's hands began to shake. It was a day after her lottery win and she had just sat down with a solicitor, who was telling her of the opportunities, responsibilities and dangers ahead. After he spoke, she looked at her hands which by now were trembling uncontrollably.

Up until that point, the mother of six from Garryowen had been a picture of composure, even if most people around her had been losing their head. Her best friend Imelda Eaton had been crying her eyes out. Her sister Deirdre O'Donovan had felt hysterical. Her neighbours at the Track Bar, where she found out she had won on Friday night, were wild-eyed with delight.

'After speaking to the solicitor, we realised she was in shock up until that point,' says Niall Purcell, Deirdre's partner. 'When she got the legal advice, it sank in. If she had won €2 million, you could deal with it. Maybe give up your job or retire. But that kind of money, it's almost dangerous. Very dangerous. She's gone away for a few days to think about it all.'

Just how €115 million will begin to affect Dolores (45), a former dressmaker, her husband Adrian, a bricklayer, their six children aged 13 to

27, and three grandchildren, is impossible to say. It is also certain to have an unfathomable impact on the wider circle of friends and neighbours surrounding her in the working-class suburb of Garryowen, a patchwork of housing estates on the southern approach to Limerick city. 'She's a very level-headed woman,' says Imelda. 'But that kind of money? Who knows … We're working-class people. We wouldn't know what to do with it.'

A day after the win there is still a giddy afterglow at the Track Bar, in the shadow of the local greyhound stadium, where Dolores and her friends realised she had won on Friday night. There are shrieks of laughter as they watch the television news on Saturday afternoon with snippets of local comment from the shop-owner, barwoman and neighbours. At the bar are Deirdre, Niall, Imelda and Dolores's daughter, Kevanne, who are laughing in rapid bursts about the frenzied chaos of the night before.

The Friday night was just another ordinary night where Dolores and her friends gathered for a few pints. Most of her friends were involved in a small Lotto syndicate, although she hadn't taken part.

There were various quirks and twists of fate which led her to buy the ticket and be in with a one-in-76 million chance of winning the jackpot. One of them was that when she called around to Imelda's house, Imelda was in bed, so she went to the shop to kill some time. 'I was in bed – I had been up since six in the morning,' says Imelda (45), who works as a shop assistant at the Fairview filling station on the Ennis Road. 'So she went over to the shop. She'd never played EuroMillions before. So she says to the girl behind the counter, "Can you do a quickpick on that?" "You can," says the girl, so she hands over her €2. That's how it happened.'

Imelda and Dolores met up later in the evening. Dolores wasn't in good form and they talked about a few problems she was having. They ate two cream buns, joked about putting on weight and decided to go to the Track Bar for a few pints before closing.

It was 10.30 p.m. After ordering two pints of Heineken, the pair sat down with some friends of theirs in the lounge of the Track Bar. They got round to talking about the lottery draw and Dolores asked one of the women to check her numbers. 'She asked Pauline [Greer] to check them,' says Imelda. 'We'd all done a quickpick between us and hadn't won. Then Pauline says to her, "They're the right numbers." Dolores says, "Yeah, right". Next they checked the numbers at the bar and everyone's checking them. It was pandemonium … then Dolores says, "I'm going for a fag!"'

As word spread that she had won, the pub was filled with shrieks of laughter and roars of celebration. Cameras flashed and mobile phones began to ring. Imelda started crying. Outside in the darkness, Dolores smoked a cigarette, still trying to absorb what had just happened. 'When she finally realised she had won,' says Imelda, 'she turned to me and said, "I'm going to buy a house for Kevanne" [her 21-year-old daughter], who's renting a house and has kids herself.'

Amid the celebration, there was sudden panic about the lottery slip. What do you do with a piece of paper worth €115 million? Where do you put it? How do you keep it safe? 'We met my son who said to me, "Where's the ticket?"' says Imelda. 'I said, "It's here, in my pocket." He asks if the whole pub knows, and I said they did. "Get in the car – now," he says.

'We rang the guards for advice, who wouldn't believe him. He was getting annoyed, so I took the phone. I was roaring crying, totally hysterical, so then they knew we were telling the truth.' When they arrived at Henry Street Garda station, the gardaí were kind and helpful, she says, but couldn't keep it in the safe for insurance reasons. Gardaí phoned around to solicitors and eventually contacted a bank manager, who arranged for it to be placed in a vault.

Back at the Track Bar, family and friends began to gather. Dolores's husband, Adrian, a bricklayer,

A happy Dolores McNamara from Limerick after collecting her Euromillions cheque for €115 million. Photograph: Frank Miller.

who is recovering from a triple cardiac bypass operation, joined in the celebrations. Paddy Tobin, one of a family of pub owners, produced bottles of champagne and the group partied late into the night. 'She bought a round of drinks,' says Imelda, 'and got worried when she realised she only had €35 on her. Of course it didn't matter, they were on the house, but she was still thinking that way.'

At a quiet breakfast the next morning at the Moose Head, a pub owned by the Tobin family, Paddy Tobin organised for her to meet a solicitor at a nearby hotel. As well as advising them of the impact such money could have on their lives, the solicitor recommended they go away for a few days, out of the public gaze and gather their thoughts. 'Reality won't kick in until she gets the cheque,' says Niall, who met her shortly before she left. 'Then she'll turn around and say, "What the hell do I do?" She'll need all the best advice in the world to deal with it.'

Wealth is not something to which Dolores McNamara's family are accustomed. Her father, a tailor, and her mother, a nurse, emigrated to England in the 1950s, but returned to Limerick several years later. 'They were lovely, caring parents,' says Deirdre, a mother of four. 'They worked hard all their lives.'

Dolores inherited her father's tailoring skills and became a dressmaker. After leaving school she set up her own shop, Buttons and Bows, at William's Court Mall. She married and left the job when she had the first of her six children, Dawn (27). Gary was next (26), followed by Kim (24), Kevanne (21), Dean (15) and Lee (13).

Dolores, her husband and younger children live in a modest semi-detached house in St Jude's Park on St Patrick's Road, an estate close to Garryowen. 'This isn't what you'd call a very well-off area. There are lots of plumbers, plasterers, that kind of thing,' Niall says. 'There used to be a lot of unemployment, but the Celtic Tiger and Dell computers have helped a lot.'

Neighbours say Dolores is very popular and they are delighted a person so well-liked scooped the prize. Deirdre says: 'Everyone knows everyone else here and I think people are really and truly genuinely happy for her.' Kevanne adds: 'As a mother, she's been great. She's always there for me. Whatever we needed. She's brilliant.'

Among friends, she is appreciated for her capacity to listen and offer advice. 'She's always there for me,' Imelda says. 'You can tell her anything and she'll never repeat it. And she's honest – she tells you things you don't necessarily like either.'

Dolores returned a few weeks ago from a package holiday to the Turkish resort of Kusadasi, where she avoided the recent terrorist attack. She had been talking about returning to work, according to friends. For Dolores, who is so shy that she normally protests at being included in a photograph, they are hopeful she can adjust to her new-found wealth.

The requests from family members so far are reasonable enough. Kevanne is looking forward to a new house, while Lee has asked for a white horse.

'She is sensible, although that amount of money is a lot for anyone,' says Imelda. 'That will be difficult to deal with. It's not so much what she'll do with it, but how people will deal with her from now on.'

Claire Kehoe (right) and Ceri Collinghorn with puppeteer Andy Colleran promoting the opening of a beekeepers' conference in Dublin. Photograph: Matt Kavanagh.

WEDNESDAY, 10 AUGUST 2005

In the Hot Seat . . . Facing the Instant Wrath of the Texters

Hugh Linehan

For some people, August means sitting in the sun, relaxing with a cool beverage while letting the cares of the world fall from their shoulders. But for a few benighted souls like myself it means sitting alone in a darkened room, frantically shuffling pieces of paper, with one eye permanently fixed on a ticking clock while trying to conduct a telephone conversation with three people I've never met.

August sees the annual migration of bewildered print journalists across the great media divide to radio, where they discover that, actually, this broadcasting lark isn't as easy as it's cracked up to be. Firstly, there's the technology of live radio – headphones and microphones and cue buttons and cough buttons and producers talking into your ear when you're trying to hear the answer to the question you've just asked and my God what's happened to my throat, my eyes are starting to water, I have 17 pieces of paper in front of me and one of them has the name of the person I'm interviewing in three seconds' time.

Then there's the interviewees, who refuse to recognise the fact that the function of the modern Irish radio show is to fill the space between ads for property abroad, and who finally hit their oratorical stride just when the producer on the other side of the glass wall is making throat-cutting gestures with increasing desperation.

Worst of all is the infernal text machine. In the genteel world of print, we get our fair share of abusive letters and e-mails, but they usually arrive a couple of days after we've penned the offending article. The text machine is, of course, instantaneous. And frequently incomprehensible: 'I c dat yr slaggin sf, y dont u f*** off, ya west brit.'

It's an article of faith among the radio-presenting fraternity that the text machine has changed talk radio irrevocably for the better, turning it into a marvellously interactive experience for the listener. At times this is almost true, with haiku-like pearls of wisdom popping up on the screen and adding appreciably to whatever debate is going on. Frequently, though, it's like being stuck onstage in a club where the audience's mood has turned irrevocably sour. There are usually a few variations on a simple theme: 'Get that idiot off the air.' Sneakier and more dangerous are the ones which suggest you're 'better than that idiot who's usually on'. You don't want to read those out, if you hope to be invited back.

If you work for this particular newspaper, you'll inevitably find yourself being accused of pinko wishy-washiness and liberal posturing. But to balance things out there's always someone who believes you're a crypto-fascist neo-con. Worryingly, a sizeable minority think you're the same guy who's always on, and address you as such. This minority can include your regular contributors, especially the soccer pundits, who are inevitably on dodgy mobile phones at airports. And there's always someone who misses the point entirely and texts in with a request for Mariah Carey's latest for Sharon who's on the late shift in Tesco.

The radio stand-in season lasts from mid-June to early September in RTÉ, and for three weeks in August in the normal world. Go figure, licence-payers. As this writer appears courtesy of the good graces of *The Irish Times*, it would be pushing my luck a bit to take on a two-month gig, if such a thing were to be offered. Far better to dip one's toe into the radio waters for a few brief days, and retreat to the sanctuary of print before the summer stand-in radio critics get their teeth into you. The only real problem is the time of year. There is no news. Now, this is not strictly true. There is always news. But, barring natural or unnatural catastrophes, it's fair to say that the news can be a bit thin and unexciting.

There are three possible ways of dealing with this: one is to grasp the opportunity of covering those vital yet tedious issues for which the regular incumbent just hasn't found time in the preceding 11 months. The plight of the Inuit. That sort of thing. Alternatively, you can ditch the hard news agenda in favour of fluffier stuff: the latest gimcrack diet craze or celebrity pratfall. This is just too depressing to contemplate and, fortunately, usually causes howls of outrage from the texters. Finally, and most probably, you can just flail around in a panic and end up falling back on the old reliables, which are, in ascending order: 'Has reality TV gone too far?', 'Aren't Americans weird?' and 'Get Sinn Féin and the DUP on the line'.

The fact is that any radio presenter is only as good as his or her production team, who actually come up with the goods all year and have to watch in horror as this incompetent who's been foisted upon them turns their carefully-constructed programme to mush. They're the ones who have to pick up the pieces; they are the true professionals.

Me? I'm just on holidays.

THURSDAY, 11 AUGUST 2005

Everyone has a Right to Ramble

Mary Raftery

After years of beating around the thorny bush of access to private land for those walking the hills of Ireland, farmers have finally come up with a proposal. The Irish Farmers' Association claims that its Country Walkways Management Scheme 'addresses the issue of wider access to the countryside'. In reality, it does no such thing. Much of the Irish landscape is dotted with forbidding signs ordering trespassers to keep out, asserting loudly that property is private. Many habitual walkers simply ignore these, but they nonetheless have the effect of creating unease or even fear.

When a farmer was jailed last year for threatening a walker on his land, representatives of the main farming organisations met him at the prison gates on his release and publicly supported his stand against trespassers. But Sligo farmer Andy (known as 'Bull') McSharry made it clear in newspaper interviews that the issue was really about money. 'It's private property,' he said at the time. 'I'd let them through if they paid.'

That is precisely what the IFA's Country Walkways Management Scheme is also about. That each hill-walker would pay individual farmers to cross their land is clearly impracticable. The farmers' solution is, as always, to make the State pay, meaning of course the taxpayer. The cost of this scheme, we're told, will be €15 million. Recent activities by the IFA have shown that the issue of access to land is not confined just to hill-walkers. As the ESB proposes to upgrade its pylon network in a number of areas, farmers are seeking substantial compensation for having the poles on their land – up to €18,000 for each pylon, according to one report. Already these demands have delayed one upgrading scheme in Kerry.

There are two distinct and separate issues here. One is people's right of access to the countryside, the other is whether it is fair or appropriate to compensate landowners for work undertaken on pathways, signage and so forth for those walking across their land.

On the issue of right of access, the IFA's country walkways proposal is entirely silent. Even if farmers secured payment under it, there is no mechanism to legally force them to remove signs or barriers and to permit access. This absence of legislation to enshrine the right of people to walk the land is at the heart of our difficulties here in Ireland. It is a problem which was equally fraught in the United Kingdom. However, recent legislation there has now firmly established that the principle of the common good is best served by giving the public the right to walk across private farmland.

Ger Byrne (left) of Abbeylawn Timber Stables in Tinahealy, Co. Wicklow, preparing for the Dublin Horse Show. Photograph: Dara Mac Dónaill.

The Land Reform (Scotland) Act of 2003, finally introduced earlier this year, is a revolutionary piece of legislation which fundamentally alters the balance between public and private interests over most of the hills, lakes and rivers of Scotland. It gives local authorities far-reaching powers to enforce public access and to remove any attempt to block pathways. All of the arguments we have heard from farmers in this country were employed by Scottish landowners against the reforms. According to Ian McCall of the Scottish Ramblers Association, they tried insisting on getting payment for access to their land and they also argued that they should be fully indemnified by the state in the event of accidents occurring on their property.

However, in Scotland (as indeed here), landowners already enjoy considerable protection against legal action, which was considered adequate by the Scottish legislature. On the issue of payment, Scottish landowners do receive subventions for work carried out on pathways, gates, stiles and signage, but this is in no way tied to the issue of the right of people to cross their land.

Crucially in Scotland, this right of access was established before there was discussion of payment for maintenance. In this country, we appear to be approaching the matter backwards, by discussing payment before we have even begun to address the issue of right of access.

In Ireland, such debates invariably end up stymied almost before they begin, by invoking the clincher to all arguments about private property – the Constitution. Landowners have always argued that their constitutional private property rights allow them to determine who is allowed or not allowed on to their land. However, such rights are in fact far from clear and are tempered by the 'exigencies of the common good', as the Constitution expresses it. This point was reinforced last year by the report of the Oireachtas All-Party

Committee on the Constitution, which stated that 'no constitutional amendment is necessary to secure a balance through legislation between the rights of individual owners and the common good'. It is therefore a matter for the Dáil and legislation to decide where on this issue the common good lies.

Rather than muddling about, discussing means of giving farmers more money, the Government should establish once and for all the legal right of each Irish person (and indeed visitor) to tramp the hills and vales of this country in peace.

SATURDAY, 13 AUGUST 2005

Burial of the Ford Closes a Bridge to Nature

Another Life: Michael Viney

The Monday morning sunshine brought a swelling automotive glitter to the edge of the strand and, by afternoon, a new and strange burbling sound came drifting up from the sea. Binoculars found SUVs right out at the tide's edge and beyond them our very first jet skis, ploughing circles in a mackerel-calm Atlantic. A few days before, I had watched the local bottlenosed dolphins passing there: a serene procession of arching fins, seeming to make no noise at all.

The dolphins will be back, and spring tides will wipe the strand clean of tyre-marks. But recent weeks have brought another change, a permanent, man-made erasure of a little bit of what the Romans called *genius loci* or spirit of place. Topographically, our corner of coast is a tangle – even, in gleaming, mid-winter floods, quite a mess. Rock, sand and water interleave in a windswept sprawl beneath Mweelrea. An arm of the sea used to reach right in behind the dunes, a scene re-enacted now in great spring tides that join up the lakes and leave seaweed up the boreen giving access to the strand. 'Road liable to flooding', says a sign beside the bulrushes.

One of the more unruly elements of this landscape has been the river from the mountain, the Owennadornaun (a name we have failed to unravel, even with the evocative flights of Dinneen). Its upper reaches run through deep clefts in the bog and spill around bleached white boulders. Further down, picking up volume and speed in a flash-flood, it cuts through the skirt of farmland between the bog and the sea. From time to time it has broken its banks and scattered its burden of cobbles across a grassy field.

It has also been in two minds about its final exit to the strand. For a long while it entered the big lagoon behind the *machair*, scouring out the sand brought in by the spring tides. Then, one night half a century ago, it refused to take a corner in a meadow and charged on, tearing out a new course beside the salt marsh and traversing, in the process, the boreen to the strand.

Thus it created first a shallow waterfall across a sill of rock, then a pool, then a ford across the boreen: rarely any obstacle to a tractor and only sometimes, in the wake of a storm, to us in our wellington boots. The trick then was to keep one's eyes on the far shore and not look down at the rush of water, the dizzying, coppery flood. There was something ecstatic in the crossing, even if – as could happen – I needed to carry the dog.

The ford was the first line of defence for the wildness of the shore. In summer, when the stream was a mere babble over stones, it sorted out the people who would never think of taking off their shoes: their cars retreated in laborious six-point turns between the field banks. Beyond the ford, too, the boreen was rocky and rutted in a final stretch to the sand. There, the tidal channel to the lake set a second watery barrier.

But the ford was much more than an awkward quirk of a river: it set a threshold to the natural world. One never knew, walking down to it, if a heron might be standing in the pool. Dippers once

Killorglin goat catcher Frank Joy with this year's King Puck, captured near Glenbeigh, Co. Kerry. Photograph: Don MacMonagle.

nested at the waterfall, and sand martins annually in holes in the bank above. Sandpiper, grey wagtail and pied wagtail were all part of the sparkling and airy spirit of the place. Some feel for it may come across in my painting, executed at the ford in its heyday, so to speak, and bought, at a time of penury, by a passing American art dealer from Vermont.

Changes began some months ago as machines addressed the river's untamed flow and continued even as summer left the ford a totally dry stretch of stones. First the little waterfall was hacked away, as if to smooth the riverbed. And then, the other morning, I found the boreen closed to all but 'local traffic'. Down where the ford had been, a digger of Wellsian proportions was heaping rocks over twin sections of wide sewer pipe.

This created an instant hump-backed bridge, which in turn disappeared beneath many more tons of stones scooped from the bed of the river and dumped at either end. Relays of lorries brought massive glacial boulders from the stacks cleared from fields many miles away and these now armour the new, high riverbanks as they narrow to the pipes. It's a logistically impressive achievement (even, if you count the great carting of boulders, an ingenious use of natural materials), and carried out with extraordinary dispatch on the eve of the holiday week-end.

Campers and SUVs can now sweep down without hesitation to the tidal apron of the strand. The ford is left to memory. In a world where people and nature lead parallel lives, it was a crossing-place, in several more senses than one.

An athlete limbers up for the Galway 8km run. Photograph: Joe O'Shaughnessy.

MONDAY, 15 AUGUST 2005

Unique Attraction of Irish

Pól Ó Muirí

Who says tourists don't come because there are signposts in Irish? Did the good citizens of Dingle/An Daingean, Co. Kerry (but never Co. Chiarraí) wake up last Wednesday morning to this paper's lead story – about the calamitous drop in tourist numbers outside of Dublin – and think 'It's all the fault of the Irish language'?

How thin those arguments about signposts deterring visitors must seem in the light of cold, hard empty beds. Tourists are voting with their wallets. Dublin abú! The fall in numbers of visitors outside of Dublin is due to many things – bad food, bad weather, dear drink, poor facilities. The Irish language is well down the list – if it is on it at all. Ironically, I read the bad news while on holiday in the Donegal Gaeltacht – one of the few places where tourism was steady this summer, due in no small measure to parents visiting their children at Irish-language summer colleges and dedicated Irish-language courses for adults.

Since 2000, Donegal has lost 100,000 tourists but you would never realise that while Oideas Gael's courses are running in Gleann Cholm Cille. The area is remote even by the standards of Donegal and has only two natural resources – its landscape and a small Gaeltacht of native Irish speakers. Since its foundation in 1984, Oideas Gael has attracted visitors year after year who want to avail of those two resources. Classes it runs in the Irish language, dance, music and hillwalking are aimed at adults who come from all over the world – Germans, Dutch, Belgians, Swiss, Japanese and Americans. They rent accommodation, eat and

Rose of Tralee hopefuls Ashley Stanbury (Southern California), Caitlin Burke (New York), Esther Budding (New Zealand), Kerrie Doherty (Midlands UK), Michelle Emery (Queensland), Jane Bretin (Luxembourg) and Dublin rose Elena McGivney. Photograph: Dominick Walsh/Eye Focus.

drink in the locale. And they come back to Gleann Cholm Cille because it has something they want – language and traditional culture – and because it is fun.

Gleann Cholm Cille is by no means one of the strongest Gaeltacht regions in Donegal, never mind the rest of Ireland, and whether it survives another 20 years is an article for another day. However, what they have done remarkably well is to make the best of what they have; they have marketed their uniqueness in a global arena and have established a thriving business because of it.

Another example of trying to offer something new and old is Tory Island, off the Donegal coast. It is running its first ever Maritime Film Festival at the end of August, a modest event that will last only a weekend. Tim Severin's *The Brendan Voyage* will be screened and Severin will be in attendance to talk about his work. A Breton film, *The Voyage of the Saint Efflam*, will also be shown and there will be traditional music, a céilí and a boat-trip around the island. Given that it rains a lot in Donegal, spending a few hours watching a film and talking with its director will be of interest. Tory is an Irish-speaking island (pop. 180) and is associated with the likes of Saint Colm Cille. (Yes, he did get around.) Folklore and film is an unusual combination and an honest attempt to tie modern and traditional together. It is different and it is appealing. (Of course, we must not get too romantic. There is the issue of hard cash. Tourists will only stay – and rightly so – if they get good value for their euros.)

There are two templates for tourism: Planet Dublin and Ancient Ireland. Planet Dublin is doing very, very well and its attractions are many and varied. What then of ancient Ireland? There are Gaeltacht regions in seven counties out of the 26 in the State and they are to be found in all four provinces. Unquestionably, many are very small and all are under constant threat.

However fragile some may be, they are all a unique attraction. Yet they are not marketed in any meaningful sense. In fact, more often than not, any coverage of Gaeltacht regions is usually negative – it is about how much Irish costs and rows about planning. In tourism terms, however, it is clear that they have great potential to make money – if promoted properly, sensitively and intelligently.

Ireland is not Ibiza, though Temple Bar likes to think it might be. Cultural, educational and recreational tourism is obviously Ireland's niche. The Gaeltacht, with its traditional arts, crafts and (for the most part) unspoilt landscape, provides all three. Those areas without a Gaeltacht will benefit too. Language can tie hillwalking to folklore and folklore ties into the ancient archaeological sites that are scattered throughout the land. Irish is the glue (even in translation) that binds so many other aspects of our heritage together. Of course, the Gaeltacht is not the be-all and end-all of tourism but it is a starting point, something uniquely ours, a choice that only we can offer visitors.

The people of An Daingean should go down on their knees and thank God and Government that they have a resource very few others do – living Irish. It's money in the bank – if only they had the wit to open an account.

TUESDAY, 16 AUGUST 2005

Diehard Settlers Dig in for Last Stand

Nuala Haughey, in Gush Katif settlement, Gaza

Shortly before 9 a.m. yesterday, a phalanx of black-clad Israeli police officers and unarmed troops marched down the main north-south road of Gaza's Jewish settlement blocs towards the largest community of Neveh Dekalim. The residents were waiting for them and had barricaded the entrance to prevent the troops distributing eviction notices to householders, signalling the start of Israel's historical pull-out from land it has occupied since 1967.

And so began a day-long stand-off as a line of unarmed police officers, trying to look inscrutable behind sun glasses, faced a line of mostly teenage girls who sang songs and told them how, as fellow Jews, they loved them. The sweet words were accompanied by free pastries and candy lollipops, all part of the settlers' strategy to induce the security forces to refuse orders.

'The point is to show the army that we love them and ask them to don't do it,' explained Esti Hababo (15), one of some 5,000 non-residents who have swarmed to the coastal strip in recent weeks to show their support for its embattled residents.

Israel's first uprooting of settlements – all 21 in the Gaza Strip and four of 120 in the West Bank – is deeply traumatising for religious Jews, who see the occupied land as their biblical patrimony. As part of yesterday's Operation Hands to Brothers, busloads of Israeli troops entered several of the strip's more secular settlements, informing people they must leave by tomorrow or face eviction and forfeiture of some of the handsome compensation payouts. But in an apparent bid to avoid early confrontations, the army said yesterday it would not go into five settlements, including Neveh Dekalim, where they will face resistance, until evacuation day tomorrow. While some residents packed their belongings into moving vans yesterday, teenagers and families lolled around in the shade of date palm trees eating ice cream.

Every now and again, the community's public address system would burst forth with instructions for protesters; go to the gates, clear away from the gates. The atmosphere was not quite festive, but was certainly good-humoured, with people praying and singing songs about their love of the biblical land of Israel.

But there is an edginess to the ultra-nationalist teenage youths who have infiltrated the strip recently. Around midnight on Sunday, youths attacked military vehicles just outside the gates of Neveh Dekalim, smashing headlights and a windscreen and scuffling with soldiers. Yesterday, they were running around in their knitted skull caps, with the tassels of their prayer shawls flapping in the sea breeze, blowing whistles and blocking the main road with industrial size wheelie bins, tyres and curls of razor wire. 'We are just kids,' said one teenage boy to the police officers. 'Look into our eyes and see if you want to fight us.'

When settler leaders asked the crowds around Neveh Dekalim's front gate to part yesterday to let in lorries carrying freight containers to people's homes, there were grumbles from some youths that these could be Trojan horses sent in by the army.

While both settlers groups and the army expect that half of Gaza's residents will have left by the expiry of the deadline tomorrow, there are fears that diehard extremists will hole themselves up in public buildings and confront evacuating troops.

'I'm from Texas originally and I'm worried about this turning into Waco,' said one visiting settler, referring to the siege of the Branch Davidian cult in Texas in 1993. 'Some of these young people have very strong beliefs.'

An Israeli settler in Neveh Dekalim runs past a fire lit in a futile bid to deter Israeli soldiers evicting people from settlements in the Gaza Strip from which Israel withdrew in August. Photograph: David Guttenfelder/AP.

MONDAY, 22 AUGUST 2005

Hayes Lifted as Galway Dazzle

Tom Humphries, at Croke Park

Old men with leathered faces and eyes which have seen everything twice, stood and gazed out at the turf upon which the tribes were dancing. The best game ever, they said, the best game ever. Nit-picking purists and dreary scholars will argue, of course, but for context and excitement and sheer wonder, Croke Park yesterday was the place to be. The centre of the universe. There were just under 40,000 there but in years to come at least five times that amount will claim to have breathed the same northside air through these 70 minutes of hurling.

What we saw was a Galway team who were humiliated to the tune of a 19-point margin by Kilkenny last summer come to Croke Park on a big day and drive five goals past Kilkenny. The last time that was done to Kilkenny was 33 years ago (an 80-minute game and they managed a draw) and it's something which one could go a hurling lifetime without witnessing.

And Galway conceded four goals as they rode the carriage to the top of the hill and then hurtled into the valley below. They led by 11 points at one stage and were clinging on with white knuckles at the finish.

Niall Healy of Galway shrugs off John Tennyson of Kilkenny to score his third goal in their thrilling all-Ireland hurling semi-final victory at Croke Park. Photograph: Dara Mac Dónaill.

Picking stories out of the game is like scooping fish from a teeming barrel. When young Niall Healy saw Kevin Broderick warming up on the sideline early in the second half he can only have assumed that his own number was up. He was scoreless and making little impression. Broderick warmed his hamstring for the longest time. He did indeed replace Niall Healy. By then Healy had scored three goals. You've never heard such crazy boasting.

'I was lucky for the first one,' said Niall. 'Richie (Murray) took a shot and McGarry made a good save. For the second one I had a bit of space. I couldn't miss. Couldn't miss the three of them, really. I was lucky for them all.' And when he came off, did he reflect on the glory of the hour? 'Sure it doesn't matter who scores them,' he said. 'Just being in a final is what counts. I couldn't watch. I lay down and just listened to the crowd roaring. Eddie Brennan was on fire. And DJ. I just couldn't look.'

Ah. Days like this. The stories just come out with their hands up. Surrendering en masse. Ger Farragher, who had a wonderful underage career, has made the senior breakthrough this year and all winter and summer people have looked at him and said, 'Yeah he's good, but he ain't Eugene Cloonan.' The last time Galway beat Kilkenny on a big day was four years ago – same greasy sod, inferior game. Cloonan scored 2-9 that afternoon. Yesterday Ger Farragher matched that amount. 2-9 v Kilkenny. A made man. 'Words can't describe it,' he said. 'They were never going to be easily beaten. They're a super team. For us, though, next Tuesday and we're back out again. We've a final to train for.'

Galway with an All-Ireland final to train for. It feels as if the season itself is owed an apology. Freighted with inevitability, it seemed we wrote the season off as banal and grey and depressing. Cork and Kilkenny saving themselves for each other. Instead on 11 September, Galway bring the best minor side of recent years to Croke Park to play Limerick, and their seniors surf in on a wave of confidence to play a Cork team who are struggling with their form. We were watching perestroika all along, without knowing it.

'An incredible game really,' said Conor Hayes who played in a few of them himself. 'The speed, the scoring. It was open and fast. To be honest, we're a bit flabbergasted by it all.'

So was every witness to it. We'd settled back into our seats early on when Eddie Brennan, dusted down and re-inserted into the Kilkenny line-up, ran around like a crazed arsonist lighting up everything he touched. A goal and two points in the opening nine minutes. Galway having to switch Damien Joyce off him before he'd broken sweat. By the end of the half the game had gone crazy, though, and Brennan was a vanishing sub-plot. From the 31st minute of the half until the whistle to take a break Farragher had his two goals, David Tierney had a point, Henry Shefflin had a goal and so had John Hoyne.

When we settled again we looked at the scoreboard. Kilkenny had scored three goals and trailed by three points. It was a day for strange, magical things. Niall Healy had scarcely touched a ball. We lacked the equipment to make any sense of it all but assumed that Kilkenny didn't suffer the same deficiency. They would come out and make short work of the second half. Order would be restored.

It was not to be and afterwards Brian Cody was as calm and gracious in defeat as he has been on the days of so many victories. 'Amazing game, really. On the sideline it was just going every way. At the end of the day it's an All-Ireland semi-final. They're in a final and we're not. I don't attribute the loss to any of our players. The commitment and love of hurling is there in every player. These fellas are used to being in All-Ireland finals every year but life's not like that.'

It's not but we'd come to expect it too. Yesterday's absurd and beautiful turn in events changes the way the game looks and how the summer feels. A little drop of history.

THURSDAY, 25 AUGUST 2005

How Middle-Class Political Correctness Holds the Sway of Power

Under the Microscope: William Reville

Fundamentalism is defined as strict adherence to the fundamental principles of any set of beliefs. The term is commonly associated with certain brands of Christianity or Islam and, in politics, with extreme right-wing movements. However, as the definition sets out, fundamentalism can be practised in many different areas, including science and left-wing politics. In my opinion it is equally unattractive wherever it is found.

Certainty and intolerance are the hallmarks of fundamentalism. Positions that differ from the fundamentalist position are condemned as false, in many cases, evil, and are to be opposed and, if possible, defeated. Dialogue, mutual understanding and compromise are not seen as viable options.

Of course, we are all entitled to interpret the world according to our lights and to argue for widespread adoption of the conclusions we reach. And, we will hold some of these conclusions with great conviction – eg, which of us will not passionately believe that it is wrong to deliberately harm children? To a greater or lesser extent, most of us can live with a situation where others reach conclusions that we do not agree with.

One well-known fundamentalist stereotype is the fundamentalist Christian who believes that every word of the Bible is literally true. But, it

Actress Lisa Lambe and Rebel prior to her taking to the stage in the Watergate Theatre in Kilkenny in Dog Show. *Photograph: Dylan Vaughan.*

doesn't seem to be widely appreciated that fundamentalism also exists in brands of scientific, secular and left-wing ideology. Secularism, the attitude that religion should have no part in civil affairs, is strongly in the ascendant in Europe. Some prominent spokespersons for secularism speak with the certainty and intolerance of the fundamentalist.

The treatment of the Italian Rocco Buttiglioni, a committed Catholic and candidate to be a European Commissioner in 2004 is a case in point. Buttiglioni's attitudes to abortion, family, and sexual practices are predictable, but he agreed to leave his private convictions outside the door on entering the Commissioner's office. Nevertheless, left-wing European MEPs forced him to withdraw, thereby highlighting a worrying trend. Even though it claims to greatly value 'tolerance', the cutting edge of the liberal left is quite prepared to adopt aggressive, intolerant measures in pursuing its agenda.

Progressive liberals have traditionally championed the idea that the personal and the political can coexist even when at odds with each other. Now it seems our personal opinions are monitored by the 'thought-police' and rejected if they conflict with the politically correct norms of the day.

Secularists would totally frown on evangelical religion, but they are enthusiastic about evangelical Darwinism. The high priest of evangelical Darwinism is Richard Dawkins, the well-known zoologist and author. Dawkins believes that Darwinian evolution fully explains the biological world and that science will eventually explain everything about a world in which the only ultimate realities are matter and energy. In particular, Dawkins and his followers hold that all forms of religious belief are symptomatic of mental backwardness. In a 2003 article in *The Guardian*, the author Martin Amis succinctly summarised this way of thinking. 'We are obliged to accept the fact that Bush is more religious than Saddam: of the two presidents, he is, in this respect, the more psychologically primitive.' Using this reasoning we could also conclude that Mother Theresa was more psychologically primitive than Hitler.

I fully accept the fact of evolution and the mechanism of natural selection, but I don't believe that science can explain absolutely everything about humanity. Science is entitled to propound its findings and to expect them to be respected as valid descriptions of the natural world. But it is not entitled to declare that the scientific sphere is the only sphere of reality and it is not entitled to denounce thoughtful religious thinking as backward nonsense.

Over the course of the 20th century, the Western European political left had little to say about abuses of human rights in Russia and its satellites but never missed an opportunity to criticise the smallest perceived flaw in the liberal free-market West. Many European intellectuals visited Stalinist Russia, eg George Bernard Shaw and JD Bernal, and blinded themselves to what they saw there. Indeed I remember once hearing that icon of the Irish left, Dr Noël Brown, being pressed in a radio interview to give his opinion on atrocities perpetrated by Joseph Stalin, and his reply was: 'You can't make an omelette without breaking some eggs.'

The fundamentalist left has come to command great influence in the media and powerfully moulds public opinion. Paradoxically this 'liberal' media influence seems to exert a tighter grip on public opinion than the old-style thundering Catholic bishops ever did. Where the old-style clergy had to actively patrol the 'flock' to ensure compliance, the middle classes now obligingly police themselves to ensure that they conform to the latest canons of political correctness announced via newspaper columns, radio and television talk shows.

We should be wary of all fundamentalists and remember the words of Bertrand Russell: 'The fundamental cause of trouble in the world today is that the stupid are cock sure while the intelligent are full of doubt.'

SATURDAY, 27 AUGUST 2005

The Baying for 'Colombia Three' to be Jailed

Mark Brennock

The Progressive Democrats and Fine Gael have been baying for over a fortnight now for the Government to come up with some pretext upon which to jail the 'Colombia Three'. It would have to be a pretext, because at this point nobody has identified a legitimate basis in law for doing so. There is the possibility of a conviction of one of them for a passport offence. But the demands for the men to be arrested, for the 'full rigours of the law' to be applied, for Ireland to show it is 'tough on terrorism' are code for just one thing: those making these demands want the men to be put away for a long time.

But how to do it? Lawyers and politicians agree that extradition cannot happen. So the Tánaiste has raised the possibility that the men could be made serve their sentences here. But it is doubtful whether Irish courts would tolerate this notion, seeing as those sentences emerged from a process which any lawyer here would regard as, well, dodgy. The latest idea to do the rounds in political circles this week is that they could be charged with IRA membership. The word of a senior garda is accepted as evidence in the courts, so we could bang them up in no time. Sure we all know what they were at over there, eh?

Well why stop there? Last Wednesday Michael McDowell emerged to suggest that Gerry Adams, Martin McGuinness and Martin Ferris TD had been party to sending the three to Colombia on IRA business in the first place. If the Minister believes this, then there must be a senior garda who would tell a court that he or she believes it too. So presumably those who believe the 'Colombia Three' should be charged with IRA membership believe Adams, McGuinness and Ferris should also be charged. The pursuit of these men could become absurd.

Whoever trained Colombia's Farc guerrillas to use mortars in urban areas is guilty of truly revolting activity. On the day of the current Colombian president's inauguration in 2002, Farc mortars killed more than 20 civilians. This was in the year after the 'Colombia Three' were arrested, having returned from the Farc-controlled area.

So the shrill demands for the Government, the Gardaí, anybody, to do something to lock up these men arises from anger at the belief that three bad guys are getting away with it. More generally, these demands arise from a deep hatred of the Provos and of what they spent 30 years doing on this island and in Britain. But the Provo-haters often forget perhaps the most important aspect of what the conflict was about. The Provos would have it that it was about the struggle to free Ireland from 800 years of etc, etc. But for those within nationalist Ireland who opposed the Provos it was about something deeper.

It was that we were different from them. They believed in killing, maiming and torturing: we did not. They believed they could decide themselves upon whom to impose summary punishment, and just go ahead and do it. We believe instead in a refined legal process which had a necessity for solid evidence, for convictions to be obtained beyond reasonable doubt, for a right of appeal, and only then for the imposition of punishment.

In short, they imposed terrible suffering upon whoever they felt deserved it. We insisted we only imposed punishment on those against whom it had been proven, beyond all reasonable doubt, that they had done wrong. They believed in military victory, we believed in negotiation and compromise. They killed, we didn't. At times our societies gave in to temptations to cut corners with our police and legal processes, but generally they stuck to these values.

Of course the Provos didn't see it like that. They dismissed as neo-unionists, west Brits and

Free Staters not only those who despised them for what they stood for, but those who despised them for what they did. They said we opposed them because they were republicans, while most of us only opposed them because they were killers or supporters of killers. Of course there was more to them than that, but it paled into insignificance beside their central point of difference with the rest of us.

And the good guys won, or so it seems. The thinking Provos have copped on to the fact that you will not get the support of the mass of decent people here if you kill and maim to make your case. It is a triumph for a whole range of democratic values which include the right to life, rule of law, due process, the presumption of innocence and so on.

So here we have three guys who, many believe, were involved in nasty activity in Colombia. But after a lengthy trial they were acquitted. Not only that, the trial judge suggested that the two main prosecution witnesses should be investigated for perjury. And then came a twist in the legal process which we simply would not tolerate here: a tribunal, sitting in private, where the men were not allowed to be represented, overturned the verdict, decided it believed the evidence after all, and sentenced the men to up to 17 years each.

Our notion of due process includes the right to be represented in any hearing which could end up in your being jailed for a quarter of a lifetime. It includes the notion that if a trial judge has been convinced that certain evidence should not be believed, then no other judge can decide, without hearing the evidence, that it is to be believed after all.

It seems out of the question, therefore, that the Irish courts could allow sentences imposed in this way for a conviction obtained in this way to be served in Ireland. Such standards and safeguards occasionally let guilty people walk free: they are also the mark of a civilised society.

However, there has been no let-up in the threatening-sounding verbal onslaught against the men, almost entirely from the PDs and Fine Gael. Early after they announced their return to Ireland, Tánaiste Mary Harney demanded that they give themselves up, and PD Senator John Minihan demanded that they be 'arrested immediately'. They were not specific about why this should happen.

Enda Kenny said the Government should explore 'the possibility of agreeing a bilateral arrangement which could see these men serving their sentences in Irish jails if their extradition is not possible'. Really? Does Fine Gael accept without question the legitimacy of the process that

Brendan O'Sullivan in a skirmish with Kerry's Séamus Moynihan just before the end of the first half of the all-Ireland Senior Football Semi-Final at Croke Park. Photograph: Alan Betson.

brought about these sentences? The dissenting judge in the appeals tribunal (the not-guilty verdicts were only overturned by a two-to-one majority) described some of the evidence against the men as 'unreal, fantasy-like and contradictory'. 'I was overwhelmed by the countless amount of technical evidence used in this case that was questionable,' said Judge Jorgé Enrique Torres. He said it was not possible to condemn the men unless there was 'certainty'.

Happily for Enda Kenny, he is not plagued by such uncertainty.

Mr McDowell says the rule of law must apply. Well, it is the rule of law that has – so far – kept these men out of jail in Ireland. Defending that rule of law is what three decades of resistance to the Provos was about. That great victory should not be sullied by seeking to contrive a ruse to put a few people behind bars just because we think they may well deserve it.

THURSDAY, 1 SEPTEMBER 2005

'You Just Can't Imagine that Something like this Would Happen in This Day and Age'

Carl O'Brien

They gathered for the loneliest of burials in Newcastlewest, Co. Limerick, yesterday, for a child no one knew, who was born in the most isolated of circumstances, writes Carl O'Brien in Newcastlewest, Co. Limerick. The body of the baby boy was discovered in a skip in Killala, near the village of Broadford in Co. Limerick, on 4 August by a 21-year-old Polish worker while the skip was being emptied. Evidence suggests the baby boy, who had been a full-term birth, had not lived long after his delivery. Despite appeals from the Garda for the mother to come forward in confidence, there has been no response.

Yesterday, members of the Garda, the health services and the local community gathered on an overcast August morning for the baby boy's burial at the Calvary Cemetery. The burial, without a funeral, felt eerily empty in the absence of family mourners. Sgt Martin Kelly carried the tiny white coffin in his gloved hands to the graveside, where it was dwarfed by the large floral tributes laid out on the grass. One group of blue flowers read: 'Sleep peacefully little angel in God's arms. And we'll pray for your mammy.'

The baby, christened Aidan by local gardaí after the saint who died on the same day hundreds of years ago, was lowered carefully into the ground by three undertakers. Without direct family or mourners, the group of about 30 people stood back from the graveside, some of whom wiped their eyes and sobbed quietly as the burial took place.

The plot, which normally costs around €500, had been paid for by the county council, while the local health services took care of the rest of the burial arrangements. A local sculptor is due to donate a headstone with the simple inscription: Baby Aidan, 2005. Two local community welfare officers, Seán Griffin and PJ Guinane, representatives of the Health Service Executive, said health services were available for the mother, who could still come forward in confidence. Supt Tom Gavin of Newcastlewest Garda station also appealed for the mother to come forward. 'The woman will need professional care and medical attention. We are asking her to come forward, where she'll be treated with compassion and sensitivity.'

Workers at White's skip hire, where the baby was discovered, were represented yesterday by company owner Ita White. 'It's very, very sad … It's tough on the young man who found him too. It's just very, very sad,' she said. Many of the local people gathered at the cemetery yesterday spoke in hushed tones of the circumstance of the child's death. 'You just can't imagine that something like this would happen in this day and age,' said Julia Walsh, with some emotion. 'I'd have hoped we'd have gone past that,' added her neighbour, Michael Kinelly.

The burial had a particular resonance for Mary Barry, a mother of five in her 50s, who wiped her eyes as she rested her hands on her five-year-old

Garda Sergeant Martin Kelly from Newcastlewest in Co. Limerick carrying the remains of baby Aidan to the graveside at Calvary Cemetery. Photograph: Alan Betson.

grandson's shoulders. 'I had a stillborn baby 30 years ago, and this brings it all back to me. Anthony John. He would be 31 today. I was in hospital at the time of the burial. My husband had to go through it all on his own.'

'What kills is there are people in this town, and what they'd do to have a child,' says Myra O'Brien, a local resident. 'There is still a stigma, there's still something there, whether it's in the family or whatever. Who knows? No one knows. We're all just thinking, now, about the mother of this child and how she is now.'

Lillian O'Mahony (40), a mother-of-three in a blue raincoat, clutched a bunch of flowers and looked out across the graveyard. 'People are just heartbroken for the mother,' she said. 'You'd love to put her in your arms and tell her that everything will be all right.' Ms O'Mahony, who works at the local Statoil station, paused, and then spoke more quietly. 'I know, I've been there before. I buried a four-week-old child with a heart defect. And this brings it all back.'

SATURDAY, 3 SEPTEMBER 2005

Heartbreak in the Bayou

Denis Staunton, in New Orleans

As a born worrier, Richard Friedman always knew his house in New Orleans could disappear one day. But as he left the city last Sunday with his wife, their son and two dogs, he didn't expect to be gone for more than a few days. Now this fastidious, silver-haired, fiftysomething businessman thinks they'll be lucky to return to New Orleans in four months – and he has no idea what has happened to his house. 'People talk about the "Big One" – which this turned out to be,' he says.

Hurricane Katrina has taken lives and wrecked property throughout southern Mississippi and Louisiana, but in New Orleans, where the dead lie floating in the streets, thousands remain stranded without food, water, power or sewerage and armed looters run riot, the disaster could spell the death of one of the world's best-loved cities. As President George W. Bush struggles to assert control over the crisis in New Orleans, many Americans are asking why the rescue effort has been so slow and ineffective, why warnings about the city's vulnerability were ignored and why the poorest, black citizens of New Orleans have paid the biggest price.

Along the 290km (180 miles) from Jackson, Mississippi's state capital, down to the gulf coast, Katrina's legacy is everywhere – in uprooted trees, tangled signposts and blown-away billboards. The damage becomes progressively worse as you approach the coastal towns of Biloxi and Gulfport, where entire seafront buildings were swept away.

Almost a week after the hurricane struck, close to a million people in Mississippi and Louisiana remain without electricity and thousands still have no running water. When previous hurricanes hit the coast, many evacuees took refuge in Jackson, but much of that city is still in the dark. Throughout southern Mississippi, mile-long queues form outside service stations that are still selling petrol and word spreads quickly if a station receives a new tanker delivery. Nobody talks of anything but the disaster that has happened, how they are coping and how much worse off others are. A local country music radio station has become one long phone-in, with listeners exchanging tips on how to survive and help others out. For many callers, the most important element in their survival kit is religious faith. 'I really don't know how people can get through something like this without God,' the presenter says.

Much of southern Mississippi is under curfew as police and the National Guard seek to stamp out looting and keep order among the fraught drivers queuing for petrol for hours at a time. Unrest is spreading, however, as homeless survivors become desperate in their search for food, shelter and an idea of what to do next. For many, the hurricane

Floodwaters fill the streets of New Orleans as fires burn in the background. Photograph: David Phillip/Reuters.

took not only their homes but their livelihoods too. A lot of the businesses that employed many low-paid workers along the coast have been wiped out. With no home and no future, most survivors know they have to move elsewhere, but many simply don't have the money to go anywhere.

Most of New Orleans' better-off residents left the city last weekend, crawling along highways for hours and seeking refuge with friends or in hotels. Others, such as the very poor and the disabled, had no such option, with no car of their own and no money for hotels. To make matters worse, the city's Greyhound Bus station closed on Saturday afternoon, before it was clear how strong the hurricane was likely to be when it came. This left poor citizens with no affordable option for escape, dooming them to the hell that has taken over the city during the past five days.

At first, the city appeared to escape Katrina's worst impact, as the hurricane changed course at the last minute and battered the Mississippi coast instead. But it soon became clear that the end of the hurricane was just the start of New Orleans' troubles. Built on a swamp in the lower Mississippi river, New Orleans is almost surrounded by water and most of the city lies well below sea level. Environmentalists have warned for years that decades of flood control measures and the gulf region's huge oil and gas developments were eroding the coastal wetlands that could offer protection against hurricanes.

Three years ago, the daily New Orleans *Times-Picayune* warned that the city was becoming more vulnerable every day. 'It's only a matter of time before south Louisiana takes a direct hit from a major hurricane,' it wrote. The paper outlined a number of steps the city and its surroundings should take to protect itself against events like Katrina. The report won a number of awards but was comprehensively ignored by the authorities.

Bob Anderson (centre), Pauline Powlack (right) and Jennifer Murrow pass the time at sunrise outside the remains of Anderson's home in Biloxi, Mississippi. Photograph: Win McNamee/Getty Images.

By Tuesday evening, when two of the levees that protect the city burst under pressure from the flooding that followed the hurricane, 80 per cent of New Orleans was flooded. Thousands of people were stranded in attics and on rooftops, and thousands more who had sought refuge at the city's Superbowl sports stadium found themselves in a dark, overcrowded, stinking sea of lawlessness.

Outside, groups of looters – some of them drug addicts desperate for relief from withdrawal symptoms – broke into supermarkets and department stores, many of which stock guns. Armed and very dangerous, they shot at a helicopter as it tried to evacuate sick people from the Superbowl and spent much of Thursday night taking potshots at police officers on the roof of their headquarters. The police lost control of the city almost immediately, and by the end of the week officers were handing in their badges, giving up hope of restoring order. Other police officers simply ran away.

Throughout the week, Louisiana's governor, Kathleen Blanco, and President Bush promised New Orleans all the help it needed to complete the rescue effort and start rebuilding the city. By Thursday, the city's mayor, Ray Nagin, had lost patience with the politicians, whom he accused of spinning for the cameras instead of saving lives in New Orleans. 'They flew down here one time two days after the doggone event was over with TV cameras, AP reporters, all kind of goddamn – excuse my French everybody in America, but I am pissed,' he said.

Yesterday, as Congress rushed through a $10 billion (€8 billion) aid package and President Bush flew to the gulf coast to inspect the damage, thousands of National Guard troops were heading

Hurricane survivors taunt a US National Guardsman for arriving too late to help, five days after Katrina. Photograph: Jason Reed/Reuters.

to New Orleans with orders to shoot to kill if necessary. Meanwhile, unrest was spreading beyond New Orleans with reports of looting and violence in Baton Rouge and in Jackson.

For those lucky enough to get out of New Orleans, the next few months will be anxious as they consider if and when they should return. George Nahas, who runs a shipping company in New Orleans and has taken refuge in Jackson, is impatient to get his office running again. He considered moving its headquarters to Baton Rouge but news of violence there has made him think again. He had hoped to go back to New Orleans next week to find out what has happened to his home but has now decided to stay away. 'What would I do there? I couldn't get in anyway, but if I could, I couldn't do anything,' he says.

Jack Zewe, who trains electricians around the US but lives in New Orleans, believes there is no point in trying to rebuild a life in the city. 'It's gone. It's just gone. We're talking about knocking it down and it's a brand new city in 20 years,' he says. Zewe knows four people who have already decided to move away from the city for good and are looking for somewhere else to buy. 'They're not even going back to look at their houses. They know the city's just gone,' he says.

As many residents are leaving New Orleans and other affected cities, American business is preparing to move in. By Thursday, teams of real estate agents had arrived in Jackson and were preparing to head south to snap up hurricane-hit bargains.

Once the rescue and recovery operation is complete, it will take at least three months for New

A makeshift tomb at a New Orleans street corner conceals a body that had been lying there for days in the wake of Hurricane Katrina. Photograph: Dave Martin/AP.

Orleans to become habitable again. Even then, most of the buildings may have to be demolished. The city's port is likely to be working within a few weeks but other businesses could take years to recover. Tourism, which has long been one of the city's biggest industries, will be hit especially hard, not least because so many hotels have been destroyed. The New Orleans convention centre, which brings hundreds of thousands of visitors to the city each year, will not be a popular conference venue for a long time.

Searching for a comparable disaster, some American commentators have recalled the destruction of Pompeii and the earthquake that wiped out the Japanese city of Kobe a decade ago. But most have focused on the earthquake and fire that almost destroyed San Francisco in 1906, killing up to 3,000 people and reducing the 'Paris of the West' to a city of refugees' tents.

Friedman is determined to return to New Orleans and to help rebuild the city, no matter how long it takes or how difficult the task appears. 'The people of San Francisco came back. One hundred years from now, people will say that the people of New Orleans came back,' he said. New Orleans occupies a place in the American imagination unlike any other city and few can conceive of the death of the 'Big Easy', the spiritual home of jazz that served as a muse to William Faulkner and Tennessee Williams and serves up some of the most delicious food in the world. Even those who have never visited New Orleans feel an affection for the city the journalist RW Apple described as 'a Caribbean city, an exuberant, semi-tropical city, perhaps the most hedonistic city in the United States. You see more orgies (and more nuns) in New Orleans than anywhere else in the nation.'

Friedman describes fleeing the city and talking to fellow evacuees as 'an almost spiritual experience' which has left him more certain than ever that New Orleans will survive the disaster and will emerge stronger than before. Then, as he considers what losing New Orleans would mean for America, he starts to cry. 'America would lose part of its soul, part of its heart,' he says.

SATURDAY, 3 SEPTEMBER 2005

Always Right on The Money

John McManus

Micheál Martin and his colleagues in Government have good reason to feel aggrieved over Eddie Hobbs. Three months ago the Minister for Enterprise, Trade and Employment appointed his fellow Corkman to the board of the National Consumer Agency, a long overdue initiative to give consumers a say in government policy.

Despite being a signed-up member of what the Government likes to see as a genuine attempt to combat the sort of profiteering that's inevitable in a fast-growing economy, Hobbs has spent the past three weeks tormenting the Government about its failures in this department via his role as front man of RTÉ's *Rip Off Republic* series. The programmes, which cast Hobbs in the role of televangelist for consumer rights, have been a massive success, with last week's episode attracting more than three-quarters of a million viewers.

The final episode goes out on Monday, and one suspects that if the Government has anything to do with it, it will be the final final episode. The series has tapped a rich seam of public resentment over the rising prices and deteriorating public services that appear to have accompanied the past 10 years of spectacular economic growth.

But Martin really should not be surprised at Hobbs nibbling the hand that feeds. If one thing characterises the 42-year-old father-of-four's journey from insurance salesman to media celebrity it's the desire and ability to have his feet in both camps and come out on the winning side. He first came to prominence in the early 1990s when he was working as an investment adviser. He became a vocal critic of endowment mortgages, a type of mortgage that was popular in the booming equity markets of the late 1980s but quickly proved disastrous when the stock markets reversed.

The problems with the products were widely reported in the UK, but Hobbs was the first to really draw attention to the issue in Ireland. The associated publicity was the making of the fast-talking and acerbic Hobbs. Even then he appeared to have little problem reconciling the business of earning his living selling financial services products with publicly running down some of the major players in the industry in which he had worked since leaving school at 16.

Eddie Hobbs by Peter Hanan.

One of the major beneficiaries of the publicity was Hobbs's employer at the time, Tony Taylor's Taylor Asset Management, which he joined in 1991 from insurance company Eagle Star, where he had worked his way up to marketing director. Hobbs was a director of Taylor Asset Management when it went spectacularly bust in 1996 with some millions of pounds of clients' funds missing. Although Hobbs claims he had left the business some time before that, he was still a director and had a 24 per cent stake when Taylor absconded and the group collapsed.

Some nine years on, the Taylor liquidation remains unresolved, and the issue of whether Hobbs bears responsibility for the events – and should be restricted from acting as a company director – has not been settled. The liquidators of the company still have to decide whether or not Hobbs has a case to answer in relation to his duties as a director. If he does, then Hobbs will have to explain to the High Court why he should not be restricted.

Meanwhile, Taylor – who was convicted of fraud in 2001 and served a jail term – protests his own innocence and makes serious and unproved allegations about his former colleague. Hobbs, for his part, characterises himself as the whistle-blower who helped bring a stop to Taylor's activities by informing the authorities. He also claims credit for Taylor being brought to justice by employing private investigators to track him down to his bolt-hole in England. The Taylor affair did Hobbs considerable damage, not withstanding his role in bringing him to justice, and the fact remains that he was a director of a group that collapsed with millions of pounds of clients' money unaccounted for.

Hobbs's return to the public eye really came by way of his involvement with the Consumers Association of Ireland, a somewhat anaemic and underfunded version of the powerful UK consumer lobby group, the Consumers Association. Hobbs had been the CAI spokesman on financial matters since 1993, when he was asked to join on foot of his endowment mortgage campaign. Despite the association's articles precluding directors of companies involved in marketing goods and services from being members of its council, Hobbs was admitted to the ruling body.

His apparent inability to see any conflicts between these two roles meant that he prospered in both. While some in the CAI were less than happy about Hobbs double-jobbing, they could see that the articulate and financially literate Corkman was a media godsend. At the same time, the connection lent credibility and publicity to his new venture, Financial Development and Marketing (FDM), which has about 150 corporate clients. The symbiotic relationship has continued ever since, despite the fundamental conflict of interest at its heart. Few raised any objection when in 2001 Hobbs devised the CAI's vetting scheme for the Special Savings Incentive Accounts. This was despite the fact that by that stage Hobbs had become an adviser to many financial services groups – including the Quinn Group and Friends First – who were planning to launch these products.

In many ways the controversy surrounding *Rip Off Republic* represents the apogee of Hobbs's career-long tactic of having a foot in both camps where possible. Apart from the obvious difficulties in reconciling his role as member of the national consumer agency with the role of tormentor-in-chief of Government Ministers, there is another, and in some ways far more interesting conflict that Hobbs has side-stepped.

It is remarkable that a television series devoted to exposing profiteering in the Irish economy is not scheduled to devote at least one episode to the financial services industry. It is not as though there is no shortage of material. The Competition Authority is nearing the end of two mammoth investigations into the banking and insurance industries. Its reports are very critical of the way banks treat both small business and more importantly the men and women in the street that form the constituency that *Rip Off Republic* has so successfully targeted. The authority has also produced a report that is highly critical of the insurance industry and in particular some of the practices adopted by brokers and intermediaries. But perhaps the biggest target of all is Allied Irish Bank and the other retail banks. Over the past 18 months the industry has been rocked by scandalous allegations about overcharging, profiteering and possible tax evasion.

None of this appears to have been deemed suitable material by Hobbs for his knockabout style of television. The explanation may lie in the activities that Hobbs squeezes in between his television career and the tireless work on behalf of the consumer at the Consumers Association of Ireland. Hobbs is an 18 per cent shareholder in a company called 3Q Solutions, which provides consultancy to banks and other financial services businesses. Its clients include a life assurance and pensions company, a building society, a financial adviser and a mortgage broker association.

3Q solutions 'builds visionary wealth management products' that enable its clients 'to maintain and increase financial services revenue from their high net worth and affluent customer base'. According to its website, 3Q has taken its clients 'on a journey which allows them to maximise their capacity and increase existing share of wallet'.

Could the wallets in question be those of the punters sitting in the studio audience of *Rip Off Republic* laughing as Hobbs takes pot shots at politicians and other soft targets? The interesting question that they might care to ask themselves is: who is Hobbs laughing at?

Education and Science Minister Mary Hanafin slips while posing for a photograph inside a model of a molecule when she paid a visit to the British Association Festival of Science in Trinity College, Dublin. Photograph: Frank Miller.

SATURDAY, 3 SEPTEMBER 2005

Sparkling Reflections in the Wake of The Master

Sideline Cut: Keith Duggan

He arrived in the colds of December, 1928, and by the time he passed away on 27 August last, the life and times of Seán Purcell had come to assume significance far deeper than his storied feats across the football fields of Ireland. In so far as there can ever be a joyous funeral, the gathering at the Cathedral in Tuam last Wednesday was more celebratory than mournful in tone as many hundreds came to salute 'The Master' of Gaelic football in the middle part of the century.

Many – including GAA president Seán Kelly – were too young to have ever seen him play in the flesh and as film footage of his athletic supremacy is negligible, many in the congregation had pieced together a vision of Purcell through newspaper reports, word of mouth, imagination and boyish imitation. As his brother-in-law Monsignor Tommy Shannon gave his homily, Purcell's boyhood friend Frank Stockwell, with whom he formed perhaps the most vivid and charismatic partnership in Gaelic games, listened from his sick bed. 'The Terrible Twins' is an unforgettable sobriquet to begin with and the fact they were born within the same lunar cycle to the same street in the steadfastly West of Ireland town of Tuam enhanced the notion they came as some sort of gift. In a society where sport was the only suitable medium for exuberant self-expression, Purcell and Stockwell were a pair to crow about – not that you would ever hear them talking about themselves.

After being waked for two days in St Jarlath's College – for whom Purcell's first flush of greatness was realised in the snowbound winter of 1947 – Tuam's favourite son was laid to rest on Wednesday last. Because Gaelic football played such a central part in Purcell's life, it was an unusual funeral service, in part a sporting reminiscence and in part an exceptionally brave and tender reflection on an ordinary, modest man who lived a somewhat public life because of his extravagant talent.

There is always the danger at these occasions Irish sentiment might place a false gloss on the departed. But through all the fond reminiscences spoken from the pulpit, the acknowledgment of his son John that there had, at times, been pain in theirs, as in so many households, anchored the tributes and kept us mindful that this was, ultimately, a mere man, with shortcomings.

Frank Purcell, elder brother of Seán, spoke of their formative days in Tuam of the 1920s and 1930s, even then a football hub, with the Kerry of the great Con Brosnan coming to play semi-finals there (against Mayo and Leitrim). Frank believed Brosnan was the Kerry footballer his brother most resembled and Seán Kelly later explained how Purcell and Stockwell were the only two exotic names to feature in the boyhood games in which they would mimic their heroes. He said a photograph of himself and The Terrible Twins is one of his most prized mementoes.

Seán Purcell's football career is reflected not so much in silverware – he has one All-Ireland, from 1956 – but in the transcendent effect he had on those who remember him playing, most of whom insist he was the greatest ever. That is an argument that will rage as long as the GAA survives but it seems clear that as well as his startling versatility Purcell had that rare, casual mastery of style and balance which set him apart on any football field he graced.

But as his son John also observed, the pleasing thing about the long wake in the school of his youth was that most spoke about the man rather than the footballer. Through John's wonderful eulogy, through Frank's distinguished reflection and through the resounding and poignant stories told by his great friend Jack Mahon, the details of a warm life filled that vast cathedral.

And it was a life of pattern, of ritual and of a great respect and love for his community. We heard about the daily drive over to Strawberry Hill NS, eight miles from Tuam, and how he would stop for students along the way. He enjoyed the conversations so much that the children devised a code to keep his attention on the road, periodically shouting 'bus' or 'dog' whenever he seemed to forget he was in control of the car. One ex-pupil said he was like a 'modern' teacher, with sweets on the first and last day, a gentle manner and no caning, ever. The pattern of his later life as a newsagent was recounted, from his early rising to the Wednesday night ritual when he would collect the *Tuam Herald* hot off the presses and deliver it to a few friends and acquaintances, including his son John while he boarded in St Jarlath's. 'But I', boasted John from the altar, 'was the only one who got lamb chops and chips with my *Herald*.'

He enjoyed racing and visiting friends and had innumerable houses where he could sit in his regular seat and assume proprietary rights to the remote control. As well as being the godfather of Galway football, he was its greatest fan. When his daughter-in-law Sheila enquired whether he would support the Dublin team managed by his son-in-law Tom Carr or his local county in a league match, a look of disgust crossed his normally pleasant features and he replied: 'A savage loves his native shore.'

Crowds gathered outside the famous boarding school and the cathedral and lined the main street, where the businesses had all locked their doors and shuttered the windows, as if it were a Good Friday of yesteryear. The great thing about 'real' towns like Tuam is that physically they cannot change much, and as the hearse carried Seán Purcell through High Street for the last time, the feel of the place was surely much the same as when he took his first tentative steps from Bishop Street.

It was only in death that they could praise him lavishly because, famously, he was genuinely uncomfortable when his own deeds were voiced. Jack Mahon, a born orator – as so many good teachers are – captured his deft way of deflecting praise. In 1996, Mahon and Purcell travelled north to honour the St Patrick's, Armagh, school team against whom Purcell's Jarlath's had played epic finals in 1946 and 1947. The wine flowed and one of the Devlin boys took the microphone and was waxing lyrical about Purcell until the Tuam man could stand it no more. Purcell leapt up, took the microphone, said 'Don't mind me,' and began to tell of his short, unhappy life as a politician. In the 1950s, he was prevailed upon to run as a Fine Gael candidate along with John Donnellan, the great Dunmore footballer and TD. The theory was that Donnellan's surplus would see Purcell through.

'I was a terrible electioneer but John's votes saved my deposit if not my pride,' Purcell said. It was a close thing and after one of those marathon counts that make Irish politics unique, he was eliminated. As he went to take the stage after the final count a Fine Gael woman from Donnellan country was overcome with emotion and grabbed him by the arm. 'Ah Seán-een,' she wailed, 'it's an awful pity you never played a bit of football.'

THURSDAY, 8 SEPTEMBER 2005

Not the End of the World – But Close

Mark Lawrenson

It's not the end of the world, but it'll feel like it a bit this morning. There was really nothing between the two sides on the night, Ireland tigerish and strong in the first half but without managing to create any clear-cut chances – a handicap that ultimately made France's night a little more comfortable.

A moment of real quality separated the sides at the end, Thierry Henry's strike, beautifully executed, but France will know that they were slightly fortunate to get more than the draw. Brian

Kerr will have to pick his team up now and try to secure second place. That's got to be the focus as there's no point dwelling on the past. It was a rip-roaring contest from the start; the passion and intensity that we expected was very much evident on both sides. Neither side shirked in the tackle, especially the Irish players, who made it uncomfortable for any French player that dwelled on the ball.

In the first half there was a ferociously high tempo that seemed impossible to sustain, but for those 45 minutes there was plenty of punch and counter-punch. Clinton Morrison epitomised Ireland's determination. He gave Jean Alain Boumsong a very tough time, purely by being physical. The Newcastle defender didn't know when to drop off Morrison and when to pick him up and conceded several needless fouls because of that uncertainty. The only disappointing aspect of that half was our inability to create any clear-cut chance – Andy Reid's free-kick notwithstanding. And those who questioned Reid's defensive qualities received their answer.

Ireland's front two, Morrison and Robbie Keane, set the defensive tone by mixing up closing the French defenders down and dropping off and letting Wily Sagnol and William Gallas have possession but no outlets, except the sideways pass. The French midfield were operating within a narrow, confined structure and that meant when they did get on the ball they were more often going from touchline to touchline rather than managing to penetrate what must have looked like a green wall before them. Zinedine Zidane and Henry couldn't get on the ball for much of the half, with the obvious exception of the former's superb free-kick and Henry's couple of early runs. Shay Given made a super save that was a little more comfortable than it looked.

Brian Kerr would have told the team at half-time to keep playing the same way while demanding a little more from Kevin Kilbane in terms of getting forward. He would also have wanted to see Reid and Damien Duff get on the ball a little more going forward. Roy Keane was an authoritative presence in the first half, breaking up French attacks and, despite mistiming a couple of tackles, making it uncomfortable for the visitors in that sector. His performance over the 90 minutes was immense.

The real danger for Ireland was that they'd drop off their men and allow the French to weave neat patterns facing the Irish goal. They were given a couple of early reminders of the visitors' class soon after the interval when Ireland were guilty of sloppy passing and diving in recklessly. One upshot of the latter was the three yellow cards Ireland picked up that ensured the players concerned – Morrison, Roy Keane and Reid – will miss the game against Cyprus; the Tottenham man's caution as needless as it was disappointing.

The problem for Ireland after the interval was that, though they continued to close down the French, they were creating very little and that meant the French were getting more possession. In fairness to France, they were as comfortable in the second half as we had been in the first. We weren't being outplayed in any way, but on a night like this you need your best players to be exactly on top of their game – and Damien Duff and Robbie Keane struggled to get on the ball. As a result it was always going to be difficult for Ireland.

The goal came out of nothing. You could be a little critical about not pressing the ball quickly, but it was a really classy effort by Henry. If you needed a final reminder of the difference in the depth of the respective squads all you had to do is look at the substitutes that were available to the respective managers.

It was a good hard-working performance from Ireland that was imbued with many qualities, but, on the night, Ireland didn't get that little slice of luck. It's not the end of the world, but it just makes the next two matches must-win games. It's not beyond them, but it will define this Irish team.

Zoo keepers Ken Mackey and Ger Creighton with elephants Judy and Kirsty waving a final farewell just before the process of their transportation to their new home at Neunkirchen Zoo in Germany. Their departure will open the way for the redevelopment of the elephants enclosure which will be completed by 2007 with the addition of two breeding elephants from Rotterdam, accompanied by a calf. Photograph: Alan Betson.

SATURDAY, 10 SEPTEMBER 2005

Childcare Argument is Nowhere Near Settled

Breda O'Brien

Maureen Gaffney appears to have a certainty that the rest of us lack. During the week, it was reported that she had said in relation to childcare, 'the argument was now settled'. She told the Fianna Fáil conference that 'irrespective of the amount of time in childcare and the age of entry, the proportion of children with secure emotional attachment was exactly the same at 62 per cent as those reared at home by their mothers'.

If the argument on childcare is settled, why do major longitudinal studies suggest that it is anything but settled? The National Institute of Child Health and Development (NICHD) in the US, starting in 1991, is following more than 1,000 children from birth onwards. The first results published dealt with ages 0–3 and, unsurprisingly, found that children were less likely to be securely attached if they had mothers who were poor, or if their mothers were less sensitive and attuned to the baby. However, the headlines tended to focus on one finding. By age three, no negative effect was found on mother-child attachment for kids with sensitive mothers in high-quality childcare.

Ah, but the devil is always in the detail. The headlines mostly neglected to point out that the study also found that longer hours in childcare 'predict less harmonious mother-infant interaction and less sensitive mothering at six, 15, 24, and 36 months of age, even when quality of childcare and family variables are controlled'. There was a slight improvement in cognitive functioning for children who spent time in childcare. However, as child development specialist Penelope Leach pointed out, it's easier for an infant to catch up on cognitive skills later on. Insecure attachment is not so easy to overcome. It can lead to poor relationship skills, and even affect ability to learn.

NICHD research then focused on children aged four and a half. It found that those children who had spent more than 30 hours a week in group childcare were almost three times as likely (17 per cent as against six per cent) to show aggressive behavioural problems than those who had spent 10 hours or less, regardless of the quality. A Dutch study re-examined the data this year, and found that the NICHD data had underestimated the link between commercial childcare and aggression.

How glibly we use the words 'high quality' when it comes to childcare.

Prof. Ted Melhuish is a highly respected figure in childcare research in the UK. He conducted an audit of all available research on childcare for the UK's National Audit office and a major study on the effective provision of pre-school education. He concludes that children under the age of 18 months need almost one-to-one care. It is possible to provide it in childcare, but it is so expensive that it is just as cheap to provide paid parental leave for 18 months to two years.

Parents have a built-in connection to and emotional investment in their own children that is hard to replace with any kind of paid care. Parents will literally kill themselves for their own children. It appears that this is exactly what they are doing. A fascinating piece of Australian research shows that parents who work outside the home do everything possible to maximise their time with their children. Using data from the Australian Bureau of Statistics Time Use Survey 1997, researcher Lyn Craig showed that parents managed to squeeze in as much time as possible with their kids by 'reducing time devoted to other activities (principally sleep, leisure, bathing, dressing, grooming, eating)'. I bet it rings true to the harassed commuter-belt parents for whom Fianna Fáil is belatedly showing such concern.

What is the best way to ease the pressure on a family where two people commute daily and their children spend eight to 10 hours in institutional childcare? Prof. Ted Melhuish makes the perceptive comment that in Sweden, high-quality infant care has long been available. It was widely used during the 1970s and the 1980s, but when parental leave improved during the 1990s, demand for childcare for small children dropped dramatically. Given the option, Swedish families voted with their feet.

The British government also backed off from plans to provide nursery places for all, largely because of Prof. Melhuish's research. They have now decided to increase maternity leave to a year by 2007. Given a real choice, most Irish parents would opt for flexible work practices and longer leave, rather than longer hours of childcare.

What about those who want to raise their own children full-time? Are they to become even more economically disadvantaged when their counterparts who go out to work receive all sorts of help? The only equitable solution is a refundable tax credit that allows parents to decide whether they want to invest it in childcare, or in helping to finance one parent to work part-time or not at all.

However, Fianna Fáil can't sell that one to ISME and IBEC, who seem to be increasingly setting the agenda for this country. IBEC is now mouthing platitudes about the value of early childhood education. Certainly, there is strong evidence for the value of pre-school education after age three, particularly when children are already disadvantaged. But listening to IBEC, you get the horrible feeling that children are supposed to be academically advanced so that they can provide a

Frances Maguire with her pet dog as she packs her belongings before leaving her home in the York Street Flats, Dublin city centre. Photograph: Bryan O'Brien.

better quality workforce, and the happiness of children or parents does not feature at all.

With their new-found focus on childcare, Fianna Fáil is neatly managing to divert attention from the fact that its policies created most of this mess in the first place. It was under Fianna Fáil's stewardship that Meath, Kildare and Wicklow were rezoned for expensive residential housing. The builders and the developers loved it, but what has our society been left with? Sweden spends 2 per cent of GDP on childcare, and it is rare for a child to enter it before 18 months. Ireland spends 0.2 per cent of GDP, and it is becoming a privilege reserved for the very rich and the very poor to actually raise their own children. We are richer than we have ever been but when it comes to quality of life, we have lost our way.

If the 'settling of an argument' requires pushing more and more children into longer and longer hours of institutional childcare, it is clear that we have a lot more arguing to do.

TUESDAY, 13 SEPTEMBER 2005

'I Suppose I'm a Bit of a Refugee Too'

Paul Cullen

Frances Maguire gives a hoarse laugh as she waves in the direction of the 'refugees' with whom she shares her one-roomed flat – her dogs, Sandy and Bobby, and her two canaries, Eggnog and Harold. 'I call them refugees because they came to me from somewhere else,' she says. 'But now, I suppose, I'm a bit of a refugee too.'

After 47 years, Frances was leaving her home in York Street yesterday. Not because she wanted to, but because Dublin City Council wants her side of the street cleared for redevelopment. That means no more walks with the dog in St Stephen's Green, just a stone's throw down the street. Her daughter Caroline lives downstairs and her two brothers are nearby, but now the family is being dispersed in different flat complexes. 'We fought them for years, but no one wanted to listen. You can't argue with money, I suppose,' she says, as the removers leave with a lorry-load of her belongings.

Across the road are the buildings of the Royal College of Surgeons. 'They never did anything for anyone on this street,' says Caroline. Emptied of furniture, Frances's flat looks shabby and ill-equipped, but the ceilings are high and there is a secret garden behind the building. The other houses on the block are boarded up and most of the windows are broken. 'The council have been running down these flats for years,' she says. 'They wouldn't give us central heating because they had a plan to get us out.'

Her new flat near Aungier Street boasts modern appliances and central heating, but Frances isn't interested. 'There won't be as much room and it isn't home.'

TUESDAY, 13 SEPTEMBER 2005

Palestinians Savour End of Israeli Presence

Nuala Haughey, in Gaza City

Palestinians swept into Gaza's abandoned Jewish settlements yesterday to savour the sweetness of the day when 38 years of Israeli civilian and military presence inside the coastal enclave came to an end. Most

A Palestinian flag is waved as Palestinian youths swim at a beach in the former Jewish settlement of Shirat Hayam in the southern Gaza Strip after Israel withdrew following 38 years of occupation. Photograph: Goran Tomasevic/Reuters.

were merely curious to peek behind the security fences and concrete military towers which had protected their unwelcome neighbours, but some also came to scavenge amid the debris of the former luxury villa homes which the evacuated residents had already picked clean of valuables.

Initial outbursts of celebratory gunfire by Palestinian militants and security forces alike gave way to a day of family celebration, with hundreds revelling in the simple pleasure of breezing past dismantled Israeli checkpoints and playing in the waves on beaches which hours earlier were exclusively reserved for settlers. Public buildings, water towers and synagogues were draped with flags of the ruling Fatah movement and Gaza's many different militant groups. Islamic Jihad militants in black balaclavas cruised along the beach-front road in open-top jeeps, keen to declare the Israeli pull-out a victory for their resistance.

At Gaza's southern border with Egypt, Egyptian troops who have assumed control of the frontier from Israel allowed people to stream across for impromptu family reunifications, but insisted this was a once-off concession. Egyptian officials did not comment on local reports that border guards had shot dead a Palestinian man at the border yesterday.

In the town of Dir-al-Balah, the Bashir family was yesterday adjusting to life without the Israeli troops who have occupied the upper floors of their cinderblock home almost constantly for the past five years. The soldiers, who had turned the building into a military outpost to protect the adjacent Kfar Darom settlement, left abruptly yesterday morning as part of the final pull-out of all remaining troops from the strip. 'They just said bye and stole the computer webcam,' said Sa'ad Bashir (40), explaining that for the past month her family had been forced by the soldiers to sleep and live in one downstairs room, which they had even labelled 'The Jail'. 'It's like a rebirth for the whole family,' she added.

Further south, in the synagogue of the former Neveh Dekalim settlement from which hundreds of mostly teenage right-wing religious Zionist protesters were carried out of less than a month ago by Israeli troops, people milled around yesterday morning while Palestinian troops guarded against vandals.

'This is like a field day for all Palestinians,' said Ibrahim Abu Subayah, a 21-year-old English student from nearby Khan Younis who had formerly worked in the settlements as a farm labourer. 'Of course this is our dream and we are very happy today to see our land which the Jews robbed from us. They came from different cultures and robbed our land and praise God because we got it back so I can't express my deep and warm feelings about this day.'

Neveh Dekalim's former synagogue was one of 26 which the departing Israelis refused at the last minute to demolish themselves. While Palestinians attempted to set fire to several other synagogues during the day, the Palestinian Authority later said it planned to bulldoze them all.

FRIDAY, 16 SEPTEMBER 2005

A Silent, Unhappy Majority Arrives at The Tipping Point

Marc Coleman

It appears that the Celtic Tiger has awoken a sleeping tiger. According to recent opinion polls, 89 per cent of us believe we are being ripped off and that government is significantly responsible. As a result, support for Fianna Fáil has fallen to 32 per cent. This is roughly the level of support Fianna Fáil received in last year's local elections and if maintained at the next election would see it returned to the Dáil with around 15 fewer seats.

Maybe the reasons for this are short term and curable. But maybe not. Perhaps the Celtic Tiger is combining with social change to do more

A clinched fist salute from protesters who are opposed to the changing of the name of Dingle in Co. Kerry to An Daingean. Photograph: Ted Creedon.

permanent damage to our traditional political system. After years in which bales of the stuff have been mounting on the camel's back, Eddie Hobbs has put the final straw on top of the pile, producing the sound of a spinal crack.

Although economic change can drive political change, this is usually a glacial process. But – rather like leaving a camera in front of a budding flower for weeks and then fast forwarding it – an examination of poll evidence from recent history can make such slow processes discernible to the eye. Most pollsters are interested in shifts of support between the two main parties. But what is interesting in this context is support for the traditional party divide. The combined vote for the two Civil War parties, Fianna Fáil and Fine Gael, has fallen from 84 per cent of the vote in 1982 to just 57 per cent now.

In the last quarter of a century, one quarter of the electorate has switched away from the traditional parties. But over this period we have moved from being an economic basket case to being, according to the UN at least, the world's second wealthiest country. So why are people deserting the two parties that have dominated government since the foundation of the State? Allow me to offer a theory.

The first reason is that there is a growing divide between what we might call the 'competitive classes' on the one hand and the 'protected classes' on the other. Take benchmarking for example. This exercise was motivated by the feeling of public servants that they had been left behind by the Celtic Tiger. But when its awards were paid, many in the private sector pointed to public servants' job security, pension entitlements and public sector

Marilyn Manson at the RDS in Dublin. Photograph: Matt Kavanagh.

inefficiency as reasons why it should never have been undertaken.

In spite of this, the Government awarded significant pay increases to public sector workers. Benchmarking does have some merits. But by not publishing the results of the benchmarking survey, the Government made a costly error. It asked the private sector to foot the bill for benchmarking, but refused to trust the private sector with information needed to justify the exercise.

Rip-off Ireland, or the perception of it, is another factor damaging the political system. The Government is seen as the friend of vested interests. By contrast, most in the private sector face intense competition due to immigration, globalisation and the pressures of a single market. Closed shops and protected sectors are increasingly seen as privileges enjoyed by a pampered elite, and paid for by the rest of us who have to make our way in the real world. Economic reforms have been achieved, of course. But whether they go fast or far enough is another question.

So to many the question 'who gets the lion's share of the economic tiger?' is answered not by 'those who worked the hardest', but by 'those who shout the loudest'. Fine Gael and Fianna Fáil are particularly vulnerable to this trend. The declines they have suffered in their party membership since the 1990s makes it more difficult for those parties to stay in touch with the silent majority.

The growing urbanisation of Ireland may also be a factor. In last year's local elections support for Fianna Fáil was significantly lower in many urban areas than in adjoining rural areas. Urban voters may be less loyal to traditional party brands. Urban TDs may also be less susceptible to lobbying by local interests, such as publicans, as those interests may not play the important social role that they often do in rural areas. The recent sight of rural TDs from both Fianna Fáil and Fine Gael lobbying effectively against café bar licences may have been perceived strongly negatively in urban areas. Further factors add grist to the mill, including a younger, less patient and more educated electorate as well as the fact that the relevance of the Civil War divide is receding in political importance.

However deep and strong the forces driving it, realising political change usually requires a defining event to happen. Enter Eddie Hobbs. In 2000 Malcolm Gladwell wrote a number one bestseller called *The Tipping Point*. The idea is that change accumulates slowly but remains inactive, until a certain point where it accelerates and is unstoppable. On its own, his programme may have done nothing overly serious, other than vent short-term spleen. But the Government's reaction reinforced an image of an establishment that is running scared and out of touch.

Now Fianna Fáil faces the challenge of recovering lost support from the 'competitive classes', especially in urban areas. Its strategy so far is to call on outside experts and gurus. This was tried by Fine Gael in the 1990s without success. But basic management theory dictates that such approaches usually fail. Rather, an organisation seeking solutions to strategic problems must draw from its own heritage. In 1958 Seán Lemass courageously faced down opposition as he ended external protectionism. As Fianna Fáil faces the policy challenge of internal protectionism in our economy, it could do a lot worse than recalling the vision and boldness of Lemass.

And there are questions for other parties: Why has the Labour Party failed to garner significantly more than 10 per cent of the vote when one third of the vote is going to the left, broadly defined? How consistent will Fine Gael's central theme of 'Rip-off Ireland' be with the policies that will emerge from its meeting in Portlaoise? Will the Progressive Democrats enter the next election with their radical ethos vindicated or fatally compromised? A final, tantalising question is: if none of the parties is able to recapture Middle Ireland, could an entirely new party emerge to represent it?

SATURDAY, 17 SEPTEMBER 2005

Sister Pact

Róisín Ingle

My sister Rachael doesn't get out much. This is apparently because she is an actuary with two small children. Sometimes I ring her up and I say Rach let's go out tonight, there is this party/premiere/envelope opening we really must attend together. If the timing is right she will say something like, ok but do you have any lipstick on you, which is a bit like Paris Hilton's sister asking her whether she has any spare designer handbags. I told you she doesn't get out much.

We had one of our rare nights out together last week at a drinks party hosted by Today FM. We ended up sharing the table with a Radio Head who took a bit of shine to her on account of them both having the maths thing in common. He came first in his class at Probability, which meant nothing to me but impressed Rachael who can add up big numbers in her head. The very happily married Radio Head and the very happily married actuary bonded happily about managing the Irish population's increasingly unrealistic pension expectations. I don't know what it means either and anyway I was more interested in the mini bagel burgers. They hit it off by working out how long the other had to live. I should mention at this point that she's very attractive, my sister, for an actuary.

After a few drinks and a bit more chat Radio Head said he reckoned he had the measure of us siblings. If we were both paintings, he said, then I was a Rothko all colourful and warm and fuzzy at the edges. The sister was not amused. 'If she is a Rothko then what does that make me?' she hissed getting that black look in her eye, the one that will be familiar to ex-girlfriends of my brothers whom

Putting the final touches to the Nissan Art Project exhibition at the Royal Hibernian Academy in Ely Place in Dublin featuring over 100 paintings by artist Stephen McKenna. Photograph: Jason Clarke.

she has cross-examined almost to death on occasion. 'You are an Escher painting, all straight lines and unusual architecture.'

'Oh great,' said Rach cutting him off. 'She gets to be all colourful and blurry and I get to be all black and white with stairs that go nowhere. What are you trying to say?' I suppose I should have told Radio Head to leave well enough alone at this point but I was rather enjoying the unfolding drama. 'Escher paintings are very beautiful,' he ventured hopefully. Rachael's stern face was, appropriately enough, a picture.

There follows an example of how Radio Head's extremely perceptive Escher/Rothco comparison plays out with my sister and me. Earlier that evening I had picked her up from her office in a taxi. She was wearing one of her sharp trouser suits with a white tee shirt underneath. I was wearing sparkly black eyeshadow and a coleslaw stained floaty dress and carrying my usual assortment of grubby looking carrier bags.

We were off to a wine tasting in a fancy hotel. I needed someone with a bit of gravitas to accompany me around Superquinn's latest wine sale. In addition to being rather good at sums she knows her Bordeaux from her elbow where I just know I like fizzy stuff, Mad Fish and a nice Sancerre. She is also quite good at persuading me not to eat my way through large containers of duck mousse paté just because, like Everest, it is there. She wasn't as successful with the big pile of melty Brie and crackers fortunately. Yum.

Then later in The Porterhouse she talked business and people management with Radio Head while I quizzed the American date of my friend – a piano player in the Liberace Museum in Las

Vegas if you wouldn't be minding – about how he got into music in the first place. At which point everyone listened open mouthed as Wes Winters, yes that's his real name, described seeing a Liberace programme on the telly at the age of five and teaching himself to play piano like Liberace for the next eight years. Then Rachael came over all Rothko and asked him did he have any Deano in his repertoire. And of course being the pro that he is Wes Winters had a lot of Deano, lots of Elvis and quite a bit of Judy Garland as well. If you have never had a sing-song led by someone who actually knows the words and sounds like the people who used to sing the songs I would advise going to Las Vegas to meet Wes immediately if not sooner.

It's only natural that there are times when Rachael would like a bit more of my Rothko and I could do with more of her Escher, but most of the time I am perfectly happy with the way things are. It means that when things get a bit too blurry I can ring her for advice on a contract I am supposed to sign or a tax form I am supposed to fill. It means that when things get a bit black and white she can rely on me to force her to put on make up and try on stunning dresses in Barcelona boutiques. That night though, the lines between Escher and Rothko blurred beautifully as we sang our hearts out with the very wonderful Wes Winters. It's times like these when my sister Rachael and I are a real work of art.

Index

WATERFORD CITY AND COUNTY
WITHDRAWN
LIBRARIES